GHOSTS OF TSAVO

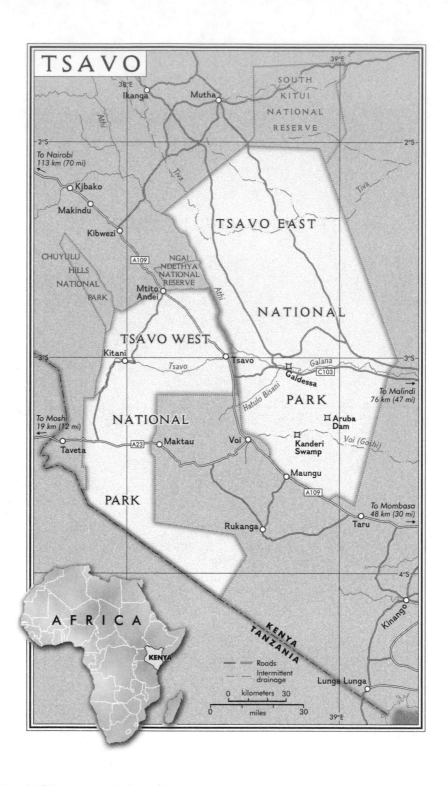

TSAVO

IKANGA
Mutha

SOUTH
KITUI
NATIONAL
RESERVE

38°E
39°E

2°S
2°S

To Nairobi
113 km (70 mi)

Kjbako

Makindu

Kibwezi

Athi

Tiva

Tiva

TSAVO EAST

CHUYULU
HILLS
NATIONAL
PARK

A109

NGAI
NDETHYA
NATIONAL
RESERVE

NATIONAL

Mtito
Andei

Athi

TSAVO WEST

Kitani

Tsavo

Tsavo

Galana

3°S
3°S

Galdessa

C103

Hatulo Bisani

To Malindi
76 km (47 mi)

To Moshi
19 km (12 mi)

NATIONAL

A23

Maktau

Voi

PARK

Aruba
Dam

Kanderi
Swamp

Voi (Goshi)

Taveta

Maungu

A109

PARK

Rukanga

To Mombasa
48 km (30 mi)

Taru

4°S

AFRICA

KENYA

KENYA
TANZANIA

Kinango

Roads

Intermittent
drainage

0   kilometers   30

0   miles   30

Lunga Lunga

39°E

PHILIP CAPUTO

GHOSTS OF TSAVO

STALKING THE MYSTERY LIONS OF EAST AFRICA

ADVENTURE PRESS

NATIONAL GEOGRAPHIC
WASHINGTON, D. C.

Published by the National Geographic Society

First Printing, June 2002

Library of Congress Cataloging-in-Publication Data

Caputo, Philip.
    Ghosts of Tsavo : stalking the mystery lions of East Africa / Philip Caputo.
        p. cm.
    ISBN 0-7922-6362-6
    I. Lions--Kenya--Tsavo National Park. 2. Lion attacks--Kenya--Tsavo National Park.
I. Title.

QL737.C23 C345 2002
599.757'096762--dc21

                                                                        2002022642

Interior design by Bea Jackson
Typesetting by Melissa Farris

Printed in U.S.A.

One of the world's largest nonprofit scientific and educational organizations, the National Geographic Society was founded in 1888 "for the increase and diffusion of geographic knowledge." Fulfilling this mission, the Society educates and inspires millions every day through its magazines, books, television programs, videos, maps and atlases, research grants, the National Geographic Bee, teacher workshops, and innovative classroom materials. The Society is supported through membership dues, charitable gifts, and income from the sale of its educational products. This support is vital to National Geographic's mission to increase global understanding and promote conservation of our planet through exploration, research, and education.

For more information, please call 1-800-NGS LINE (647-5463) or write to the following address:

NATIONAL GEOGRAPHIC SOCIETY
1145 17th Street N.W.
Washington, D.C. 20036-4688

Visit the Society's Web site at www.nationalgeographic.com

To the memory of my mother,
Marie Ylonda Caputo
April 30, 1915 - August 9, 2001

CONTENTS

PROLOGUE

THE MAN-EATER OF MFUWE *

The old inhabitants of Europe, or of Assyria, or Asia Minor...looked
to the King or chief, or some champion, to kill these monsters for them.
It was not the sport but the duty of Kings, and was in itself a title to be
a ruler of men. Theseus, who cleared the roads of beasts and robbers;
Hercules, the lion killer; St. George, the dragon-slayer, and all the
rest of their class owed to this their everlasting fame.
—*from* The Spectator, *March 3, 1900*

---

* This account is based on interviews with Wayne Hosek and on a written narrative he supplied
to the author.

IT WAS THE FACE of the new Africa that made him decide to kill the lion. He didn't decide by weighing pros and cons before arriving at a conclusion; rather, he answered a summons that announced itself as he lay on his cot one afternoon, in a tented safari camp in the Luangwa Valley of eastern Zambia. Wayne Hosek was a man of faith, and the words that ran through his mind had the ring of a religious imperative: "To him who knows good and doesn't do it is sin." A lean man of average height, with receding brown hair, Hosek was three days into a two-week hunting safari, something he'd dreamed of doing since he was a boy. So far he'd bagged a large kudu, a Cookeson's wildebeest, and a Sharpes grysbok, but he wasn't thinking about them as he rested through the hottest part of the day, his mosquito net furled above him and the tent's front flaps rolled back so that he could see the Luangwa River and the village beyond, where the lion had killed a woman named Jesleen three nights ago. He'd heard about this killer cat on his first day in camp, and although he intended to hunt lion, he'd wanted no part of tracking down a man-eater. Now, he was reconsidering. Jesleen was the lion's sixth victim in two months, and the people in her village and in several others up and down the Luangwa were terrified in a way Hosek's neighbors in California could never fathom, because in their America of shopping malls and theme parks and supermarkets and endless suburbs linked by freeways posted with signs directing you to FOOD GAS LODGING and sometimes the nearest hospital, a predator that devoured humans was a threat even more remote than famine or plague, pretty much on the same level of possibility as an invasion by extraterrestrials. If they could imagine what life would be like if a psychopath were roaming their neighborhood, killing at random, they would get an idea of what these Zambian villagers were enduring. Hosek recalled the stories the villagers had told him about the man-eater's raids. Mostly, he thought about the children he'd met, suffering from bilharzia, malaria, guinea worm, and malnutrition. Theirs was the collective face of the Africa never shown in travel books and tourist brochures, in movies and TV travel documentaries, cameras panning over the symphonic landscapes of the old Africa of Isak Dinesen, Ernest Hemingway, and Robert Ruark.

Considering all their daily afflictions, it seemed, well, wrong, for the villagers to be tyrannized by a man-eating lion, and a compulsion to intervene swept over Hosek, like the sear dry-season wind blowing through camp. "To him who knows good and doesn't do it is sin," might sound like bullshit, dressing up blood sport in altruism's frills. But Hosek's feelings were sincere.

He got up and walked across camp and told his guides, Charl Buekes and Willie Cloete, that he was going after the man-eater. He had confidence in them and in their three Zambian trackers, Gilbert, Boniface, and Ken. He was also confident of his own shooting abilities. Still, he felt that he was taking a step into the unknown; a man-eating lion was a different thing altogether from a kudu or wilde-beest or grysbok.

If Buekes and Cloete were surprised by his announcement, they didn't show it. Nor did they try to talk him out of it. Explaining his decision wasn't necessary, but he explained it regardless, pointing out the lion's virtues as a trophy—it had been described by some vil-lagers as a large male with a huge mane—and adding that killing it also would be a sort of public service. The two professional hunters (the term "white hunter" long ago fell out of usage because of its colo-nial connotations) agreed on the second point but expressed doubts about the first. They suspected that the lion's impressive mane was a fantasy concocted by a few locals to lure trophy hunters into the Luangwa Valley. The more people they could draw into pursuing the lion, the greater the chances that someone would rid them of it. Under the circumstances, the deceptive advertising was under-standable, but Buekes and Cloete were sure the man-eater was not fully maned, if it was maned at all; eyewitnesses they considered reli-able had described it as maneless, which had led to the mistaken belief that it was a female, which in turn had led game rangers and profes-sional hunters to kill six lionesses since the attacks began. The lionesses' deaths had been a pointless waste; the attacks continued. That fact, combined with the reported size of the cat—it was said to be huge—had convinced Buekes and Cloete that the marauder was an unmaned male.

A maneless lion would be a remarkable creature to most people, accustomed to the gloriously crowned "king of beasts" that adorns countless African postcards and roars at audiences from the MGM screen, but Hosek had seen two such lions before, mounted as exhibits in the Field Museum of Natural History in Chicago, where he was born and raised. His father had taken him to the museum when he was in grammar school, more than 35 years ago. There, in Stanley Field Hall, he saw the stuffed replicas of the feline pair, poised on a slab of papier-mâché sandstone, one crouched, the other standing, right paw slightly raised, both looking intently toward the bronze castings of Masai warriors, one of whom had thrown a spear and missed. His weapon was stuck in the ground next to the standing lion, and the warrior was kneeling on one knee behind his buffalo-hide shield, a hand on the short sword hanging from a cord around his waist. The printed legend at the base of the statue explained that the Masai hunted lions with spears, both as a manhood ritual and to protect their cattle herds, and that when a warrior's cast missed its mark, he received the lion's charge on his stout shield and battled it hand to claw with his sword while his comrades waded in with their spears. The young Hosek marveled at the courage and nerve of the Masai, but he was more captivated by their quarry.

Those two lions, he discovered, had attained mythic status by literally stopping the British Empire in its tracks back in 1898, when they killed and ate some 135 Indian and African laborers building a railroad bridge over the Tsavo River, in what was then British East Africa, later the Republic of Kenya. Work on the bridge came to a halt, forcing the army engineer in charge of the project, Lt. Col. John Henry Patterson, to pursue the man-eaters. It took him nine months to track them down and kill them, a saga without equal in the annals of big-game hunting. Many years later, while lecturing in the United States, Patterson donated the lions' skins and skulls to the Field Museum. A taxidermist turned the hides into life-size mounts, and they were put on exhibit in 1924, a source of grim fascination to countless visitors and notably to Hosek. The lions' fearsome history was matched by their appearance; the absence of manes made them look more sinister than majestic; it was as if nature had dispensed

4

with distracting ornamentation to show the beasts in their essence—stripped-down assemblies of muscle, teeth, and claws whose sole purpose was to kill. But it was their eyes that impressed most. They were glass facsimiles, yet they possessed a fixed, attentive, concentrated expression that must have been in the living eyes when they spotted human prey decades before, on the plains of Africa. Hosek stared at them, awestruck by their great size, by the power evident even in their lifeless imitations. The exhibit awakened in him a fascination with Africa and an ambition to go there, an ambition that would not be fulfilled until he was nearly 50 and that would lead him to almost repeat Patterson's experience.

Naturally, he had no way of knowing that in the mid-1950s. What he did know now, on this early September day in 1991, was that standing face to face with a taxidermist's dummies was absolutely no preparation for the real thing. After announcing his decision to his PHs, he felt a range of conflicting emotions, excitement wrestling with dread. He'd read *The Man-Eaters of Tsavo*, the best-selling book Patterson published in 1907 about the lions' deadly raids and the ordeal he went through hunting them. To call it sobering would be like calling Dracula interesting; it was a chilling account of two killer cats almost supernatural in their ability to overcome the defenses thrown up against them and to outsmart their pursuer.

Working as a team, the pair sneaked into the construction camps at night, snatched men from their tents, and consumed them, often within the hearing of the victims' fellow workers. Patterson, who'd had considerable experience hunting tigers in India, used every trick in the big-game hunter's playbook and devised ingenious traps and ruses to bring the killers to bay. They outwitted him time and again, proving so crafty that the workmen—mostly contract laborers imported from India—came to believe ancient legends about body-snatching demons told by local tribesmen. They added an anti-imperial spin to the myth: The lions were the incarnate spirits of African chieftains angered by the building of a railroad through their ancestral lands. "Beware, brother! The devil is coming!" the men would call to each other on nights when the lions' roars fell silent, for silence meant they had begun to stalk.

Patterson's description of the aftermath of one attack reads like a gothic novel. His Sikh *jemadar,* or servant, Ungan Singh, had been seized by one of the lions in the middle of the night. The next morning, Patterson found, "The ground all round was covered with blood and morsels of flesh and bones, but the unfortunate *jemadar's* head had been left intact, save for the holes made by the lion's tusks.... It was the most gruesome sight I had ever seen."

Singh was one of the lions' early victims, and his ghastly death was what sent Patterson after the lions. He didn't know what he was in for, but found out soon enough. The construction camps were scattered up and down the railroad right-of-way. The lions would strike at a particular camp one night and Patterson would stake it out the next night, waiting with his .303 rifle, but they always seemed to know where he was and would attack elsewhere.

The workmen meanwhile surrounded their camps with high *bomas,* or protective fences, made from thorny commiphora shrubs. For a while, the attacks stopped. One night, a few workers figured it was safe to sleep outside their tent but inside the boma—a bad decision. One of the lions leaped over the fence (a lion can make a vertical jump of 12 feet) and grabbed a man. His friends threw stones and firebrands, but the lion calmly dragged its victim through the thorns. Outside, it was joined by its partner, and the two savored their meal within earshot of the dead man's friends. Some were armed and fired at the lions through the fence, but the bullets missed, and the cats, not in the least disturbed by the gunshots, leisurely finished dinner.

Perhaps Patterson's worst memory was of the night when he was in a tree stand and both lions carried their most recent kill close to him. It was too dark to aim and fire. He sat up there, listening to the crunching of bones and to what he described as a contented "purring"—sounds that he could not get out of his head for days.

The cats did not confine themselves to humans. In December 1898, they killed a donkey. Scared off by Patterson, they abandoned the carcass. Patterson, inspired by his tiger-hunting days in India, built a *machan,* or platform, with four poles and a wooden plank, from which he could shoot in relative safety. He used the partially eaten donkey as bait, lashing it with wire to a nearby tree stump. That night, Patterson stood vigil. Soon, he heard a twig snap and a lion sighing with hunger. It ignored the donkey, however, and began to stalk Patterson, circling around and around his rickety perch. All it had to do was knock out a pole or jump, and Patterson would have been a dead man. The lion growled, then moved in for the kill. Patterson fired. The lion snarled—it had been hit and ran into the bushes. Patterson blazed away into the brush; the snarls grew weaker and finally ceased. The first man-eater was dead.

The next day, its body was recovered. Measuring nine feet, eight inches from its nose to the tip of its tail and forty-seven and a half inches at the shoulder, the male was so heavy it took eight men to carry it back to camp. (A lion of those dimensions would weigh an estimated 475 to 500 pounds, roughly 100 pounds more than average.)

To dispatch the second lion, Patterson tried one of his tricks. After the cat killed a goat near the railroad inspector's shanty, Patterson tied three live goats to a length of railroad track, then entered the shanty and waited. The lion came just before dawn, killed one of the goats, and began to carry it away, along with the other two goats and the 250-pound rail. Patterson fired, missing the lion but killing one of the goats.

The rail left a trail easy to follow; the lion escaped nonetheless. The dogged Patterson stalked it for almost two weeks and finally managed to wound it. He and his gun bearer followed the blood spoor, or trail, for a quarter mile and at last spotted their quarry, glaring back at them with bared teeth. Patterson took careful aim and fired. The lion charged. A second shot bowled it over, but it got up and charged again. Patterson fired a third time without effect, reached for his second rifle, and saw that his gun bearer had fled into a tree. Patterson had no choice but to join him; if one of the bullets had not broken the lion's hind leg, he never would have made it. Once in the tree, Patterson grabbed the rifle and shot the lion again. It fell heavily. Patterson foolishly climbed down—and was stunned to see the lion jump up and charge him again. He put a round in its chest and another in its head, and the lion went down for good, snapping at a branch even as it died.

The second man-eater measured nine feet, six inches in length and forty-five inches at the shoulder, and its death ended the reign of terror. In a short time, the huge cats became international celebrities, gaining the distinction of being the only lions ever to be referred to in the House of Lords, when the Prime Minister at that time, Lord Salisbury, made a speech describing the difficulties in building the Uganda Railway:

"The whole of the works was put to a stop for three weeks because a party of man-eating lions appeared in the locality and conceived a most unfortunate taste for our porters. At last the labourers entirely declined to go on unless they were guarded by an iron entrenchment. Of course it is difficult to work a railway under these conditions, and until we found an enthusiastic sportsman to get rid of these lions, our enterprise was seriously hindered."

Now, nearly a century later, Hosek was aware that the "Man-eater of Mfuwe," as it had come to be called, after a village where it had claimed its first victims, had displayed a cunning almost equal to that of the Man-eaters of Tsavo. One of its pursuers was a professional named Carr, who had made several attempts to get within rifle range of the lion, but it always managed to evade him. Another was a Japanese hunter and naturalist who had killed one of the lionesses, only to discover, after Jesleen was taken and eaten, that he'd shot the wrong animal. Buekes theorized that the females belonged to the man-eater's pride and that witnessing their deaths had made him still more clever. He'd learned that human beings with weapons were dangerous.

For two days, Hosek, Buekes, Cloete, and the trackers visited various villages, looking for signs of the lion, collecting descriptions of him and his activities—a kind of intelligence-gathering mission to build a picture of the man-eater's patterns and range. They were going to war against a solitary, elusive foe, in terrain that favored their adversary. The Luangwa is a rift valley 350 miles long, running roughly parallel to the Tanzanian border between two low mountain formations, the Tern in the east and the Muchinga in the west. Most of Zambia is rolling, lightly wooded savanna, but the Luangwa is more densely vegetated—scrub brush thickets and mopane tree forests alternating with patches of grassland—and is cut up into a puzzle of ravines and gullies formed by the streams and rivers that flow into the Luangwa during the rainy season. The lion had its choice of hiding places, or of ambush sites should it decide to turn on the hunters.

In the village called Ngozo, where the woman Jesleen had lived, the men got up-to-date information on their quarry. The villagers, belonging to the Kunda tribe, told a frightening tale—the day after devouring Jesleen, the lion walked into Ngozo in broad daylight, entered Jesleen's house, and came out with her white canvas tote bag, filled with some of her possessions. He then paraded through the village, roaring and playing with the bag as a house cat does with cat-nip. The villagers shouted, banged sticks together, and pounded on pots and pans, but the lion went on with his fun and didn't leave until he was good and ready, carrying the bag in his jaws.

The next day, several women went down to the Lupande River, a tributary of the Luangwa, to do the family wash. The Lupande was dry, as were most of the smaller rivers, and the women intended to do their laundry by digging until they found water. Wash day, however, would have to be put off, for they saw the lion, contentedly toying with Jesleen's bag in the sandy riverbed. The following day, villagers cautiously approached the spot. The bag was gone, but paw prints led to its rediscovery a few hundred yards upstream. The morning after, the villagers found the bag in a new location, and then the lion reappeared with it in the middle of town, roaring once again, batting his plaything back and forth. He seemed to delight in tormenting the people with his bold, bizarre behavior. One man inadvertently came within yards of the cat as it cavorted in the riverbed. The lion paid no attention to him, obsessed with Jesleen's bag. The village elders counseled among themselves and concluded that the bag must be bewitched to so captivate the man-eater, which they told Hosek, Buekes, and Cloete was possessed by a demon, if not a demon itself. Hosek recalled the words from *The Man-Eaters of Tsavo*: "Watch out, brothers! The devil is coming!" The parallels between his experience and Patterson's 93 years before were more than a little disturbing.

A game scout from the Luangwa Game Reserve offered some information, reporting that he'd seen the man-eater stalking through

the long, golden grass near Ngozo. He confirmed that it was a male
and without a mane. The scout then led the three hunters and their
trackers to the Lupande to show them Jesleen's tote bag. He pointed
to it from the riverbank, but would go no farther; like the rest of the
villagers, the scout was convinced that the bag was bewitched and
refused to get near it. Hosek and Buekes, guns at the ready, went down
into the riverbed for a look, and it was then that the American realized he was becoming "Africanized" even though he'd been on the
continent less than a week. Myth and reality had become so fused
he could barely distinguish between the two; as he looked at it, the
white bag seemed to cast a spell over him. His blood drained from his
body, congealing at this feet, his stomach dropped, and he shivered
despite the 100° heat. If that was what was meant by one's blood
running cold, then, Hosek thought, "I want to keep warm forever."
His resolve and confidence deserted him, fleeing out of his mouth
with each breath. He cradled his .375 Holland & Holland and wondered what had made him think that he, Wayne Hosek, an estate
planner by profession, was ready for a venture like this.

The professional hunters and the trackers were meanwhile
studying the pugmarks (footprints) in the sand. Shaped like scalloped
saucers, they led down the riverbed and then into the tall grass alongside. Everyone was frowning, tight-lipped, and their somber mood
seemed to thicken the air itself, an atmosphere that overpowered
Hosek's thoughts and emotions except for one: fear. He asked Cloete
where he thought the lion might be.

"Could be there," Cloete said, pointing at the shrub-shrouded
riverbank a few yards away. "Could be five miles away. No telling."

Gilbert would not look Hosek in the eye, and Boniface and Ken
wouldn't speak to him; it was as if the trackers resented him for getting them into this. Buekes, his huge .458 Winchester at his side,

gazed down at the paw prints, mesmerized. "He's big, he's big," he murmured, almost to himself.

No one yet realized that Buekes had just uttered the understatement of the year.

The three men followed the lion's spoor up the riverbed. Buekes and Cloete proposed laying a bait on the riverbank between a couple of mopane trees, some 50 or 60 yards from the bag, which they now called "the lion's bag," for it did belong to him and him alone. After studying the lay of the land, the PHs chose a site for a blind another 50 yards from the bait. That done, and with dusk approaching, everyone returned to camp for dinner. There was none of the lighthearted conviviality and small talk that marked previous meals; conversation focused on tactics and contingencies—if the lion does this, we'll do that. When it was time to turn in, Buekes took Hosek aside and said, "Remember to follow up hard after you make your first shot," meaning that he was not to linger even for an instant to see if the first shot had done the job; he was to chamber another round and fire immediately.

Hosek retired to his tent, propped his rifle against a post, dropped the mosquito net over his bed, and tried to sleep. He barely noticed the night chorus of hyena whoops and elephant trumpets, of jackal laughter and a leopard's two-toned roar, like a crosscut saw being drawn back and forth across a board. He fell asleep, woke up thinking about the lion, slept again, woke up again, and prayed. He dismissed all thoughts of backing out. He'd conferred upon himself a duty and an obligation that he could not ignore and still be able to face himself in the mirror. He dozed once more, then heard a voice outside his tent telling him it was time to wake up.

In the morning, the trackers built a blind from bamboo poles and elephant grass cut by the villagers—their contribution to the effort.

Buekes and Cloete shot a small hippo and cut off a haunch and laid
it at the base of a fever tree near the riverbed and covered the haunch
with branches. At half past three in the afternoon, they and Hosek
entered the blind, knowing that they could not leave until the next
morning. Like all cats, lions are primarily nocturnal, so there was no
question of vacating the blind at night. Hosek settled in, observing
that he had a clear field of fire to the bait through a corridor in the
undergrowth 60 feet wide. He could see beyond to the opposite bank,
where a swale of open grassland lay burnished by the afternoon light
and ended in a patchwork of shrubs and thornbush.

Nightfall in the tropics lacks the lingering twilit preambles of
northern latitudes. It really does fall, suddenly, as if a shroud has
dropped over the Earth. The hunters took turns on watch. Nothing
happened until Hosek heard the laughter-like call of a hippo, grazing in the riverbed. He whispered a warning to Buekes and Cloete,
who paid no attention until the hippo brushed against the blind and
then, catching human scent, trotted noisily away. Bats flew into and
out of the blind; insects buzzed, whined, hummed. Cloete saw a genet,
an odd little creature with a long, striped tail and a body spotted like
a leopard's, visiting the bait, but that was all.

The trio got a surprise in the morning, when the trackers, arriving in the Land Rover to pick them up, found fresh pugmarks only
50 feet from the blind. There were more a short distance from the
bait, still more downriver around the white bag, which the lion had
moved yet again. Hosek was amazed that the man-eater had come
so close to the blind without his two experienced companions ever
hearing or seeing it.

A quick breakfast at camp, a morning spent hunting zebra as a
kind of diversion, another strategy session over lunch. Buekes
pointed out that rangers who'd attempted to kill the lion had laid baits

in the Lupande; so had the Japanese hunter. The cat had his choice of dining spots. If there were only one, the chances of luring him in would be increased, so Buekes and Cloete decided to consolidate their bait with the others. They set off by vehicle, collected the baits, tied them to the rear bumper, dragged them down the riverbed past the "bewitched" carry bag to leave a trail of scent, and then placed them beside the hippo haunch to make a single pile of rancid meat. Once again, Hosek and the PHs settled into the blind at 3:30 p.m. Buekes and Cloete said they were sure that they would make contact tonight, a confidence Hosek did not share. "Is this really me doing this?" he thought, feeling as though he were watching himself in a movie.

The feeling of separation continued even in his sleep. His eyes were closed, his mind unconscious, and yet he'd acquired the ability to listen to every sound. He later recalled "it wasn't a half sleep or a light sleep or any kind of sleep" he'd ever experienced. He seemed to be in two equal and opposite states at the same time—soldiers in combat know this sensation of being fully alert and fully asleep simultaneously.

He heard a sharp crack above his head, in the low trees beside the blind. Instantly, his brain processed where the sound had come from, and it told him to move very slowly as he turned his head to the right to see through the blind's grass walls. He made out a pair of elephant legs, only six feet away, and raising his eyes, saw the whole great bulk of the creature, standing virtually over his head as it grazed on the tree branches, breaking them off with its trunk. With utmost care, Hosek shifted his glance to the left. Crouched, motionless, Buekes was pointing the .458 straight up at the tusker's chest. The elephant fed for several minutes, then moved on in complete silence, as if its three or four tons were without substance.

In the morning, the trackers again returned with the Land Rover to drive the three men back to camp. Gilbert, Ken, and Boniface had disquieting news: The lion had entered the village where they'd spent the night and killed and ate a bush pig. The hunters were silent for a minute or two, musing on the lion's astonishing ability to elude them. "This one is crafty. He's really a crafty lion," Buekes remarked, staring at the ground. He looked up, straight into Hosek's eyes, and added, in a tone of mingled dread and bewilderment, "He knows what we're doing."

That morning's breakfast was as cheerful as a post-funeral supper. Frustrated, worn out from two nights of fitful sleep, Hosek realized that in this *danse macabre,* the lion had become the dance master, choreographing his mood and the mood of his companions—and they had yet to see him. It was as if they were dealing with a presence rather than a creature of blood, bone, and muscle, an invisible menace that was carrying each of them to a spiritual plane none had visited before. The villager elders' belief that the lion was a demon no longer seemed like superstition.

Later, the men again went hunting lesser game, and their sport lifted them out of their gloom and apprehension and stimulated them to devise a new strategy. Since the lion appeared to know that the blind was a trap, they would set up a new blind in a different location, with fresh bait, and leave it vacant for two days to lull the cat into a false sense of security. If the deception worked, he would return to the bait on the third day, supposing the blind to be empty, but it wouldn't be. Buekes chose the site; it was two and a half miles from the Lupande, between two water holes where the lion had been seen drinking in the recent past, and only a few hundred feet from a small village. That could also work to the hunters' advantage—possibly, the lion would mistake the blind for a villager's hut.

While driving to the new spot, Hosek, out of curiosity, asked about the elephant of the previous night.

"That was bad," Buekes commented, offhandedly. "If he'd caught our scent, he would have stomped us to death."

Hosek was unfazed by what might have happened. Nothing mattered but the lion. He was their adversary, the center of their thoughts and actions, and all else was incidental.

Buekes made a prediction: If the ruse failed and the lion sensed their presence, he would not permit the men to see him standing still. He would be moving. Hosek would have two to three seconds to make his shot.

"He'll be on the move," Buekes repeated for emphasis, and gave his client a long, penetrating look. "You've got to make this shot, Wayne. No matter what you think of it, make it. I'll be ready to follow up with the .458 regardless of any follow-up by you, but make the shot."

"I'll make it," Hosek replied, and his self-assurance wasn't faked.

The next day, Gilbert, Boniface, and Ken built the new blind and hung a zebra haunch from a tree about 60 yards away. While the three hunters observed the work, a group of village boys hung around, asking questions. Hosek photographed them and was much affected by the eldest, a 14-year-old boy missing one arm. It had probably been cut off in some accident or other, or had been amputated as a result of gangrene. Looking at him reminded the American of all the other barefoot, diseased, and crippled children he'd seen in the Luangwa Valley. From the village boys, he learned that one of their friends, also 14, had had a narrow escape only the day before. He'd been relieving himself in the bushes near his hut when he heard something moving in the undergrowth. Without a second's hesitation, he ran full speed for home, with the lion charging after him. Somehow, he won the race, literally slamming the door in the lion's face. The man-eater paced around the hut, looking for a way in while the boy's neighbors, barricaded in their houses, shouted and made noises to drive him off. The tale aroused an outrage in Hosek. It represented a subtle but important shift in the emotions that had inspired him to go after the lion in the first place. In *The Man-Eaters of Tsavo,* Colonel Patterson often referred to his quarry as "brutes" and "outlaws," as if they had violated some ordinance of nature by making prey of human beings. It had seemed a strange, almost juvenile characterization—those lions, after all, were obeying the fundamental law of nature, which is survival. But now, Hosek was inclined to sympathize with Patterson. In his mind, the Man-eater of Mfuwe came to embody all the hardships and sufferings the kids had to endure. He found himself thinking of the big cat as a "foul beast," even as evil, as if it were deliberately victimizing the weak and downtrodden.

Hosek confessed to Buekes that he was beginning to hate the lion. The professional looked at him with bloodshot eyes and nodded to say he understood.

The pressure on the three men mounted during the next 48 hours. Local authorities imposed a 5 p.m. curfew on an area encompassing 65 square miles. Most of the villagers obeyed, but on the way back to camp that evening, Hosek observed that some were venturing out past curfew, either out of necessity or under the illusion that the lion would not attack them. Even so, ordinary life had almost halted; the whole region was in a thrall of fear, and hundreds of people were looking to him, Buekes, and Cloete to liberate them. Hosek could almost feel their eyes on him and his guides, pleading that they succeed where others had failed.

He barely slept that night, anticipating the moment when he would again enter the blind with his rifle. How had Patterson endured so much tension and exhaustion for nine months?

The first 24 hours of waiting passed. The trio once more stalked other game to give themselves an emotional break, as well as to convince themselves that the lion wasn't controlling every moment of their lives. But of course he was. They couldn't get their minds off him. No matter where they were—in camp, in the Land Rover, out in the field—the great cat seemed to be with them, watching them. At dinner, Hosek asked Cloete what would happen if the lion decided to attack them inside the blind, a distinct possibility if he thought it was a shelter for some helpless villager.

"There will be three guns waiting for him and he'll be killed," Cloete answered, matter-of-factly. Hosek would later learn that the veteran professional hunter was not as sure of himself as he pretended to be.

They scouted the new site after sunrise. The man-eater had come to the bait, torn off a chunk of meat, and devoured it a few yards away, on a footpath leading to a nearby creek. Hosek took out his camera to snap a photo of the pugmarks. Incredibly, the shutter froze. His view through it was black. He smacked the camera with his hand and shook it but could not get it to work. Buekes and Cloete were as astonished as he, but they refused to say a word about what had happened. They, like Hosek, seemed to accept the broken camera as an omen, though of what they didn't know. Did it mean "lights out," and if so, lights out for whom? One of them, all of them, or their quarry?

On the appointed day, there was no talk of the coming afternoon's work. In the future, thinking back, Hosek would be reminded of a baseball team's dugout when their pitcher is throwing a no-hitter. "Don't talk about it, don't even think about it." Nevertheless, he did think about it, craving relief from the pall of oppression that had settled over him, from the fear and anger that constantly competed for his attention.

At the usual hour of half past three, he entered the blind with Buekes and Cloete. The trackers instructed the villagers to remain in their huts to avoid distracting the lion from the bait as well as to protect themselves in case Hosek merely wounded him. If that happened, Gilbert, the chief tracker, would be in charge of following his blood spoor until, in pain and fury, the lion decided to attack his pursuers—an appalling prospect, but one they had to be prepared for— or became weak enough to allow Hosek or one of the PHs to put him down for good.

They waited in the blind, speaking in the softest undertones. An oddly lighthearted mood had descended on them, but it ended less than an hour later. Buekes raised a finger to his lips. With hand signals, he indicated he'd spotted movement in the long grass. He peered through the walls and practically kissed Hosek's ear, whispering that the lion was circling the blind, not more than 40 feet away. All three men turned themselves into statues. The mossy cliché from the literature of big-game hunting "We dared not breathe" suddenly did not seem quite so clichéd. A new terror visited Hosek. What if he or one of the others dozed off at a critical moment and began snoring? That seemed an outlandish possibility, what with the man-eater only yards away; but, dazed from lack of sleep and the relentless heat and the assault of powerful emotions, he found himself fighting off attacks of sleep. As the brief equatorial dusk enveloped the blind, he succumbed, passing out for a sliver of a second.

His eyes popped open on instinct. Buekes and Cloete were standing, motioning to him to get up. He jumped to his feet and peered through the blind's firing window.

"See him? He's behind the tree!" Cloete whispered, meaning the tree from which the bait was hung.

Hosek at first saw nothing, because the lion was approaching in a straight line with the tree. When Hosek did catch a glimpse, he noticed that he wasn't moving at a casual pace, but at a quick stride, almost a trot, and was using the tree trunk to mask himself. Despite all the careful plans and preparations, the cat had once again sensed that something wasn't right and was taking every precaution. Buekes's characterization of him as crafty did not suffer one bit, but when he stepped out from behind the tree and the three men got their first good look at him, Buekes's earlier description, "He's big," did suffer. The lion wasn't merely big, he was enormous, his tawny hide paled by the fading light. Ignoring the bait, he turned to face the blind and snarled, absolute confirmation that he knew the men were there. As Buekes had forecast, he wasn't going to allow them to see him standing still. He picked up speed, now at a full trot, and his one mistake was to offer Hosek a full broadside view of his body. Resting the .375 on the firing slit, the American put the scope on his stomach, jumped the crosshairs to below and just back of his shoulder, a perfect sight picture. Sweeping the scope to keep pace with the lion, he could not allow himself to think about what he was doing; it had to be all experience and training and instinct now, as he followed the marksman's ancient formula: Breathe, aim, squeeze the trigger as you let out the breath. The rifle seemed to go off by itself just as the man-eater extended his legs to go into a full run. Hosek heard the solid thunk of the bullet striking home and, in the same instant, caught the orange flash from Buekes's .458 delivering the follow-up. A .458 makes a tremendous blast, yet Hosek didn't hear it. The whole world went silent as he jacked a fresh round into the chamber and watched the lion sprint with greyhound speed into the grass, too quickly for him to get off a second shot. Now his hearing returned. The sound of the lion crashing through the grass was distinct, and sickening. Somehow, neither he nor Buekes had fired a fatal shot. A moment later, they were grateful to hear a low gurgling sound and then something like a sigh and then a welcome silence.

Buekes and Cloete, however, weren't ready to concede that the Man-eater of Mfuwe was finished. For all they knew, this intelligent cat had faked the sounds of its own death.

"We're going to check him; you stay here," Buekes said. This was in accordance with the one great commandment of African big-game guides. When a dangerous animal is wounded, the guide must go in after him first. Getting a client killed is very bad for business and also could result in the loss of a professional hunter's license.

Shortly, Buekes called back that the lion was dead. Hosek stood trying to savor the moment, but his heart remained in the state it had been in when he fired—devoid of emotion except for a residue of fear.

The trackers drove up in the Land Rover. They'd heard the shots from the nearby village and had come immediately, not knowing what had happened. They went past Hosek to where Buekes and Cloete stood, some 40 yards from where the lion had been hit. Gilbert looked down at the carcass and began singing a haunting melody in a strong clear voice. Hosek would later learn that it was called the "Kunda Lion Song." "*Moto-moto anamata, Nkalam sa funna nkondo*—Fire, fire young man, The Lion does not want a war." Gilbert's operatic bass reached the village. The people there knew its meaning, for the song is sung only when a lion has been slain. The Kunda believe that if it's sung when a lion has not been killed, whoever sings it will be killed by a lion. Very soon, a flickering orange light rose in the near distance. The villagers were lighting bonfires in celebration, and they too began to sing and shout and beat drums, signaling to their neighbors that this man-eater's reign of terror had ended. In the out-side world, wars were being fought, parliaments debated, the Earth's billions went about their ordinary days, but in that remote corner of the Luangwa Valley, September 9, 1991, was a day that would be remembered. It was an unforgettable moment for Hosek as well. The scene was something out of the earliest ages of the human race—drumbeats, a chorus of celebratory voices, dancing figures silhouetted by bonfires leaping in the darkness against the backdrop of the tall grass on the skyline.

As Hosek started toward the lion's body, illuminated by the Land Rover's headlights, the trackers ran up to him and hugged and kissed him. Over and over, Ken said, "I say today you get your lion." Hosek now allowed himself to feel joy, mixed with enormous relief that he and the others had not had to track the man-eater's blood trail in the middle of the night.

When he was about 25 feet from the dead lion, he stopped. Something, some force or power, would not allow him to go any farther. He couldn't get near the carcass in any case. Children poured out of the village and swarmed around it, and Hosek was astonished to see them spitting on the beast that had tormented them for so long, beating it with sticks, casting out their fear and rage. More people arrived, one an old woman with a cane. She went up to Buekes, who was leaning against the Land Rover, and asked who had shot the lion. He gestured at Hosek. The old woman approached the American, looked at him with a fierce expression, and squeezed his hand. "*Zikomo kwambli,*" she said. "Thank you very, very much." Hosek would later learn that she was held in high esteem by the villagers and that to receive her deepest thanks was a high honor. After her recognition of his achievement, dozens of other people, men and women, old and young, jubilantly crowded around him, touching him, offering their hands in thanks. He might have been Beowulf after slaying Grendel, but Hosek did not see himself in any such heroic light. He was a hunter who had shot a lion, though it was no ordinary lion. Even in death, it seemed to bewitch him. Looking at it, lying as if asleep, except for the blood-rimmed hole behind its shoulder and the chunk taken out of its left rear leg by Buekes's snap follow-up, Hosek continued to feel the strange paralysis.

The celebration continued. More songs were sung, speeches made, thanks given. An assistant school principal who'd been held hostage in his house for a day and a half because the lion was prowling nearby praised Hosek's mother for giving birth to him. Villagers carried him around on their shoulders, and someone told him he could spend the night with any woman he chose, married or single, for among the Kunda, as among the Masai and Turkana and Samburu, it is an honor for a woman to make love to a man who has killed a lion. Hosek declined the offer.

Now he gathered the nerve to approach the lion, going up to it from behind. He tentatively touched its muscled haunch and then stepped back. Buekes, recalling that Hosek's camera had broken, said he would take a picture with his, but it also failed to function, for no reason except the one neither man could voice.

It took six strong men to drag the cat to the Land Rover and load it on board. Hosek and his guides and trackers returned to camp, where the skinners opened the man-eater's stomach to see if any identifiable human remains could be found. This gruesome operation was as ceremonial as it was forensic, because the Kunda believe that the body parts of a person devoured by a predator must be given a proper burial; otherwise, the deceased will not enter heaven. Unfortunately for the souls of the hapless Jesleen and the lion's other victims, no remains were discovered. Jesleen's white bag, however, was left undisturbed in the riverbed, as a sign of respect.

Buekes took out his measuring tape, extending it from the lion's nose to the tip of its outstretched tail. Ten feet six inches. He measured its shoulder height, four feet even, half an inch taller than the bigger of Patterson's two man-eaters. No scales were available to weigh Hosek's lion, but much later, experts from the Field Museum in Chicago estimated that the lion went upward of 550 pounds. Indeed, the Man-eater of Mfuwe would turn out to be the biggest man-eating lion ever recorded, a fact that would come to light seven years later, when, following the script of Patterson's saga, Hosek donated the lion's mount to the Museum.

The camp staff were in as festive a mood as the villagers. Hosek, riding on the excitement, stayed up till past midnight. Some six hours after shooting the lion, he approached it again and was able to bring himself to touch its huge, maneless head.

The next morning, at breakfast, Cloete, smiling broadly, made a confession.

"Y'know, I'd made up my mind to never put my head down or doze off, because I was afraid. This lion, being a man-eater, just might decide to creep up and suddenly come into the blind."

Later, Hosek returned to the blind, which had been dismantled by the villagers, its grass thatch and bamboo poles saved as souvenirs. Hosek found a souvenir of his own—the spent cartridge from his rifle. It seemed to reflect his own mental and emotional condition. Looking around, he noticed how the landscape, so filled with menace just a short while ago, now appeared placid, dull, and lifeless, as if the absence of danger had somehow drained its vitality. He recalled a peculiar, poignant moment from the previous night, after he'd returned to camp. A young English woman, working as a wildlife researcher in the Luangwa Game Reserve, arrived to join in the festivities. Her name was Kathryn, she was from Oxford University, and she'd been in the bush for four years, sufficient time to learn that the rationalities of science are not all they're cracked up to be, that there are forms of knowledge not to be acquired by the examination of evidence or the testing of theories and hypotheses but only by listening to the older voices in the human mind. Certainly there was no evidence of a scientific nature to support the notion that the lion possessed supernatural powers, but Kathryn acted as if it were as true as Newton's laws of motion. Afflicted by the same spooky paralysis that had gripped Hosek, she looked at the animal from a distance, unable to draw closer. Hosek walked over to her and asked if she would like to inspect the lion, perhaps touch it. She said something odd—"I want to meet him.... No, not yet, but I will." The American told her that she didn't have time to wait; in a few minutes, the carcass was going to be skinned in preparation for the taxidermist. Kathryn remained motionless and kept murmuring "I will" as she stared at the lion. Finally Hosek asked if he could escort her, and she said, "OK." But only after he took her hand in his would she step forward to "meet" the legendary beast.

Man-eaters die hard, Hosek thought, slipping the cartridge case into his pocket. He drove back to camp, where Buekes presented him with the lion's skull and some of its bones. Hosek had been "Africanized," Buekes said, meaning that he'd discovered what it's like to live with sudden danger, lethal threats, and constant uncertainty, and those bones were symbols of his Africanizing. Hosek held them and felt a familiar rush of adrenaline, as if the man-eater still lived. And in his mind, it always would.

ACT ONE

LEGENDS

If the whole body of lion anecdote, from the days of the Assyrian Kings till the last year of the nineteenth century, were collated and brought together, it would not equal in tragedy or atrocity, in savageness or in sheer insolent contempt for man, armed or unarmed, white or black, the story of these two beasts.... To what a distance the whole story carries us back, and how impossible it becomes to account for the survival of primitive man against this kind of foe!
—from The Spectator, March 3, 1900

THERE ARE SOME similarities between Wayne Hosek's background and mine. I am also Chicago born and raised. And one weekend when I was in grammar school my father brought me to the Field Museum, a long drive from the suburb where we lived, through the three-flat and brick-bungalow neighborhoods on the west side into the Loop's shadowy canyons and the sunlit expanses of Grant Park beyond, then south down Lake Shore Drive to a vast, neoclassical building that, with its soaring Ionic columns and broad staircases, looked like the temples I'd seen in books or in Cecil B. DeMille's epics: a magical structure promising all the wonder absent from my quotidian life amid the split-levels and new shopping centers sprawling into the Illinois prairies beyond the smoky city. The museum delivered on its promise. Stanley Field Hall was another world, where under a vaulted ceiling three stories high the mounts of two African elephants stood on a pedestal, ears flared, tusks curving like enormous scimitars, and the Masai warriors in their bronzed immobility awaited with upraised spears the charge of the two big lions poised on replicated rock on the opposite side of the hall. The Masai's courage and the legend of the Tsavo man-eaters captivated me as much as they had the young Hosek and ignited a desire to someday go to that part of Africa on safari, a desire that was likewise not fulfilled until I was well into middle age, 58 years old, to be precise.

I was also in pursuit of lions, but there the similarities end. I went armed with a camera and notebook instead of a rifle because my purpose was not to shoot a killer cat but to lift the veils of legend that had shrouded the lions of Tsavo ever since Colonel Patterson's book made them notorious. Not to put too high a tone on it, my quest was to find out the truth about one of humankind's oldest myths, the myth of the rogue beast, the man-eater.

That word man-eater is profoundly disturbing. Instantly it dissolves hundreds of thousands of years of human progress and carries us back to our beginnings, when we were puny hominids, slouching across the African savanna where man was born, huddling in fireless caves, waiting for death to rush at us from the long grass. The thought of being devoured offends our sense of human dignity, subverts our cherished belief that we are higher beings—"the paragon of animals," to borrow a line from *Hamlet*. The man-eater's actions say to us, "I don't care if you're the President of the United States, the Queen of England, the inventor of the microchip, a bankable movie star, or an ordinary Joe or Jill, you're no paragon in my book, but the same as a zebra or gazelle—a source of protein. In fact, I'd rather hunt you, because you're slow and feeble."

Sharks and crocodiles attack and eat people. Among the big cats, leopards are more efficient killers of human beings than lions are, and as the citizens of rural India and Indonesia know very well, human flesh is a staple of the tiger's diet, which isn't believed to be true of the lion. Nevertheless, as a creator of primeval terror, the man-eating lion

resonates most powerfully in our minds, probably because the lion figures so deeply in our folklore, going back to a time long before man began
to write down the legends and tales grunted around the tribal fires:
Images of lions were painted on the cave walls of Pleistocene Europe.
Proceeding into recorded history, we read of Hercules subduing the
Nemean lion in hand-to-hand combat to demonstrate his superhuman
strength, of the prophet Daniel cast into a lion's den, of the Psalmist
who cries out, in the 22nd Psalm, "Save me from the lion's mouth."

Viewed in this light, Colonel Patterson's *The Man-Eaters of Tsavo*
can be seen as a saga that welds myth and reality. It describes actual
events, yet it reads like fiction, which may be why it has inspired two
Hollywood fantasies, *B'wana Devil* in 1952, the first 3-D movie, and
The Ghost and the Darkness in 1996. (Legend has it that those were
the nicknames the Indian laborers had given the Tsavo man-eaters.)
Today, 95 years after publication, it remains in print.

I read it for the first time when I was 16, after paying another
visit to the Field Museum. It gave me nightmares. I reread it 42 years
later, before leaving for Kenya's Tsavo National Park, and found that
it had not lost its power to terrify, to seize my imagination. That
seemed odd at first, for the prose in *The Man-Eaters of Tsavo* probably sounded a bit antiquated even in 1907, when Ezra Pound and
T. S. Eliot were laying the foundations for the modernist movement
in literature. To contemporary readers, its style is as far from the hip
postmodernism of, say, Don DeLillo as ultraviolet is from the black
end of the spectrum. It's a Victorian drawing room of a book,
scluttered with unnecessary adjectives, covered in the damask of dated
figures of speech, darkened by the heavy drapery of melodramatic
phrases. Yet that style, harking back to gothic tales like *The Castle
of Otranto* or *Frankenstein*, partly accounts for its ability to scare the
hell out of you and keep you turning the page.

Partly. The action and the subject matter more fully explain the book's appeal. It doesn't give you a transitory fright, like a good ghost story or a movie about the occult, but stays with you, infiltrating your subconscious, because you know it isn't a screenwriter's make-believe. Those were real lions, their victims were real people, and, oh, how you can picture their legs thrashing as they're dragged off into the darkness, just as helpless as a vole or mouse in the jaws of your pet cat; how you can hear their final screams as the lion crushes their skulls or delivers a thoracic bite, and then the sounds that Patterson listened to when he sat up in the tree: bones being crunched, the disgusting slurp of entrails ripped out and gulped down. The next morning, you gaze with Patterson at what's left—a complex human being, with a unique identity, with hopes, ambitions, and desires just like yours, reduced by a creature with a brain slightly larger than your fist to nothing more than a few fragments of bone and a bloodstain on the grass, speckled with bits of flesh. Beyond nausea and horror, you suffer a kind of metaphysical shock. Are we really the paragon of animals if a cat, a cat, for Christ's sake, can turn us into mere prey with so little effort? Or is our glorious self-image a delusion of our overblown egos? It's an insult even to ask such questions, much less to answer them. And the belief that lions generally turn man-eater only when they're too sick, old, or injured to pursue their normal prey adds to the insult. That is why Colonel Patterson referred to the marauding pair as brutes, savages, outlaws: They not only refused submission to man's supremacy but also refused to acknowledge it, a notion that I suspect troubles us as much as it did him. In our postindustrial, hyper-technological, hyper-urbanized world, we are accustomed to being in control. It's difficult to bend our minds around the idea that we can be part of the food chain—and not at the top, either—because we no longer see ourselves as part of nature. Indeed, we feel sorry for the natural

world in a way, embarking on various projects to preserve it, penning
it up in national parks and game reserves and wildlife sanctuaries,
which is of course another way of exerting control.

*

Iain Allan is at the wheel, driving me, my wife, Leslie, and photographer Rob Howard up the Ngong Road out of the crumbling, smog-
cloaked heart of Nairobi into the suburban highlands that are very
green (botanically) and very white (racially). We are heading for
Karen, named for Karen Blixen, a.k.a Isak Dinesen, the author of *Out
of Africa*. Her farm was in the town before it was a town. Karen is a
sedate place today, but it once had a wicked reputation. Josslyn Hay,
a British aristocrat, was found murdered near the junction of the
Ngong and Karen roads in January 1941, creating a scandal that
exposed the depraved hijinks of upper-crust colonials and years later
inspired James Fox to chronicle their misbehavior in *White Mischief*.

If that book is an indictment of imperialism, modern Nairobi is
a condemnation of independence. The slums girdling the city center
are swamps of hopelessness. The streets and sidewalks are falling
apart, prolonged power failures plunge entire neighborhoods into
almost nightly blackouts. Muggings, murders, and carjackings are so
common they have to be spectacular to make the front pages of the
daily newspapers, and with tourism declining, security service is probably the only growth industry left in the country. Almost every
restaurant and office building in the capital hires *askaris* as protection against criminal invasions.

Old hands bemoan Kenya's decay, telling nostalgic tales about a
nation that had once seemed exempt from the social, economic, and
political dysfunctions plaguing the rest of sub-Saharan Africa. In some

ways, it still is. At least it's been spared the hideous, genocidal conflict that turned Rwanda into a mass graveyard, the famines that
starved millions in Ethiopia, the intractable civil wars that have
brought chaos to Somalia, Sierra Leone, the Congo, and southern Sudan.
Nevertheless, an exploding population (from about 8.3 million souls
at independence in 1963 to more than 30 million today) has worked
hand in hand with the kleptocratic regime of President Daniel Arap
Moi to slowly but inexorably unravel Kenya's social fabric. Tribal
chieftains calling themselves ministers of parliament stay in power
by playing off ancient rivalries between Kikuyu and Luo, Turkana and
Samburu, Kamba and Mbere, plundering the public treasury, and leaving the masses to struggle for the scraps. Some, the more vigorous and
angry, aren't willing to struggle and aren't interested in scraps and take
whatever they can lay their hands on, often with violence. "Don't go
out at night," the pretty front desk clerk at the Norfolk Hotel warned
us. "Thugs in town, bandits in the countryside."

She didn't say anything about the suburbs, though it's obvious that
bucolic Karen must be a prime target for those thugs and bandits.
Askaris stand watch by the high steel gates and walls surrounding
graceful villas with barrel-tile roofs and expansive lawns and gardens;
the larger of these estates boast stables and riding rings. The roads
are paved now, the grove of tamarind and eucalyptus that appears in
photographs from the era has been replaced by a gas station. The atmosphere in Karen is far less rural than it once was, though vestiges of
rural life remain, like the broad, undeveloped pasture where some
Masai have established a cattle camp. Smoke from cooking fires curls
into the cool, highlands air; a few young Masai herd skinny cattle
alongside the road. Dressed in shorts and T-shirts instead of the
traditional red cloak, the *shupka,* and carrying herding sticks instead
of spears, they look nothing like the statues I'd seen, decades before,

in Stanley Field Hall of the Field Museum. I am a little disappointed, but Iain tells me that Masai still maintain a semblance of their old, nomadic life in the Masai Mara Reserve, near the Tanzanian border. The government prohibits them from spearing lions, an injunction they occasionally ignore, sometimes to rid themselves of a cattle killer, sometimes for old times' sake.

An askari opens a gate and we drive into a walled compound that seems a world away from grimy Nairobi: a fine, whitewashed villa, a guest house, an office, five acres of grass and shaded garden. Iain lives here with his second wife, Lu, a physician from Australia, a daughter by his first marriage, Jody, two young sons, Duncan and James, and a Rhodesian ridgeback and a rottweiler, who are present to deter intruders, in case the askaris fall down on the job. Dinesen's farmhouse, made internationally famous by Meryl Streep and Robert Redford in the film version of her book, is just next door. It's now a museum. A brisk wind is blowing down from the hazy Ngong Hills, the air is bracing, more like northern California's than the tropics. Iain parks the Land Rover under a carport that shelters several other vehicles, all an identical dark green, with the name of his safari company, Tropical Ice Ltd., painted in white on the doors.

The name refers to his specialty—leading treks to the frozen summit of Kilimanjaro. This ruddy-faced six-footer also takes small parties on walking safaris throughout Kenya and Tanzania and, when he's not doing that, he scales mountains and rock climbs as a hobby, activities that have given him the legs of a professional soccer player. He belongs to the last generation with memories of the colonial era, having migrated with his Scottish mother and father to Kenya in 1956, when he was eight years old and the country belonged to the British Empire (upon which the sun was then swiftly setting). His father, an accountant for a British firm, stayed on after independence, and Iain later became a

Kenyan citizen. White Kenyans, who are mostly descendants of colonial settlers, compose a tribe of their own, a tribe that enjoys the privileges of their forebears, like fine houses staffed by servants, but at a price. Iain grumbles about it as we stroll toward the main house.

"I can't stand this mob in power, but I can't do or say much about it," he says in his British-Kenyan accent. "A white Kenyan had better be apolitical."

He is probably thinking about the country's most renowned Caucasian citizen, the very political and outspoken Richard Leakey, son of the world-famous anthropologist, former head of the Kenyan Wildlife Service, which under his command brought an end to elephant and rhino poaching in Kenya. Leakey was also appointed to rid the Kenyan civil service of corruption. Some years ago, he was crippled when his private plane crashed under suspicious circumstances.

We settle down in Iain's living room, which, white-stucco-walled and wood-beamed, could have been lifted from a ranch house in the American Southwest. The bookshelves are filled with Africana, including *The Man-Eaters of Tsavo* and *The Lunatic Express*, Charles Miller's account of the building of the Uganda railroad. Iain recommends it for its chapter on Colonel Patterson's experiences, which he thinks is better than the original because it's free of Patterson's purple passages. He isn't shy about expressing his none-too-lofty opinion of Patterson as a mediocre hunter, a martinet, a caricature of the imperial *pukka-sahib*.

The conversation turns from Kenyan politics to the man-eaters and lions in general. They are the reason we're here on this fine clear day, one month into a new century and millennium.

There aren't too many advantages to growing older, although publications like *Modern Maturity* would like us to believe otherwise. The images of healthy retirees pedaling mountain bikes through charming landscapes and frisky geriatrics hopping into bed for a night of senior sex are an expression more of hope than reality. Yet there is one plus to aging: Sometimes, if you're lucky, you're presented with an opportunity to live out a youthful dream and discover that you have, at last, the time and money to do it.

After the century turned and my personal calendar flipped one page closer to 60, I reread *The Man-Eaters of Tsavo*, along with *Death in the Long Grass*, an engrossing book about dangerous game by the American hunter and author Peter Capstick. Both reawakened my old yearnings to go to Africa, even though most of wild Africa had surrendered its authenticity to the tourist industry. Among the parts of the continent that had not completely lost their primeval soul was Tsavo National Park in Kenya, the least visited park in the country and at 8,200 square miles (roughly the size of Massachusetts), one of the largest in the world. The bridge that Colonel Patterson built and the hills where he tracked the man-eaters lie within the park's boundaries, so I determined to go there.

Eventually, I was put in contact with Iain Allan, who knows Tsavo as well as anyone. The region is best known for its elephant herds—Denys Finch-Hatton, Dinesen's dashing lover, hunted them early in the 20th century, and Tsavo was the battleground in the 1970s and 1980s for the wars Leakey's rangers waged against Somali ivory poachers. However, I was interested in its lions. The reputation Patterson conferred on them was deserved, Iain told me. They were more ferocious than the lions of the Serengeti Plains, and they looked different as well: The males did not sport magnificent manes but short crests resembling Mohawk haircuts and scruffy side whiskers; some had no manes at all and looked like oversize females. A research team from the Field Museum in Chicago was now in Tsavo to study the cats, an effort long overdue, Iain said. The lions of Tsavo were a riddle. No one had any idea how many were in the park; a census had never been taken, nor was much known about their natural history, ranges, and habits.

It isn't often, in our overmapped, overcrowded, overstudied world, that you hear about an animal that is a mystery. I had to see these big felines with their frightening image, shrouded in myth. Could I, perhaps, open up the shroud a little, even though I'm not a natural historian, much less a scientist? In any event, that would be my quest.

I began to do some research. I got in touch with three members of the Field Museum's research team: the leader, Dr. Bruce Patterson (no relation to the colonel), curator of mammals, Dr. Julian Kerbis Peterhans, adjunct curator of mammals, and Thomas Gnoske, whose title, chief preparator of birds, sounded out of sync with the project. It turned out that preparing birds for exhibit was what Gnoske, an artist by training, did for a living; his avocation, his passion, was big cats, lions in particular. The three were back in the United States after weeks in Tsavo. Two of their colleagues were still there, a Kenyan zoologist named Samuel Andanje and Dr. Chapurukha Kusimba, an anthropologist and the museum's assistant curator of African archaeology and ethnology. The Tsavo Research Project, which the museum was conducting in collaboration with the Kenya Wildlife Service (KWS), was an ambitious undertaking, one that already had stirred up some controversy in scientific circles. It began in the early fall of 1998 and would take 30 months to complete, its main purpose to remove maneless lions from the list of nature's mysteries.

Unmaned lions are found throughout Africa, with a heavy concentration in Tsavo, a land of arid scrub belonging to a belt of inhospitable brush that extends for 3,000 miles along the East African coast, from Somalia in the north to Botswana in the south. Throughout the month of January 2000, I communicated with

Patterson, Kerbis Peterhans, and Gnoske by e-mail and phone and learned that no one knows why some lions lack manes, in part because no one knows for certain why nature decided to furnish lions with manes in the first place. It's the only cat, wild or domestic, to display such ornamentation.

According to one theory, a mane protects a lion's neck from potentially fatal bites in battles with his rivals; according to another, lions use their manes to control prides, leonine families that usually consist of one or two males and up to 20 females and cubs. As a pride leader, a male has exclusive breeding rights, which he'll defend with his life. The trouble with this monopoly is that there are always young bachelors eager to challenge the incumbent and take over. On most occasions, this means a fight, which can result in serious injury to both combatants, and sometimes in death for the loser. If the challenger takes the prize, the first thing he does is kill any young cubs fathered by the deposed champion. Infanticide causes a nursing female to go into heat in a few days, and she will then mate with the new boss. Not a pretty picture, but it's nature's way of ensuring that the new pride leader gets an immediate opportunity to pass on his genetic legacy. What does the lioness get out of the deal? Insurance that resources will be devoted to her litter, and the fittest male to defend her and her cubs.

But male lions are reluctant warriors. Their aim in life, besides mating, is to lie around in the sun, surrounded by harems of females who do most of the hunting. They don't want to spend too much time and energy warding off youthful intruders. It is thought (though this isn't absolutely certain) that mane size correlates to physical health and testosterone levels; a sexually active male produces more testosterone than a celibate one, and, with access to plenty of females to supply him with food as well as sex, he will grow a large, imposing mane. Therefore, goes the theory, a big mane is both an advertisement and a deterrent. It announces that the pride leader is in good shape: He obviously has the resources to support a physiological luxury (rather like a human male whose new Ferrari signals a fat stock portfolio). Also, it warns potential rivals that its owner hasn't lost a battle in a long time, as male lions tend to shed their manes after a loss in combat. In short, a large mane is a sign of a lion's ability to defend his pride, and a challenger who sees a pride leader adorned with one will think twice before going to war. He may wait until he's bigger and stronger or go off in search of a pride led by a male past his prime.

Rummaging around in the annals of current lion research, I discovered another possible reason for a mane: attracting females. That theory is being developed by Peyton West, a Ph.D. candidate at the University of Minnesota. Working in Tanzania with her faculty adviser, Dr. Craig Packer, one of the world's leading experts on the African lion, West's experiments indicated that size does matter for lionesses: The bigger the mane, the more attracted she is to its possessor. Color matters as well. In lion society, ladies favor dark manes.

So where did that leave Tsavo's maneless males? If a large mane was so important, why were theirs abbreviated or nonexistent altogether? That was the question Bruce Patterson and the others were trying to answer. One idea involved the dense thickets of commiphora bushes that blanket Tsavo.

These nasty shrubs—called wait-a-bits or *ngoja kidogo* in Swahili—bristle with curved thorns that can claw the shirt off a man's back in minutes and leave his flesh looking as if he's been wrestling with a bale of barbed wire. In such an environment, a mane's liabilities could outweigh its advantages, so Tsavo lions may have adapted by getting rid of theirs. Another, simpler reason is that the thorns simply rip out mane hair.

Patterson's team, however, were tending toward a more exotic explanation: Tsavo lions are genetically different from common lions, *Panthera leo*.

This intriguing hypothesis was based on prey density and its effect on leonine social structure. In arid regions like Tsavo, prey animals are scarcer than in places like the Serengeti plains, populated by vast herds of zebra and wildebeest (as many as 1.3 million of the latter roam the Serengeti). A comparatively scant food supply would preclude lions from living in large prides, and indeed, Patterson, Kerbis Peterhans, and Gnoske told me that the prides they'd observed in Tsavo appeared to be smaller than elsewhere.

Small prides would have two consequences. One, females would not congregate in large groups that could be defended by one or two males, which would reduce the role of sexual selection in mane growth; two, the males could not rely on females to do most, if not all, of the hunting, which is how things are done on the plains. This would enhance the role of natural selection in restricting or eliminating mane growth. Being a luxury, the product of the plains males' leisured life, a mane would be less likely to grow on a working lion; his physical resources would be devoted to hunting and survival, not to developing an extravagant ornament.

To test the hypothesis, in the fall of 1998 the team collected DNA samples from dead lions culled in the KWS problem animal operations. If genetic differences account for manelessness, it would mean that Tsavo's lions represent a distinct lineage within the lion family, possibly descended from a "clan" that had lost their manes due to the evolutionary forces of natural selection.

Patterson told me in one of our electronic correspondences that tens of thousands of DNA base pairs were being sequenced and submitted for study to a genetics laboratory in the Brookfield Zoo, near

Chicago. The researchers had also hoped to gather tissue samples from living lions for DNA analysis by shooting them with biopsy darts. Finally, they'd requested permission from the KWS to remove several young male lions from the park and raise them in captivity to see if they would grow manes outside their natural habitat. If genetic causes for manelessness couldn't be found, and if the team was unable to relate mane variation to prey density, then Tsavo lions should be able to grow normal manes in a different environment.

No results were yet in, Patterson said. That's where matters stood as I prepared to go to Africa: A lot of studying had been done, but no conclusions reached. There had been some disappointments. The team had planned to conduct field surveys to census Tsavo's lion population and identify where maneless lions lived and in what size prides, but the dense, tangled vegetation, combined with the limited manpower of the KWS, conspired against the researchers. "Existing information is grossly inadequate for estimating [the population]," Patterson wrote to me, "and the park is not currently pursuing the monitoring needed to determine it." Another phase of the project—to survey lions's ranges by placing satellite collars on selected animals—had been frustrated by ecopolitics, which had likewise prevented the team from removing lion cubs from the park and from darting adults for DNA samples. The KWS strives to keep Tsavo wild, or at least to maintain an appearance of wildness for the benefit of visitors. It discourages scientists from collaring, capturing, and darting animals, under the theory that tourists don't come to Tsavo to see researchers brandishing dart guns, or lions or any other wildlife walking around with radio collars draped around their necks.

I couldn't say it was a philosophy I opposed. By definition, a wilderness should be a wild place, not an open-air laboratory. Still, I was a little disappointed that the Field Museum team, better than halfway through the project, did not know as much as I'd hoped they would. The difference between science and journalism, I suppose: The former is patient, the latter anything but.

My disappointment, however, was leavened with some excitement about a novel idea that Gnoske and Kerbis Peterhans were developing independent of Patterson. Their conjecture—it was too nascent to be called a hypothesis, much less a theory—took the possibility of genetic variation a step further. Tsavo lions could be a feline "missing link" between modern lions and the unmaned cave lions of the Pleistocene (*Panthera leo spelaea*), which went extinct somewhere between 8,000 and 25,000 years ago. Gnoske and Kerbis Peterhans were suggesting that *Panthera leo* is the most evolved of the species—the latest model, so to speak—whereas certain morphological differences in Tsavo lions indicate that they are closest to the primitive ancestor of all lions. If they were right, then the commonly held belief that all African lions belong to the same species would be disproved. The continent would be home to two distinct breeds of cat, the modern lion of the plains and a lion that is something close to a living fossil.

Gnoske and Kerbis Peterhans weren't ready to go public with their, well, let's call it a hypothesis. Further work would be needed, much of it involving measurements of lion skulls and other such morphological matters; but they promised that they soon would have the data to support it. The idea struck me as not totally outlandish: Geneticists studying African elephants, I'd learned, were on the verge of declaring that the continent's reclusive forest elephants were as distinct from the herds that roam the savannas as lions are from leopards. Two separate species of elephant, why not two species of lion? Anyhow, I found the unorthodoxy of Gnoske and Kerbis Peterhans's research appealing. The romantic in me cast them as renegades, running off the scientific reservation on a quest that would either lead to a startling new discovery or to ridicule by their peers.

I was particularly captivated by how their idea related to man-eating among lions.

Conflict between humans and big cats is one of the fields Kerbis Peterhans specializes in. It's almost axiomatic among naturalists and scientists that lions turn to man-eating only when injuries or old age prevents them from pursuing their normal prey. However, a colleague of the two researchers had come up with tantalizing hints that there may be some lions with a predisposition to prey on humans, even when strong and healthy enough to bring down a zebra or buffalo. The explanation for this behavior would then subtly but significantly shift from the pathological to the Darwinian: Conditions in a lion's environment, as much as changes in its physiology, can drive it to hunt people.

Still, such a beast poses a mystery, and the key to that mystery may be found in the lions of Tsavo. Gnoske and Kerbis Peterhans seconded some of Iain's observations. Tsavo males, in addition to absent or abbreviated manes, are distinguished from male plains lions by their size. The latter average three feet at the shoulder and weigh between 385 and 410 pounds; the former are up to a foot taller and can tip the scales at about 460 to 520 pounds, giving you a cat the size of a small grizzly bear. Gnoske and Kerbis Peterhans said there are reasons for the Tsavo lion's greater bulk: thin prey base and smaller prides. Males share in the hunting and may do most of it, not only because they lack sufficiently large harems but also because the predominant herd animal in Tsavo is the Cape buffalo. One of the largest, strongest, meanest creatures on Earth, the Cape buffalo grows up to 1,800 pounds and is armed with curved horns like sharpened concrete. As many as half a dozen lionesses would be required to bring down a mature buffalo, and a couple of them would most likely be killed or badly injured in the process. That's why, said Gnoske and Kerbis Peterhans, Tsavo's males are such bruisers; their massive shoulders and fore-bodies are suited to grappling with prey that weighs as much as a small car.

Even so, they stand a good chance of suffering a broken jaw or some other serious wound. It's true that plains lions also prey on buffalo, but they generally don't have to, what with zebra and wildebeest herds in such abundance. Tsavo lions don't have that choice. Fighting with buffalo much more often than their Serengeti counterparts, they are that much more likely to get hurt, and therefore more likely to go after domestic cattle and people as a result of injuries incurred. That fits in with prevailing explanations, but with this twist: A lion that becomes a man-eater because it's injured doesn't go back to its traditional prey even after it recovers. It has discovered, Gnoske told me in a phone interview, that eating people "is an easy way to make a living."

Interestingly, one of the Tsavo man-eaters had a severely broken canine tooth with an exposed root. The tooth was well worn and polished, and the entire skull had undergone "cranial remodeling" in response to the trauma, indicating that the injury was an old one. Colonel Patterson's book and Miller's *The Lunatic Express* record that at least one man-eater had been prowling about Tsavo before Patterson arrived with his bridge-building gangs, in April 1898. A railroad surveyor, O. R. Preston, lost several members of his crew to a man-eater near the Tsavo River early in 1897. When Preston and his men searched for remains, they found the skulls and bones of individuals who had been killed earlier. There is no proof that an injury was the lion's "motive" for turning man-eater, but it's a plausible explanation. He might have been kicked in the jaw by a buffalo and lost a tooth and stuck to preying on humans after the injury healed, having found out how safe and convenient it was. The arrival of the railroad workers, packed into tent camps, must have struck him as manna from leonine heaven.

But what about his partner, who was in prime health? The researchers speculated that an epidemic of rinderpest disease, a deadly virus that attacks cattle, may have played a role. In the early 1890s, the disease, likely to have been spread by cattle imported from India, all but wiped out domestic cattle and buffalo in parts of East Africa. With its usual prey eliminated, the starving lion had to look to villages and construction camps.

Another, more disquieting explanation lay elsewhere, with the elephants of Tsavo. Slaughtering them for their ivory is a very old story, going back as far as ancient times. Caravans once passed through Tsavo laden with tusks. They carried other "goods" as well: slaves who'd been captured in the interior for sale in the slave markets of Zanzibar and the Swahili coast.

Gnoske and Kerbis Peterhans's colleague, Chap Kusimba, grew up in Kenya with the story of the man-eaters and Colonel Patterson's epic hunt for them. Kusimba, whose specialty is ancient Swahili cultures, studied the traditional caravan routes and learned that the Tsavo River was an important stop where the traders rested their camels, refreshed themselves, and restocked their water supplies before moving on. However, Kusimba believes they disposed of unnecessary cargo—captives too sick or weak to travel farther—first, abandoning them to die.

Spinning off from that, Gnoske and Kerbis Peterhans wove another thread into their tapestry of assumptions. With so many corpses around, scavengers in the vicinity had an abundance to feed on. The scavenging most likely started with hyenas and then was taken up by lions. From there, it wasn't a big step for the cats to go after living people. That possibly explains the myths about "evil spirits"; the men who mysteriously disappeared from the caravans' campsites had been seized not by devils but by lions. The slave and ivory caravans had passed through Tsavo for centuries, and that leads to the disturbing aspect of the theory. The lion is a social animal, capable of adopting cultural traditions that are passed on from generation to generation. If a lioness is hunting people, her young will grow to regard them as a normal part of their diet and pass that knowledge on to their young. The upshot is that Patterson's man-eaters may have done what they did not because they were handicapped by injuries or because their traditional prey had been wiped out, but because they came from a man-eating lineage so long that an appetite for human flesh was ingrained in them. Stalking and devouring the paragon of animals wasn't the exception, but the rule.

Hypotheses and theories require verification through the process that's known as peer review: A researcher's assertions must be tested and examined by other scientists before they are accepted as true. Confirming evidence from amateurs, no matter how knowledgeable or gifted, is generally dismissed, but in support of Gnoske, Kerbis-Peterhans, and Kusimba, I offer the following in all humility. It comes from Peter Hathaway Capstick who had years of experience in Africa. In *Death in the Long Grass,* Capstick presents a table compiled by one Peter Turnbull-Kemp, a South African game ranger, on the age and condition of 89 known man-eaters at death: 91 percent of the killers were in either "good" or "fair" condition; 13.3 percent were old but uninjured; and a mere 4.4 percent were both aged and injured by any cause, including man.

"Aside from those lions forced through injury to a life of homicide, there are many ways that normal lions may take up man-eating," Capstick continues. "They may be the offspring of man-eating parents, weaned on human flesh and taught to hunt man as a normal activity....There are many natural catastrophes, such as plagues and epidemics that litter the bush with corpses, that may lead to lions' learning to eat man...."

Was that the case with the Man-eater of Mfuwe? I'd come across Wayne Hosek's story while visiting the Field Museum's website. Zambia's Luangwa Valley is a thousand miles from Tsavo, but his lion was maneless, and also far bigger than average. I called Hosek in California, and he told me that some experts had found possible evidence of bone cancer in the lion's jaw, but it was far from conclusive. Otherwise, there were no signs of injury or sickness, nor had any plagues depleted the numbers of its normal prey.

Was there some linkage among manelessness, big body size, and a proclivity to prey on people? Could the lions of Tsavo be a throwback to primitive lions or some heretofore unknown subspecies? Could they tell us anything new about the king of beasts? Those questions, as much as a longing for an African adventure, were what prompted me to go to Tsavo.

Not that I thought that I could even begin to answer them. If a whole team of professionals had been stumped, what chance was there for a writer who'd gotten a C in high school biology? I wanted to introduce myself to Tsavo and get in some face time with its lions as preparation for accompanying Gnoske and Kerbis Peterhans on an expedition they planned to mount within the next year.

I bounce a few of the above questions off Iain after we move outside to have tea and coffee. He is no big-cat biologist, but 28 years of leading safaris allow him to speak with the authority of direct experience. There, in a garden scented by frangipani and hibiscus, he says that there is no doubt in his mind that Tsavo lions are different. Though he can't say if they have some built-in taste for human flesh, he does paint them in dark colors.

"They're total opportunists, all lean muscle, just killing machines that will attack and eat anything, even African hares," he says, and, echoing Dr. Patterson, explains that Tsavo is a harsh, penurious place.

"So these lions have to take what they can get. They're also more cunning than plains lions, often killing from ambush instead of stalk and spring. There's something sinister about them."

I mention Gnoske and Kerbis Peterhans's observations that Tsavo males do most of the hunting.

Iain nods and responds with a story, illustrative of the males' strength as well as their cleverness.

"I was walking along the Galana River recently and came on two big male lions attacking a buffalo. One would rush it from the front and, as it lowered its horns to meet the charge, the other would come in from behind and rake its haunches. When it whirled around to meet that threat, the first lion would leap at its back and tear open another wound. That went on for a while. Buffalo aren't dumb. That one figured out what was going on and backed into thick thorn scrub to guard its rear. It was bleeding a lot. Lions aren't dumb either. Those two simply ambled off and sat in the shade of a tree to wait for the buff to grow weak from loss of blood, which it did in about half an hour. When it was too weak to use its horns and its great black head lowered, the lions charged in and finished it off."

We adjourn for dinner at Carnivore, a popular tourist restaurant near Wilson Field, the airport from which Beryl Markham flew west with the night and Finch-Hatton took off in his biplane to hunt elephant. "Tell them I'll be in Tsavo," he would say, donning his goggles, "them" being his pals at the Muthaiga Country Club, the sanctum sanctorum of colonial settlers. Carnivore serves grilled game meats. Eland, gazelle, zebra, but I don't see buffalo on the menu.

I DON'T IMAGINE "tell them I'll be in Tsavo" would sound quite so jaunty coming from me. I don't have a gram of Denys's aristocratic flair. I'm leaving Nairobi in a Land Rover, not an Avro Avian, and Tsavo is hardly the edge-of-the-Earth place it was in Denys's day but accessible to any chubby day-tripper in a budget minibus.

Clad in his bush clothes—a stained, wide-brimmed hat, shorts, sneakers—Iain is at the wheel. Clive Ward, his number two and climbing partner, is in the passenger seat. Clive is a spare man, with short, graying hair, chiseled features, and a clipped way of speaking that sometimes leaves the words trapped in his mouth. He possesses an ascetic handsomeness that reminds me of a British officer in a war movie: the quiet one who dies with pointless heroism in some idiotic attack. Clive tells us that he led safaris in Namibia before coming to Kenya and mutters something about a land-mine explosion that lacerated one of his legs—an injury that hasn't hindered him. Together, he and Iain have scaled most of the world's major peaks, from Alaska to South America to the Himalaya, and they have led so many parties up Kilimanjaro that the ascent has become to them something akin to climbing a flight of stairs. Clive belongs to a class of Englishmen I've run into over the years: Restless and deracinated, they roam a post-imperial Earth, preferring the air of lost colonies to the air of home.

We roll on down the Mombasa Highway, which parallels the tracks of the "Lunatic Express," and pass slow trucks spewing what looks like volcanic ash. The road is narrow and bumpy, a slapdash strip of asphalt that runs across the Kapiti and Athi Plains, where Teddy Roosevelt hunted but no one hunts anymore, first because big-game hunting was outlawed in Kenya in 1977, and second because there isn't much game left to shoot, thanks to poaching and the transformation of wildlands into farmland by Kenya's ever-growing population.

The hunting ban, Iain mentions, turned him from an employee into an entrepreneur.

"I got to know Bill Woodley in the mid-'70s," he says, mentioning a famed Tsavo game warden. "After talking things over, I realized I could do walking safaris like the old hunting safaris, except you shoot with cameras instead of guns. The old white hunters wanted nothing to do with photographic safaris, so I had the wide-open field to myself."

The biggest achievement of his career occurred in 1996, when he and Woodley's two sons, Danny and Bongo, led a foot safari that was something out of the annals of early African exploration: a 250-mile trek from the summit of Kilimanjaro, down through Tsavo and the coastal plains to the shores of the Indian Ocean. They were accompanied by mountaineer Rick Ridgeway, who chronicled the adventure in *The Shadow of Kilimanjaro*.

Continuing our drive southward, we enter the Kikwezi Plains, grasslands hemmed by knobby volcanic hills. A pale chanting goshawk perches on a telephone pole at the roadside, a black-shouldered kite on the wires. An exquisite bird with an iridescent blue breast flies past the windshield—a lilac-breasted roller. Iain glances at the landscape, gestures at the highway.

"This was a dirt road back in the 1950s, and when we drove down to Mombasa, we used to make a game of counting the rhino."

Leslie reminds him of all the rhino she had seen on a safari nearly 30 years ago, and he grunts an affirmation that is also a kind of non-verbal elegy. It reminded me of why I wanted her with me in Africa. She would provide more than companionship: I'd had no experience with East Africa and its wildlife; she'd had some, even though it was a long time ago. Except for a small herd in a rhino recovery reserve in Tsavo, the ugly, ponderous, yet somehow grand rhinoceros, a living relic of prehistoric times, has all but vanished from East Africa. About 400 black rhino survive in Kenya, and there are still fewer of the larger white rhino (the name doesn't have anything to do with its color, but is a corruption of an Afrikaans word, "*weit*," meaning "wide"—a reference to the width of the animal's mouth). In the 1970s and 1980s, a new status symbol arose among Arabs rich on petro royalties: Yemeni daggers with handles and scabbards made from rhino horn. They were more popular than gold Rolexes. The demand fueled a vigorous poaching trade. Efficient gangs armed with assault rifles slaughtered rhino by the thousands, and whenever the dagger-handle market became saturated, the poachers fell back on the traditional sales to the Far East, where the horns were ground up into medicinal powders and aphrodisiacs. Looking out at cattle and spotted goats grazing on the old rhino range, at the swarms of humanity walking along the road or sitting in the shade of the trees selling papaya heaped in straw baskets, I contemplate a wildlife holocaust committed to satisfy a lust for ornamentation and to stiffen penises in Asia. A familiar depression settles over me. If Thoreau was right, that in wildness do we find our salvation, then I guess we are damned. All we can do is mourn the lost wonder and wildness of the world and fight rear-guard actions to save what's left from ourselves. It isn't the free market that's at fault, or socialism or industrialism or any other ism; there are too many of us.

The road takes us into a typical rural town: a few shabby shops, a few fruit-and-vegetable stalls, a low, block-brick bar advertising Tusker beer. A sign announces the name of the settlement—Simba, which means "lion" in Swahili. It lifts me out of my melancholy, taking me back to a time, not terribly long ago in historical terms, when wilderness and wildness were considered the adversaries of civilization, and the last thing anyone wanted to do was to preserve them.

Colonel Patterson tells the story of what happened in *The Man-Eaters of Tsavo.*

In 1900, at a whistle stop on the East African railroad called Kimaa, a big male lion had taken up residence in the vicinity and developed a zest for members of the railway staff. Among others, he'd carried off a signalman, a stationmaster, a brakeman, and the driver of the pumping station. At one point, ravenous for a meal, he climbed up on the station house roof and attempted to tear off the corrugated iron plates to get at the telegrapher, who tapped out this message to the traffic manager in Nairobi: "Lion fighting with station. Send urgent succor."

Patterson doesn't say if succor was sent, but the lion gave up, its paws bloodied. Succor did arrive by train on June 6 in the form of a British police superintendent named C. H. Ryall. He was accompanied by two friends, Huebner and Parenti. They were traveling to Nairobi, but when they heard about the man-eater, they decided to stay the night and try to shoot it. Their carriage was detached from the train and bumped off to a siding near the station, where, due to the unfinished state of the line, the carriage did not stand level but listed sharply to one side, a small detail that was to have disastrous consequences.

The three men spent the afternoon looking for signs of the lion, found none, and returned to the carriage for dinner. Afterward, Patterson writes, "They all sat up on guard for some time; but the only noticeable thing they saw was what they took to be two very bright and steady glowworms. After events proved that these could have been nothing else than the eyes of the man-eater steadily watching them all the time and studying their every movement."

Later, Ryall volunteered to stand the first watch while his companions slept, Huebner on a high berth on one side, Parenti on the floor. Evidently, after watching for a long time, Ryall concluded that the lion wasn't going to appear; he lay down on a lower berth and dozed off. Colonel Patterson conjectures about what happened next.

No sooner had Ryall fallen asleep, than "the cunning man-eater began cautiously to stalk the three sleepers. In order to reach the little platform at the end of the carriage, he had to mount two very high steps from the railway line, but these he managed to negotiate successfully and in silence. The door from this platform into the carriage was a sliding one on wheels...and as it was probably not quite shut, or at any rate not secured in any way, it was an easy matter for the lion to thrust in a paw and shove it open. But owing to tilt of the carriage and to his great extra weight on the one side, the door slid to and snapped into the lock the moment he got his body right in, thus leaving him shut up with the three sleeping men in the compartment."

The lion sprang for Ryall, planting his hind feet on Parenti, his forepaws on the police superintendent. Awakened by Ryall's loud cry, Huebner leaped from his bunk onto the lion's back, in an attempt to escape through a second sliding door into the servants' quarters.

He managed this not inconsiderable feat (busy dispatching Ryall, the lion ignored Huebner) and squeezed in with "the trembling coolies." A moment later, Huebner and the servants heard a crash and the carriage lurched violently to one side: The lion had broken through one of the windows, carrying Ryall in his jaws. Released, Parenti jumped from the floor and through a window on the opposite side of the carriage, fleeing for the safety of one of the station's outbuildings. Ryall's remains—and we can be sure they didn't amount to much— were found the next morning a quarter of a mile away in the bush and taken to Nairobi for burial.

As for the lion, Patterson writes, "The terrible brute...was caught in an ingenious trap constructed by one of the railway staff. He was kept on view for several days, and then shot."

I summarize this tale for the benefit of my wife and traveling companions, and it prompts Iain to recall a missionary's memoir that he'd read in the library of the Royal Geographic Society in London.

"He and his wife were camped near the Tsavo bridge after Patterson shot the first lion but before he killed the second. They were kept awake all night by this most awful, evil, mournful wailing and moaning of the second lion. It was mourning the death of its friend."

At first blush, that sounds like excessive anthropomorphizing; however, as any pet owner can tell you, humanlike emotions aren't unknown among animals. Sage, my English setter hunting dog, expresses affection, happiness, and sadness, and our pet cat, a charming fellow named Ditto, suffers loneliness when we are gone and shows pleasure when we return. Male lions, I'd learned in some of my research, often form bachelor groups before they're ready to take over a pride, spending years hunting and wandering together. You can assume that some sort of rudimentary camaraderie develops among them. It's possible that Ghost and Darkness were a pair of hunting brothers, and that Darkness was indeed bereft after his buddy's death. His sorrow, however, may not have been devoid of the self-interest that rules the natural world. During the three weeks between the shooting of the two lions, there were no known attacks on Patterson's workers, leading some observers to wonder if Ghost, the larger and presumably the older, did the killing while Darkness merely shared in the spoils. The "awful...wailing and moaning" the missionaries heard may therefore have been Darkness expressing not grief but the loss of his breadwinner.

Approaching Tsavo, the road improves considerably. It's wider and smoother, with dividing lines and a recognizable shoulder. The Chinese had rebuilt the highway between the park and the coast, presumably to make it easier for day-tripping tourists from the Mombasa resorts to get to the park and back in time for dinner. To the west, the dark green Chyulu Hills rise to heights of 7,000 feet, and eastward, slate blue in the harsh afternoon light, the Yatta Escarpment looms over the landscape, its top as flat as the deck of an aircraft carrier—the longest lava ridge in the world, Clive informs us. The land slopes gently down toward the Tsavo River. The Tsavo bridge appears ahead, resting on stone pillars against which the reddish brown river pushes and forms dancing riffles. Diesel locomotives hauling freight and passengers still pass over it, more than a century after its construction, testimony that John H. Patterson knew how to build a bridge, and his Indian coolies how to do a job right the first time.

We stop to take photographs, trying to imagine the scene 102 years ago, the work crews lowering the steel girders and wood beams onto the stone piers, track gangs spiking down the track, their labors interrupted by flash floods that turn the Tsavo into a racing sluice, tearing trees out by the roots—"whirling them along like straws," Patterson wrote. Hard enough without the terror of being attacked by man-eating lions. I picture those anonymous Indians, hearing the news in their home villages that laborers are wanted in far-off Africa, signing up for a few rupees a day but with the hope that those few will put them ahead of life's curve for once; then the long sail across the Indian Ocean in some stinking steamer, jammed in together, cheek by jowl, until they dock at Mombasa for the overland journey to the railhead and weeks of backbreaking labor in the downpours of the wet, the heat of the dry, and endless nights listening to that sound out in the bush, *wauugh-aaraRRAR unh-unh-unh,* waiting for the roars to grow silent and the cry to pass from camp to camp, "Watch out, brothers! The devil is coming!" I wish a plaque had been erected to those men, listing the names of the dead. They, too, are ghosts of Tsavo, and I would like to know who they were, though a name doesn't tell you anything.

Between the bridge and the Chyulu Hills are the Ngulia Hills, a range of volcanic knobs, covered in scrub, through which beige slabs of gneiss protrude like the ruins of some lost city. Somewhere in them is the "Man-eaters' Den," the discovery of which constitutes one of the more peculiar episodes in Colonel Patterson's book.

After he'd eliminated the two "brutes" and work resumed on the bridge, Patterson decided to explore the hills and do some recreational hunting while he waited for a shipment of construction materials to arrive. He was in a dry riverbed, tracking a rhino, when he spotted something that stopped him cold: "I saw on the other side a fearsome-looking cave which seemed to run back for a considerable distance under the rocky bank," Patterson wrote, in typically melodramatic fashion. "Round the entrance and inside the cavern I was thunderstruck to find a number of human bones with here, and there a copper bangle such as the natives wear. Beyond all doubt, the man-eaters' den!"

After taking a photograph (which is printed in *The Man-Eaters of Tsavo*), he left his find, and from that day in early 1899 until recently its location was lost to history. Patterson's characterization of it as a lion's den has aroused controversy and skepticism among naturalists and zoologists for a century: Lions are not known to be denning animals (the tale of the prophet Daniel notwithstanding). They don't stash their kills in caves or dens because they don't have to; they eat them on the spot.

In 1996, Chap Kusimba, who was working at an archaeology site near Mombasa, took a break to visit Tsavo National Park and get permission to search for the cave. His belief was that Patterson had not uncovered a lion's den but a burial ground belonging to the Taita people, who had once inhabited the park. He got permission but couldn't find the cave. Early the next year, Kerbis Peterhans made an attempt, accompanied by his wife, Pamela Austin, and Samuel Andanje, a Kenyan zoologist. They also failed. Then, in March 1997, Kerbis Peterhans returned with Gnoske to find the cave and determine if it really had been occupied by lions. Kerbis Peterhans was fairly sure that it was a hyena den, but he couldn't be positive until he examined the bones Patterson had uncovered for the distinctive gnaw marks made by hyena teeth. He, Gnoske, and Andanje, joined by four KWS rangers, made extensive searches southwest of the Tsavo River bridge—the direction Patterson said he'd followed on his excursion. They battled ferocious heat and slashing wait-a-bits, crawled up streambeds and into offshoots on a quest that was regarded as quixotic. The hunt was even mentioned in a guidebook, which characterized it as "absurd." Indeed, it seemed so: The men found nothing that remotely resembled the cave in Patterson's book.

Having covered so much ground, they began to wonder if Patterson had erred in his descriptions of where the cave was located. One night, frustrated, unable to sleep, Gnoske decided to review the book. He made a startling discovery. Wherever Patterson gave directions, he was consistently 90° off, writing that from Tsavo he could see Kilimanjaro to the south, when it was to the west, that the Ndungu Escarpment was to the east instead of to its true direction, the north, and that the N'dii Range was to the south, when it was to the west.

The next morning, he told his colleagues about his late-night epiphany. It seemed strange for a trained engineer to make so gross an error; they speculated that Patterson, writing eight years after discovering the cave, had incorrectly oriented the hand-drawn map he was using as a reference by 90°. Either that, or the book's editors had erred in transcribing Patterson's notes.

Whatever the cause of the mistake, the team now had renewed confidence that they could find the cave. Splitting up into four teams, they worked their way up a dry streambed lined with doum palms, one group following the left bank, another the right, a third down the middle, and the fourth all three. Forty-five minutes later, Gnoske, in the fourth group, heard Kerbis Peterhans shouting from across the ravine. Clawing his way through the thorn bushes, he found his colleague standing before a cave that perfectly matched the one in Patterson's photograph. The man-eaters' den had been rediscovered after 97 years. Their feat made them heroes at the Field Museum, which hadn't experienced anything quite like it since the late 19th and early 20th centuries, when its scientists returned from unexplored parts of the world with tales of discovery and adventure.

But had the two men found a man-eaters' den? Their initial joy turned to disappointment when they entered the cave and found it empty. No bones, no copper bangles, nothing but a layer of red sand coating the cave's rocky floor. It became immediately clear why the cave was empty: In the middle of a seasonal streambed, its contents had long ago been washed away.

Undeterred, Gnoske and Kerbis Peterhans got permission from KWS authorities to excavate the cave. Work began in 1998 and is still under way as we drive toward the park's Manyani Gate. Graduate students working under Kusimba are sifting through the dirt to recover human bones and examine them for teeth marks; if there are any, the team will be able to determine if they had been made by lions, hyenas, or leopards. They are also looking for human teeth, to distinguish between Asians and Africans; Asian teeth would be all but incontrovertible proof that the victims had been the Indian railway workers.

I am to interview Kusimba sometime during our safari to learn what, if anything, all the sifting and searching has produced. Regardless of his findings, Gnoske believes that Patterson may not have been off base in calling the cave a lion's den. Some modern lions use dens, Gnoske asserted in one of our many long-distance conversations; that, he added, tends to support his and Kerbis Peterhans's theory that there are two distinct forms of lions living in Africa— the lions of the plains and lions that are throwbacks to the cave-dwelling cats of prehistoric times.

He sent me a tape of a program describing a 1998 Gnoske and Kerbis Peterhans expedition that investigated incidents of man-eating in Uganda's Queen Elizabeth National Park. There, they learned that an official of the Ugandan Wildlife Authority, one George Bwere, had been attacked by an angry lioness two years before while surveying hiking trails along the Kyambura River, a Nile tributary. The Kyambura flows through a gorge of the same name. Thickly jungled, the gorge bisects the savannas of the Albertine Rift Valley in western Uganda. Bwere was rushed by the lioness as he pushed through the dense tropical vegetation. He narrowly escaped with his life and observed a male lion retreating into a cave with young cubs. Soon after, he was joined by a second male, and Bwere (who must have been a cool customer to stick around after such an encounter) observed them patrolling the gorge while the lioness entered the cave to guard the cubs. Over the next several months, there were numerous reports of two male lions attacking vehicles and people who got too near the cave.

The stories piqued Gnoske's and Kerbis Peterhans's curiosity. Could this cave be an example of modern lions using a den? They got permission from Ugandan authorities to explore the Kyambura in October 1998. Accompanied by a ranger armed with an AK-47, they descended into the gorge until they reached the river. It was an enchanted world, wholly different from the dry savannas above, its silence broken by the whoops of chimpanzees in the trees, the cries of rain forest birds. The lush vegetation looked like typical leopard habitat, not lion country.

They approached the mouth of the cave warily, then crawled inside on their hands and knees, their hearts pounding, their flash-lights sweeping the darkness, revealing dripping stalactites and a small waterfall. What they hoped not to see was the reflected glow of feline eyes: At such close quarters, even an AK-47 would not be much defense against two big male lions and an enraged female guard-ing her young.

The flashlights' beams fell on something white—a bone. Kerbis Peterhans examined it and determined that it was a buffalo bone. Several more were lying around. None bore the gnaw marks from hyena predation, and both men recalled that Ugandan wildlife author-ities had told them of eyewitness reports of two male lions dragging a buffalo carcass down the steep bank of the gorge. Then the search turned up something that confirmed the accounts: blond hairs from a lion's mane.

"We have no doubt that this cave was a lion's den," Gnoske had told me. "It's the first modern documentation of a lion den."

But why would those lions in the Kyambura use a cave, whereas lions on the savanna did not? One answer was obvious—there aren't any caves on the open plains. Yet, even if there were, Gnoske said, the lions wouldn't hole up in them. The real answer lay in his theory that different kinds of habitat give rise to different social systems— small prides in densely vegetated regions, large ones on the savanna. Without the safety provided by big families, cubs in environments like the Kyambura are more vulnerable to predation, particularly by hyenas. Taking aggressive action against intruders (the lioness's attack on Bwere) and rearing them in dens could give them the protection that cubs on the plains don't need.

Iain is intrigued by all this—he's never seen the "den" Patterson found. He has no idea where it is. Nor do I, except that it's somewhere up in that jumble of rock and scrub, and I'm not entirely sure I'm ready to go looking for it.

We approach the Manyani Gate to enter Tsavo East (for administrative purposes, the park is divided into Tsavo West, a mostly hilly, forested region west of the highway, and Tsavo East, which is larger, flatter, more desolate). While Iain and Clive tend to such matters as permits and park fees with a park ranger, Leslie, Rob, and I watch an agama lizard doing push-ups on the exposed root of a large acacia—an *elata abyssinia* tree, the encyclopedic Clive informs us after the paperwork has been sorted out. We head down a laterite road, a gash of rust-red dust in the scrub. Golden pippets flit from the bushes, and a European roller flies past, a migrant from central Europe, its plumage a gorgeous palette of pale turquoise and white and rufous brown. The land reaches away, meadows of dun-colored grass, vast stretches of bristling commiphora scrub overlooked by acacia, their wide-spreading branches ornamented with the gourd-shaped nests of weaverbirds. No towns or farms or highways or fences, wild country at last—wild country of a particular kind. This is the Pleistocene surviving in all its primeval grandeur, the world as it looked to our remote ancestors, *Australopithecus afarensis,* hairy-bodied and small-brained, but walking upright as they wander the savanna, foraging, scavenging, copulating, evolving ever so slowly toward the creature that will develop an opposable thumb and a capacity for reason and language and art and laughter. Also for hate and war and a conscious cruelty beyond all the creatures that creep, crawl, and fly.

We pass Mudanda Rock, which thrusts up out of the level landscape above a big water hole formed by a natural dam. Finch-Hatton was killed near Mudanda in May 1931, when his plane crashed after running into a vulture, but the rock is more noted for its water hole, which draws hundreds of elephants during the dry season. A small herd is there as we pass by, dipping their trunks into the muddy water, shuffling about, their hides coated in Tsavo dust so that they are more red than gray. They cross the road in front of us with a lovely, gliding stride, and one old bull, to protest our presence, turns to face us, flares its ears, and trumpets before moving on into the trees.

I am thrilled—they're the first elephants I have seen in the wild. The sight inspires Iain to rhapsodize about the elephant, which is his favorite animal. It, not the lion, is emblematic of Tsavo: "The true king of beasts," he says—a highly intelligent, social creature that controls the fate of the environment, sometimes in subtle ways. Fifteen years ago, when the park's elephants were poached nearly to extinction, the Kenya Wildlife Service observed a big increase in the numbers of dik-dik in the park. The tiny, delicate antelope, which weigh an average of 12 pounds, had grown in population because the trees and brush cropped by elephant had proliferated to the point that the eagles that prey on dik-dik could not see them through the dense foliage. Tsavo's elephant herd has roughly doubled, to about 10,000 animals, since the Conference on International Trade in Endangered Species, known as CITES, imposed a worldwide ban on ivory sales in 1989. That was far more effective in ending poaching than the efforts of Leakey's rangers, with their helicopter gunships and authorization to shoot poachers on sight. As for the future of Tsavo's elephants, Iain can be described as cautiously pessimistic: So far, the ban is working, but powerful forces are at work to undermine it. Zimbabwe and Botswana, which periodically cull their elephant herds to control their numbers (Kenya does not allow culling), have been lobbying hard to get CITES to partially lift the ban so they can sell their ivory. Once ivory gets into the market, no one will be able to tell which country it came from or distinguish between poached ivory and culled ivory, so Iain worries that even a partial lifting will bring the highly skilled, well-equipped, and well-armed Somali gangs back to Tsavo to resume the slaughter.

We turn east onto another dirt road, then onto a vague two-track that takes us across the Voi River, waterless now in the dry season, its sandy bed printed with animal tracks. On the other side is Iain's tent camp. Like most American outdoorsmen and women, Leslie and I are accustomed to doing things for ourselves; we pitch our own tents, cook our own food, scrub our own pots, make our own beds, and lie in them. That isn't the style in Kenya, or anywhere in Africa. Iain is a firm believer in the axiom that you don't have to practice being miserable. His safaris hark back to the stylish roughing-it of a bygone age—commodious wall tents with cots, blankets, mattresses, and canvas camp chairs; outdoor showers; portable privies in canvas enclosures; laundry service; and a competent, six-man staff to do all the cooking and camp chores. We are promised that Kahiu, the cook, will do meals over an open fire equal to anything served in the best Nairobi restaurant, and we will wash them down with South African and Italian wines, making us feel pretty pukka-sahib.

We settle in, meaning that we drop our duffel bags in our tents, while Iain and Clive issue a few orders in a Swahili that bears the peremptory tones of the old White Highlands. In the capital, the Caucasian Kenyan has to keep his opinions to himself, but it's obvious that he's still the *bwana makuba* out here. Iain tells us that we will spend four days at this camp and look for lions on game drives, then we will strike camp and move to another on the Galana River, some 30 miles to the north. From there, we will go on foot into the Northern Area, an immense sweep of semiarid savanna. It is the wildest region of the park, and because the KWS is underfunded and undermanned, it is lightly patrolled and therefore closed to the general public. Only authorized walking parties are allowed into it, and they must be accompanied by armed rangers to protect them from bipedal as well as four-footed predators. In other words, *shifta,* as Somali bandits are called. That sits well with us; travel without an element of danger is mere sight-seeing.

Rob Howard, a dark-haired guy, 36 years old, with the looks and enthusiasm of someone 10 years younger, shoulders his arsenal of cameras and lenses and we set off in the Land Rover. It is late afternoon, the golden hour in East Africa. The light is like liquid butter. We meet Andanje, co-discoverer of the man-eaters' den, at a place called Aruba, where an earthen dam built decades ago has created a water hole the size of a small lake. The landscape here resembles the Serengeti, level breadths of brown grass drawn out to the horizon, the occasional acacia standing sentinel. Samuel, in a white Land Rover, with the name of the Royal Zoological Society painted on its doors, scans the emptiness with binoculars. He is now a research associate with the KWS and is studying lions and other game on a grant from the Society. He spends his nights locating the cats by their roars and his days tracking them in his vehicle. As we approach, he climbs out, an athletic six-footer with a round face and bright, easy smile, greets Iain and Clive, and tells them a group of lions is feeding on a freshly killed buffalo nearby. They belong to a pride of 23 lions, he says, pointing to a low ridge a hundred yards from the lake. I don't see anything at first; then I catch the flick of a triangular ear and make out a long beige body lying in grass that perfectly matches its color. A head rises up, then another. A pair of females. Our first look at the lions of Tsavo. Rob and I get our cameras ready, both equipped with fast 300-millimeter lenses half as long as rocket-launchers. Iain eases the Land Rover off road and slowly approaches to within 40 feet of the pair lazing in the sun, their bellies swollen with buffalo meat (A lion will consume anywhere from 45 to 75 pounds of meat at a single sitting. For comparison's sake, imagine yourself eating, say, 50 porterhouses in one meal.) As we poke our heads through the roof hatches and begin taking pictures, amber eyes gaze at us with supreme indifference. In fact, they don't look at us so much as through us. In an undertone, Iain says we are very lucky. The lions of Tsavo are "wilder" than those in Kenya and Tanzania, which have become habituated to tourists, and will hide from people in the dense saltbush thickets bordering rivers and *luggas* (dry riverbeds) or in the clumps of commiphora. Although Tsavo is under increasing pressure from visitors—roughly 200,000 a year—the numbers don't match those in other parks and game reserves. Were we now in the Serengeti or Amboseli, we would be surrounded by at least a dozen other vehicles. Ours is the only one in sight. Even if Tsavo were as popular as its sister parks, it's so vast that a lion could pass most of its life without seeing more than a handful of people. This pair, inhabiting one of the few open stretches in Tsavo, don't have anywhere to hide; and it's possible that they've encountered enough minibuses full of gawkers not to be disturbed by us.

Their tolerance depends on our remaining in the Land Rover. A human being on foot, if seen by a lion, will trigger one of two instinctive responses: It will either attack or flee. A vehicle, which it may think is some sort of creature unto itself, neither threat nor prey, makes it feel as safe from you as you from it—a fact that has led some unscrupulous, cowardly hunters to shoot lions from cars.

A movement off to the left reveals the presence of a third lioness. How camouflaged she is; if you were walking around out here, you could step on her before you saw her, and I imagine that would be the last step you ever took and the last thing you ever saw, for she is bigger than the other two, a fully mature female, the alpha girl, perhaps 300 pounds. There is another movement from behind a low bush farther to our left. Iain puts the Land Rover in gear and creeps in that direction. It's the male, the leader of the pride, and he is awesome. Awesomely big, every ounce of 450 pounds, and awesomely ugly, with sparse, dark side whiskers and a short crest for a mane—not a photogenic, Oscar de la Hoya sort of lion, but a Jake LaMotta lion, his face and hide scarred from the thorny country he lives in, from battles with rival lions, from the kicks of the zebra and buffalo he kills for food. He lies in the shade of the bush, only 25 feet away, eyes partly shut, breathing heavily beside the carcass of the Cape buffalo. Around him, two more young lionesses loll in the short yellow grass, well fed and yawning. Two cubs lick and nibble the buffalo's hindquarters, the ragged strips of meat in the hollowed-out cavity showing a bright, shocking red under the black skin. Nothing else remains of the animal, except for the horned head, the front hoofs, and a few scattered bones.

We observe and photograph the male for several minutes. I am thinking of *Hamlet,* and Shakespeare's paean to *Homo sapiens:* "What a piece of work is man! How noble in reason! How infinite in faculty! In form and moving how express and admirable! In action how like an angel! In apprehension how like a god! The beauty of the world! The paragon of animals!" It seems to me that the lion deserves a hosanna or two. How powerful in body, its bone mass light, its muscles heavy! Its forebody the strongest of all the cats, its forepaws able to break a zebra's neck with one blow! How adapted are its eyes to hunt at night, coated to reflect even moonlight, with a white circle beneath each to reflect more light into them and improve their vision in darkness! How fearsome and efficient are its teeth for killing! The canines spaced so they can slip between the cervical vertebrae of their favorite prey! How astonishing is its two-piece hyoid bone that gives it the power to roar! And how terrifying that roar, forceful enough to raise clouds of dust! How vigorous in sexuality, mating as often as 40 times a day when the female is in estrus!

The question I'm pondering is, Does the big fellow in front of us—I've decided to call him Scarface—belong to a subspecies of the Serengeti lion, *Panthera leo massaicus*? Am I looking at a living fossil that has walked into the modern age from the Stone Age? Is the bobbed, scruffy mane the result of genetic variation? Other questions about the Gnoske–Kerbis Peterhans hypothesis creep in. This is no leonine nuclear family—8 animals altogether, only part of a pride of 23 according to Samuel's count. How would the researchers explain that? Perhaps this part of Tsavo, with its savanna-like sweep, permits large prides to develop. But then, why doesn't Scarface sport a luxuriant mane? Nor can I tell if Scarface follows the Gnoske–Kerbis Peterhans scenario by doing most of the hunting. He may have killed the buffalo, but it was a young animal, judging from the span of horn and the size of the hindquarters, and may have been taken down by the lionesses. Or it could have been scavenged. Lions obtain a good deal of their food—as much as 40 percent in some circumstances—by stealing it from other predators, hyenas being the most frequent victim of lion larceny. I wish I had an expert field biologist to turn to for perspective and insight. With my long lens braced on the Land Rover's roof, I feel that I'm no seeker of facts or truth, but a glorified tourist.

I run out of film and drop through the roof hatch to fetch another roll from my camera bag. Rob, deciding he needs a better angle, boosts himself through the hatch and stands up. Immediately, the drowsy, indifferent expression goes out of Scarface's eyes that glow like brass in firelight as they focus on Rob with absolute concentration. Rob's camera continues to whirr and click, and I wonder if he's noticed that he's disturbed the lion. Now, with its stare still fixed on him, it grunts out of one side of its mouth, then the other, gathering its forepaws into itself and raising its haunches. The long, black-tufted tail switches in the grass.

"Say, Rob, might be a good idea to sit down again," Iain advises quietly. "Move slowly, though."

He barely finishes this instruction when the lion makes a noise like a man clearing his throat, only a good deal louder, and lunges across half the distance between us and him, swatting the air with one paw before he stops. Rob tumbles through the hatch, almost landing on top of me in a clatter of camera equipment, a flailing of arms and legs.

"Jesus Christ!" he says, obviously impressed. Scarface settles down again, though his tail continues to sweep back and forth.

"The short, happy life of Rob Howard," I wisecrack. "It's embarrassing to see a man lose his nerve like that."

A bit of bravado on my part. We are going to be on foot in four days, and if we are charged then, how will my own nerve hold up?

Perhaps Rob is wondering the same thing about himself. He asks what he'd done to provoke the lion.

"Standing up like that. It was the silhouette of the bipod," answers Clive, in one of his habitual malapropisms. "Lions have learned to fear and hate the bipod."

"Would he have jumped up on the roof?" Rob asks, his expression telling us that he's formed a mental picture of the appalling results.

"Could have, but he wouldn't have," Iain replies, a vague smile cracking across his rough, sun-reddened face. "That was just a demonstration, to let you know the rules. Of course, you had no way of knowing that."

Shortly after the male teaches Rob the rules, the females, with the cubs in tow, move off toward the lake to drink. They make a fine sight in the golden afternoon light, walking slowly through the dun-colored grass with movements that suggest water flowing. Scarface remains behind to guard the buffalo carcass from jackals and hyenas. As the sun lowers, the lake becomes a wildlife magnet. Two hippos wallow in the middle. On one side, a dozen elephants, creased hides reddened by dried mud, drink through the great straws of their trunks while a herd of about 30, in the far distance, shamble toward the lake. Along the shore where the lionesses and cubs crouch, their tongues lapping, sacred ibises peck the mud with their long, curved beaks: a bird of simple colors, black and white, sharply delineated, and called sacred because it symbolized the Egyptian god Thoth, who toted up the Pharaoh's good and evil deeds in the Book of the Dead.

So speaketh Clive, telling us that the sacred ibis can be seen on the hydroglyphs in Egypt.

"Hieroglyphs, Clive," corrects Iain.

"That's what I said."

"No, you didn't."

Over the years, they have developed a relationship that seems to combine war-buddy comradeship with the easy familiarity of an old married couple; they bicker now and then and needle each other, but beneath the bickering and needling, I sense an abiding bond knit on sheer rock faces and icy crags and long, hot tramps through the African bush.

Clive's disquisition on sacred ibis is followed by a series of throaty grunts from the male lion, which isn't a commentary but a call to the females and cubs to return. As they pad soundlessly through the grass, we leave—it's growing dark— and come upon a lone lioness, lying at the junction of the road and the two-track that leads to camp. She doesn't move as the Land Rover approaches, nor when we turn onto the two-track, passing within six feet of her. She's a big girl, too, and seems to regard the intersection as hers, and of course it is.

The big storks roosting in the branches of dead trees in the Voi riverbed look ominous in the twilight. Up ahead and across the river, the glow of kerosene lamps and a campfire make a more cheerful sight.

After dinner, we sit around the campfire on folding chairs under the stars, and once, when the wind turns, we hear the lions roaring in the distance. The sound inspires Iain to offer a tale of his scariest encounter with a Tsavo lion.

It happened on a safari the previous July. It was late in the afternoon, past the time when he usually checks in with his Nairobi office by satellite phone (nowadays, even safari guides cannot escape the tyranny of instant communications). Iain ambled down to the wide, sandy banks of the Galana River, where reception was better than it was in his tree-shrouded tent camp. As he chatted with his assistant, he observed a bushbuck poke its way through a saltbush thicket some distance upriver, then begin to drink. Suddenly, the animal raised its head and froze; an instant later, a lioness sprang from the saltbush still farther upriver, and the bushbuck bolted down the shore in Iain's direction, the lioness in pursuit. When the lioness was about 50 yards from Iain, she veered off without breaking stride and headed straight for him, bursts of sand flying behind her. Iain tossed the phone away, and in a microsecond that seemed like minutes, realized that he needn't worry about her teeth and claws; he was going to be killed by the impact of 300 pounds of sinew and muscle smashing into him at a speed faster than an Olympic sprinter's. When she was only 20 feet from where he stood, she veered again, kicked sand all over him, and vanished.

Iain suspects that the lioness charged him because she was confused, annoyed, or curious.

"That's the closest I've ever come to getting killed," he adds. "After she disappeared, I had the feeling that she'd run into camp, so I ran back and told my clients to get in their tents and zip them up, and warned the staff that a lion was in camp. Well, they looked at me as if to say that the old boy had had too much sun, and after I didn't see the lioness for a while, I figured they were right. I was about to tell my clients that they could come on out of their tents, when I turned around and saw eight Africans running like hell for the Land Rover, with the lioness running among them—not after them, but right in the middle of them. The men leaped up to the roof in one bound. I think that old girl was very confused—she'd started off chasing a bushbuck, ended up in a camp full of people, tents, vehicles—things she'd never seen—and must have wondered, 'How did I get into this mess?' She ran out, but stopped at the edge of camp and stayed there all day. Just sat there, like the lioness we saw a little while ago."

"What good did zipping up tent flaps do?" I ask. "She could have shredded an eighth of an inch of canvas if she wanted to."

"Lions don't like entering dark, enclosed spaces," Iain explains. "That's why it's important to keep the flaps closed at night. Only last August, in Zimbabwe, there was a young Englishman, son of an earl, on a camping safari. Seems there was a lot of drinking going on, and, after the party, he went into his tent and fell asleep without closing the flaps. Sometime during the night, a lioness got close to his tent. He woke up and, scared as hell, ran out. Lions like things that run, same as any cat. She chased him right into a mob of other lions, and when they got through with him, I don't think there was anything left."

That is not a bedtime story to tell in lion country. Or maybe it is: When Leslie and I go to our tent, we not only secure the flaps, we zip up the covers to the mesh ventilation windows—and can barely breathe the stifling air. As I lie beside my beautiful lady, listening to the muffled roars, I'm not reassured by Iain's claim that lions don't like entering dark, enclosed places. Didn't the Man-eaters of Tsavo barge into the tents of the construction crews to grab their meals? Maybe the workmen didn't close the flaps, I think. But what about the lion that killed C. H. Ryall? It opened the door to an unlighted railway carriage, opened the door, for Christ's sake. My sole armament is a K-bar, the ten-inch fighting knife issued to me when I was in the Marine Corps in Vietnam. I have heroic fantasies of defending Leslie from a predatory attack and recall the statue of the young Masai in the Field Museum, kneeling behind his shield, hand on the hilt of his *simi*. I think of stories I've read about brave men killing lions with knives or other edged weapons. There was Lord Delamere, an early English settler in Kenya, knocked off his horse by a man-eater. As he lay stunned, the lion, supposing him dead, seized him by a shoulder and trotted off with him, presumably toward a suitable dining area. Coming to, Lord Delamere drew his knife and plunged it into the lion's heart. Peter Capstick, while tracking a man-eater in the same area as Hosek, the Luangwa Valley, was ambushed by a lion, which knocked him down and sent his rifle spinning off into the underbrush. The huge male then charged Capstick's tracker, who was armed only with a spear. Slapping the spear aside with a forepaw, the lion leaped on the man and commenced to maul him. He saved himself from instant death by shoving his arm into the lion's mouth. Capstick recovered, and, unable to find his rifle, snatched the spear by its broken shaft and drove it into the lion's neck, severing its spinal cord. It collapsed as if it had been shot in the brain. In *The Shadow of Kilimanjaro,* Rick Ridgeway tells of a Kamba hunter and tracker, Elui, who wore two lion hair balls (like domestic cats, lions lick themselves clean and vomit up hair balls that result from their grooming) on leather thongs tied around his upper arms. The Wakamba, who inhabited Tsavo before it became a peopleless park, believe that the ornament gives a man the strength of a lion. Quoting Danny Woodley, the son of the Tsavo game warden, Ridgeway describes how Elui acquired his:

"One day Elui was at a water hole when he was pounced on by a lion. He gave the lion his arm, pulled his knife, and stabbed him in the aorta. The lion collapsed and spit up the hair ball onto Elui, who from then on wore it around his bicep. Later he killed a female lion and so he had that hair ball on his other arm."

Not one, but two lions. With a knife. If Elui could do it, then so can I, if I have to. I will defend Leslie with all my strength and courage, to the last breath. I touch the ridged haft of the K-bar, resting in its leather sheath on the night table next to my cot, but it seems to me that the best thing I can do with it in the event of a lion attack will be to fall on it and save the lion the trouble.

"JAMBO," DAVID, ONE of the camp staff, calls softly from outside our tent. Jambo means "hello" in Swahili.

"Jambo," we answer and get up and dress by lantern light as David fills the canvas sinks with hot water. I splash some on my face. It smells wonderfully of campfire smoke. After breakfast, and with light erasing the last morning stars, we roll out to the Aruba dam to look for Scarface and his family. Along the way, we spot baboons— fellow primates!—squatting in their night perches in the trees, and an African fish eagle, white-headed, black-winged, resembling the American bald eagle, roosting in a branch. Sand grouse flush from the roadside, a hornbill sails from a bush, letting out a plaintive cry.

The lions are not where we had left them. We drive slowly, looking for pugmarks in the soft, rust-colored earth, until we hear a deep, bass groan that ends in a chesty cough. Scarface. The sound he makes is so loud we think he's only 50 yards away. Leaving the road, we set off in the direction of the roar, bouncing over a prairie of short, dry grass tinted pale gold by the early morning sun, Clive, Rob, and I standing on the seats with our heads poking out of the roof hatches.

"Ah, there he is," says Iain, at the wheel.

"Him, all right," Clive seconds.

I spend a lot of time hiking and bird hunting in the woods and am not bad at spotting game, but I have no idea what they're talking about.

"It's the ears, you look for the ears sticking above the grass when you're looking for lion," Iain instructs, and drives on, and then I see them, two triangles that could be mistaken for knots in a stump, except they move. We're 20 or 30 yards away when he stands up, with a movement fluid and unhurried. Ugly-handsome Scarface proceeds down an elephant trail at the leonine version of a stroll, then up over a rise and down toward a marsh. We stay with him all the way, keeping a respectful distance, cameras clicking away. Looking at him broadside, I wonder if my earlier estimate of his weight was conservative. One big boy, all right, and if he were a man-eater, he would kill you in one of three ways: bite to your head, piercing your temples with his canines (this is preferable, as death is instantaneous); break your neck (death in a few seconds); or bite into your chest, driving his tusks into your lungs or heart (definitely not your first choice, as it may take you a while to die, and it's possible he'll start to devour you before your soul has departed for a better place; there are horrifying records in Africa of lions eating people alive). As far as the actual dining goes, the lion will first flay off your skin with his tongue, which is covered with small spines that give it the texture of coarse-grained sandpaper and are used to bring nutritious blood to the surface; bite into your abdomen, open you up, and scoop out your entrails and internal organs and consume them because they are rich in protein, your liver especially; his incisors will tear into your meatiest parts, thighs and buttocks, followed by your arms, shoulders, and calves, and then he'll crack open the smaller bones for their marrow. He will not eat your stomach, but bury it. Lions don't consume the stomachs of their prey, though no one knows the reason for this. Your larger bones will be left for the hyenas, which have stronger jaws. Vultures and jackals will dispose of your face and scalp and whatever scraps of flesh remain, so that, a few hours after your sudden demise, it will be as though you had never existed. There is a terrible thoroughness to the mechanics of death in Africa, and we are not exempt.

Scarface leads us right to his harem, and then, after posing on a knoll, he moves off into the marsh, the lionesses and cubs following soon after.

"That's that for now," says Iain. "Have to come back in the late afternoon. Let's look up Sam and try to find the rest of this pride."

We drive toward Sattao Camp, a safari lodge, and find Andanje standing atop his Land Rover, sweeping the horizon with binoculars. He says he'll take us to where he'd last seen the pride. We follow him along a remote stretch of the Voi, through the spiked commiphora scrub. I mention the bomas Colonel Patterson's laborers had constructed out of that stuff, and how the lions had found ways through them, with the canniness of trained guerrillas infiltrating an enemy's barbed wire. Four-footed killers with above-average IQs. A brain weighing only half a pound can do more than you might think.

"I don't doubt but that they had the whole thing totally wired," Iain remarks. "The difference between people and animals is that we can see the big picture and figure out how to survive in any environment, but within their area of specialization, most animals are as smart as we are, maybe smarter." He pauses, chewing over a further thought. "Take a look at this country.... I'm convinced that they have territories they know as well as you know your backyard, with their ambush places all staked out. They're clever. They know where to be and when."

An interesting observation, I think. It reminds me of something I'd read, to the effect that because a human being's one big advantage over a predator is intelligence, the lion that hunts man has to sharpen its wits rather than its claws to be successful. But the lions that Patterson encountered may have had keen wits to begin with to survive in their environment and honed them further as they grew more experienced, stalking their big-brained, bipedal quarry.

Capstick noted: "The brazen dedication of the experienced man-eating lion to his art can be spine-chilling. Just as a normal lion learns techniques of killing and hunting animal prey in specific manners, so does the man-eater develop modus operandi for catching humans. The fact that a man-eating feline is the most difficult animal in the world to hunt can be explained by the cat's ability to learn well and quickly."

Waterbuck freeze and stare at our vehicles before bounding off, their rumps with white circles resembling bull's-eyes on a target. Elegant Grant's gazelle, long-legged, fawn-colored hides glossy as rubbed leather, the males' horns shaped like lyres, graze in the distance. Farther on, we come upon a large herd of Cape buffalo, tar black, baleful looking, the old bulls incredibly massive—I can't imagine even a team of lions bringing one of them down. And indeed, a buffalo often kills the lion or lions that try to kill it. Samuel tells us that he saw a male stomped to death by a buffalo only last week. Far off, a lone elephant browses amid the branches of a tall tree, but there are no lions in sight, and by half past ten the quest is hopeless. It's close to 100°, and the cats are laid up, deep within the thickets.

We return to camp, have lunch, idle away the afternoon watching a Masai giraffe munch tree leaves on the far side of the riverbed. Moving from tree to tree, it looks like a crane in stately motion. A breeze springs up, relieving the dry-season heat, rustling through the coastal oaks, rattling the brown seed pods hanging tonguelike from the tamarinds. Bulbuls warble, a drab bird with a beguiling song, and superb starlings, aptly named for their stunning plumage—their crowns jet black, their backs and wings metallic blue blushed with green, their bellies chestnut—flit from shrub to shrub. Splendid, but I'm not here to bird-watch.

In the late afternoon, we return to the marsh near the Aruba dam. There, Scarface's harem lolls with the cubs on the grassy ridge overlooking the marsh, where a solitary bull elephant grazes contentedly. Iain parks a short distance from the lions and we begin observing and photographing. There isn't much action. The cats do nothing but lie around, mouths half open, eyes half shut, ears flicking every now and then.

"I'm afraid what you're seeing now is typical lion behavior," says Iain. "This is what they do 20 hours out of 24. Conserve energy."

The light is glorious, a rich copper that turns the savanna grass to a champagne color and sets the lions' eyes on fire. Two of the females, young and lean, groom each other with their tongues. They are so at ease with our presence that they allow us into their midst. One lioness rests not five feet from the rear bumper. But I am getting restless, eager to get out into the bush on foot. There is a certain feeling of removal, observing wildlife from a vehicle, a certain absence of tension. It's like looking at captive animals, though in this case, we are the captives, the Land Rover our cage.

The sun drops below the Chyulu Hills and a blessed sundowner begins to blow. Away off to the west rises a hazy mountain where Iain found seven human skulls on a climb. It was a burial ground of the ancient Taita people. The lions stir. A small herd of Grant's gazelle daintily walk down into the marsh to graze, and the biggest lioness, the dominant female, raises her head and fastens her gaze on them, exactly as our pet cat raises his head when he sees or hears a mouse crawling through our pachysandra beds. Twelve pounds or 250, a cat is a cat is a cat.

"She's looking for a slight limp in one of the gazelle," Iain observes. "Any sign of weakness, but gazelle isn't a lion's favored prey. They're so fast and there isn't much meat on them, so it's hardly worth the effort. Lions are lazy hunters." Gesturing at the marsh, he returns to the theme of feline intelligence. "A lot of thought went into choosing this position, above the swamp and with most of it upwind, so they can see or scent almost anything that comes along. It's perfect buffalo country. The sun's lowering, they're rested, and they'll be getting hungry soon."

But a kill will happen, if it does, sometime after midnight, out of our sight. The lions begin to move, and the gazelle, winding them, bound off. A tawny eagle circles overhead, and a flock of storks or flamingos—I'm too heat-dazed to ask Clive what the birds are—loft out of the Aruba lake, thick as a swarm of bees.

When we are about a quarter of a mile from camp, Iain and Clive spot the female that occupied the road junction the night before. She is with two very young cubs, hardly bigger than house cats. Her hide looks gray in the twilight, and she walks so quietly on her cushioned paws that she seems insubstantial, a wraith in the gathering night.

*

The whole Aruba pride has vanished, and we can't find sign of them anywhere in the neighborhood this morning. The one exception is a line of pugmarks in the road north of the lake, but those soon turn into the grass, where we lose them. Iain heads farther north, crossing a stark, monotonous plain toward the Galana River. Were we on a tourist safari, we would be delighted. A male lesser kudu, a fairly uncommon sight, bounds across the road in front of us, his brown flanks flashing thin white stripes, his twisting horns like a pair of serpents rising from his skull. He exudes a stunning power and energy and is so fast that we barely glimpse him; it's as if we've seen a fleeting hallucination. Farther up, we encounter a few hartebeests, an animal that looks like one of nature's failed experiments, seemingly cobbled together from the parts of other animals: a narrow, oblong head with ears too big and horns too short, sickle-shaped and confused about which way they should go; they curve forward, then backward, then outward. I'm not saying we aren't pleased to see this wildlife, but our quarry is proving elusive to us. We've journeyed nearly 30 miles without spotting a single lion. On the plus side, we've seen only one minibus, though even that lone vehicle caused Iain to grumble. Too many of them showing up on Tsavo's tracks, he muttered. A necessary evil—the fees they pay are needed to maintain the park. This leads him into a brief discourse on the dangers of anthropomorphizing animals too much. It gives rise to misanthropic feelings.

"The longer you spend with wildlife, the more you identify with them. But you can carry it just so far. After a while, you don't like people all that much."

I myself have felt that dislike, bordering on a disgust with our ever proliferating species. The fields and prairies where I hunted pheasant and rabbit in high school are now buried under endless acres of shopping malls and corporate office parks surrounded by the unnatural green of chemically treated lawns. The two-lane blacktops I drove to farmhouses to ask permission to hunt are now four and even six lanes, teeming with traffic. It's difficult, sometimes, to maintain belief in the worth and sacredness of each human life when there is so much of it. I recall the two long fishing and hunting trips I took in arctic Alaska in 1995 and 1996, when I saw so few people that I was actually happy to run into them or to come across signs of human presence, like the ashes of a campfire.

On we go. MMBA, Iain calls the arid expanses—Miles and Miles of Bloody Africa. The country goes on like this, he adds, for 300 miles, all the way into Somalia. The Galana is a different world entirely. The wide, brownish river, coursing under the frown of the Yatta Escarpment, is lined with doum palm and saltbush. That verdant cord reminds me a little of the Nile Valley in Egypt: everything lush and green near the river, then, abruptly, desert. We search diligently for lions and find none. Elephants are abundant, along with giraffes, gazelles, impalas, waterbucks, baboons, and zebras. As we turn back south, down a road bordering a Galana tributary called the Hatulo Bisani (a Somali word, Clive chimes in; amazingly, he doesn't know what it means), the bird life would keep the entire Audubon Society happy—from big tawny and Bateleur eagles to midsize hornbills to small golden pippets that fly from the bushes like dabs of butter with wings. The dry season has reduced the Hatulo Bisani to a mere stream; the exposed sedges of what will be river bottom in the rainy season are a startling green, against which feeding egrets look so white they seem to be the idea of whiteness incarnate. Two goliath herons, the largest bird in Africa, are intent on catching lunch, staring into the water with Zen-like focus. Sensing the Land Rover's approach, their heads rise on long, russet necks— they must be five feet tall.

Iain spots pugmarks at the roadside. We get out and follow them on foot for a few yards before they angle into the underbrush and vanish. Some distance ahead, and off to the left, a big buffalo herd grazes in the scrub. The backs of the animals show above the grass and through the scrub as a field of enormous black boulders.

"Those tracks back down the road," Iain says, musing aloud. "Could be a pride trailing this herd. They'll be looking for an old one, a weak one. You can have two lions on either side of a buffalo herd, and they'll be keyed in on each other, knowing which animal is the one to hunt. Could be a kill tonight. We'll come back in the morning."

*

The long drive down rutted dirt tracks in 100° heat leaves us feeling like electroshocked mullets. Kahiu's lunch partially restores us. Two hours before sunset, we're off lion hunting again. A couple of bull elephants are browsing near camp. Either one would bring an adrenal quiver to an old-time trophy hunter and cause a Somali poacher to dream of replacing his mud-walled shack with a six-bedroom villa, and trading in his horses and camels for enough BMWs to fill the attached five-car garage. One elephant's tusks almost touch the ground as he stands with his massive forehead braced against a tree trunk to give himself a break from carrying all that ivory. Iain estimates a hundred pounds for each tusk; the other elephant's might be slightly less, say 90 pounds. Three hundred and eighty pounds works out to 172 kilos. In 1988, before the ivory ban went into effect, ivory was going for $6,000 (U.S.) per kilo. To a poacher or trader, those two elephants represented a gross profit of $1,032,000, in a part of the world where the average annual income wouldn't cover an American family's monthly grocery bill. No wonder the animals were almost annihilated.

As we drive toward another meeting with Samuel on the Voi, the smaller of the elephants stages a mock charge, gliding rapidly toward us with shrill trumpets, his ears spread; then he turns abruptly and trots away, leaving a fog of dust in his wake. Iain states that it's unusual to see elephants of that size in Tsavo, the big ones having been destroyed by poachers. Not many elephants in the park are much over 15 years old, and those that are are in effect shell-shocked and unable to tolerate the proximity of human beings. The one that charged us had probably seen its mates slaughtered, spent years evading the paltry, upright apes with the sticks that spat fire and death. He has every reason to hate people.

Another drive with Samuel fails to produce a lion. We do hear baboons barking and shrieking in the trees. Clive opines that a leopard is nearby. Listening to the frantic howls, I picture the solitary cat, serene and confident in his skills as a lone hunter, and feel some contempt for the baboons. I also imagine some higher being—an angel, say—feeling the same about the villagers in Ngozo, shouting and banging pots and pans as the Man-eater of Mfuwe parades by, Jesleen's tote bag in his mouth.

*

The campfire coals glow, sparks fly toward the stars. Over by the cook tent, in the light of kerosene lamps, David and Kamal are washing the dinner dishes. Iain sips a beer and tells a tale to refute a comment I have made, gleaned from my research into animal behavior, that lions usually attack Cape buffalo that have been abandoned by the herd. The remark seems to have impugned the buffalo's capacity for loyalty and compassion toward its own kind, and Iain rises to its defense.

"I was taking a safari through the Masai Mara when I saw a coalition of seven young male lions leap on a buff, an old bull. Seven of them! They'd partially eviscerated him and had badly chewed up one foreleg before he went down. But before the lions could finish him, the rest of the herd charged and drove them off into the scrub. Some others formed a circle around the wounded buffalo, and for the next hour the most heartbreaking scene took place as the buffalo took turns licking the old bull's mangled foreleg. Literally licking his wounds. Sometimes the lions would creep out of the bushes for another go at him—they never gave up, they were hungry—but the biggest bulls would charge and drive them back. After a while, you could tell that the herd knew the wounded bull was hopeless. They began to move away, but as they did, he bellowed pitifully and they returned to his side and licked his wounds again. I had three clients with me, and they were in tears watching this. Well, I'll be damned if, after an hour, that bull didn't get to his feet, and when the herd got moving, he went with them, his intestines trailing out of the back of his belly, his bloody leg flopping. You knew he wouldn't last the night, but he'd been spared from those seven lions."

Roused at 4:30 a.m. by David's "Jambo," we breakfast under the Southern Cross and drive north again, to the buffalo herd on the Hatulo Bisani. While we're gone, the staff will strike the tents and move them to our walking safari campsite at a place called Durusikale, on the Galana. I am eager to get out of the damned Land Rover, even though that will diminish our chances of seeing the cats that have already proved difficult enough to find. I guess I'm seeking to do something more than pursue Tsavo's mysterious lions; I'm after a certain quality of experience that's undermined by confinement to a vehicle. The Africa of Dinesen and Finch-Hatton, of Ruark and Hemingway is what I want, and the best way to get it is on shank's mare; "safari," after all, is a Swahili word derived from the Arabic for "to travel on foot."

The sunrise is electric. Once more, I'm mesmerized by the supernatural white of the egrets, standing vigil in the swaths of sedge, and by the goliath herons, rising up on eight-foot wingspans. Ahead, a vast, black smear fills the riverbed. It would look like mud except that it's moving, and as our vehicle approaches, heads lift up and look in our direction. Before Iain can stop, the buffalo hear the engine, and a hundred animals break in alarm, scrambling up and over the steep riverbank. They're followed by the entire herd, 600 animals, maybe a thousand, bolting as one great mass of tossing horns, heaving backs, and lunging legs that in its upward surge resembles an avalanche in reverse. The buffalo thunder across the road into the sere scrub beyond, where the stampede stops. They mill around, cows and calves in the middle, the dominant bulls turning to glare at us through the risen dust, their flanks slathered in river mud, wet noses glistening, thick horns bent like grappling hooks. Those on one of the larger bulls are so curved, so symmetrical as to form a figure eight lying on its side.

We pause for photographs—this is the closest we've come so far to Cape buffalo. Once again, I am trying to picture a lion strong enough and desperate enough to take one on.

We proceed slowly, stopping to search with binoculars, sniffing the air for the stench of a rotting carcass. Nothing. At mid-morning, with the heat like a weight, we give up and head east, toward Durusikale, some 30 miles downstream. A small zebra herd forages on the savanna, beautiful creatures in the wild, and strong: A kick from a zebra's hind legs can break a pursuing lion's jaw. Two giraffes amble along, fanciful beasts; if they weren't so graceful, they would appear one of nature's contraptions.

Partway to the new campsite, we stop to climb one of the Sobo rocks, a series of sandstone outcrops, to scan for game with binoculars and reconnoiter our route. The Galana, fed by melting snows on Mount Kenya and Kilimanjaro, shows a brassy brown as it slides slowly between galleries of saltbush and doum palm toward its distant meeting with the Indian Ocean. Out on the scorched, rust-colored plains beyond the river, a procession of elephants are migrating to the river to drink and cool themselves in the midday heat. Postponing our lion quest for the moment, we return to the Land Rover and cut cross-country toward the herd, drawing close enough to count the animals—about 60 altogether, the calves trotting alongside their mothers, a huge matriarch out front, other old females guarding the flanks and rear.

As I've said, Iain and Clive are elephant enthusiasts. Seeing the herd shambling toward the Galana, they decide to take us to a spot on the river where we'll have a good chance of observing the animals at close hand. What the hell and why not? Can't find lions, might as well do something.

We picnic in the shade of a tamarind tree, with a broad, sandy beach in front of us. Half an hour later, the elephants arrive upwind, within a hundred yards of where we sit. They come down with a stiff-legged gait that looks deceptively slow—they're actually covering ten or twelve feet in a single stride. The marvelous thing is how silent they are, passing through the saltbush with barely a rustle to enter the river. It seems to us that we are beholding Tsavo's wild soul made flesh.

With cat-burglar creeps, we position ourselves on the shore and watch and photograph for almost an hour. It's a wondrous sight. The animals' ears flap, big as a dinghy's sails; tails switch, trunks bend into their mouths or back to spray their heads with water. An incredible organ, the elephant's trunk, says Iain, taking over for Clive as information font. It contains 4,000 separate muscles and serves as the hand that feeds the elephant, as nose, drinking straw, built-in shower, and weapon, all in one.

Matriarchs have taken up sentry positions, covering the four points of the compass. The calves are thoroughly captivating as they playfully roll in the river and submerge themselves. With the wind blowing into our faces, the herd is unaware of our presence, though the matriarch facing upriver sometimes appears to sense that something is out of the ordinary. She looks our way and raises her trunk overhead and swings it back and forth—an olfactory periscope scanning for scent of danger (elephants have poor eyesight, but their senses of smell and hearing are acute). She doesn't act alarmed, and that's good. Bull elephants make false charges, but when a matriarch comes at you, she usually means to carry the thing through. If this one does charge, she'll be on us in about three seconds flat, and there is nowhere to run.

"The usual way an elephant kills a human being is not to stick and stomp," Iain says, "but to knock you down, then kneel on one knee and lean its forehead into you and crush you to death."

I gather he does not want us to feel too charmed by these animals.

The campsite at Durusikale is idyllic, tents pitched in a meadow of Bermuda grass that looks as manicured as a country club fairway. It is shaded by doum palm and feathery tamarind and fronts the river. A hippopotamus wallows on the far side. On the low ridge above, zebras stand outlined against the bright sky. I marvel at the camp staff's work; in just a few hours, they've dismantled the whole outfit, moved it 30 miles, and set it up again, so efficiently that the camp looks as if it's been here for weeks. Two new members have been added, and we meet them, Sergeant Adan and Corporal Hassan, garbed in the green camise and beret of the Kenya Wildlife Service, armed with G-3 semi-automatic rifles, NATO caliber, 7.62-millimeter. They will be our guards on the foot safari into the Northern Area across the river. They are Borana tribesmen from northern Kenya, near the border with Ethiopia. The Borana are a Cushitic tribe, and Adan and Hassan have the handsome, well-defined features and wiry builds of Ethiopians,

Adan much the taller of the two at six feet three. Standing about five feet eight in my hiking boots, I feel childlike beside him.

But there will be no hiking until tomorrow morning. Car-bound once again, we head downriver, following a little-used sandy track, the Galana appearing and disappearing. At a broad bend in the river, Iain recounts a day when he saw a large male baboon squatting there on the rocks. In the next instant, it was dead; a lioness had leaped from the thick scrub behind him and killed him before he knew what hit him.

"I love it here," he rhapsodizes. "It's raw and primitive, Africa without any fat on it. It doesn't tolerate fools or forgive mistakes."

I take him to mean that the baboon was either a fool or had made a mistake. Maybe he was a fool because he made a mistake, though I'm unsure what he did wrong. Strayed from the troop, perhaps, sat out in the open presenting himself as a target, let his guard down for one critical second.

The track winds, following the river's course. We pass alongside thicket after thicket of saltbush. The stuff looks like cedar and grows to between ten and twenty feet high, with game paths running through like narrow, twisting corridors in a garden maze. Something creepy about those thickets, something that touches the old part of the brain, our inheritance from the puny hominid who quaked in the predator's night, feared the dark coverts concealing sudden death. I am reminded a little of Vietnam and the long jungle patrols when our gazes would swivel right to left, left to right, turn up, turn down, seeking trip wires, snipers, ambushes, the glint or flicker of movement, the perception of which could mean the difference between spending another day aboveground or going home in a box, if there was enough left of you to fill one. "If I die in a combat zone / Box me up and ship me home." We were both predator and prey, keen as hunters, wary as the hunted.

The track makes a hairpin turn. True to the Tsavo's mysterious ways, a lioness appears, with a suddenness that suggests she's been conjured up by some sorcerer's trick. She is walking purposefully down the road in front of us, and we swing off, driving parallel to her, Rob standing on the seat, his head through the roof hatch, his camera's motor drive whirring. There is nothing beautiful about the lioness; old scratches and cuts mar her skin like sewn rips in a threadbare sofa, and her ribs show, though not in a way to spell starvation so much as a spare, sinewy toughness. If the sleek lions of the Serengeti are the haute bourgeoisie of the leonine world, Tsavo lions are the proletariat, blue-collar cats who have to work hard for a meager living. I recall Iain's comment about Tsavo. This lioness is perfectly suited to her habitat. Certainly no fat on her; nor does she look tolerant or forgiving, but very focused.

We trail her, but she shows no alarm. Now and then, she throws a sidelong glance at us, just to check on our distance or our behavior. If we edge too close, she angles away, maintaining a critical space of perhaps 15 yards. A lady with a mission, she goes through the saltbush and commiphora with the steady, unflagging pace of a veteran foot soldier.

Half a mile, a mile, two. The lioness, pausing, begins to call with low grunts. We figure she's trying to locate her pride, but if they answer, we don't hear them. Another quarter of a mile, and she stops on a rise and calls more loudly—a sound that seems to come from her belly instead of her throat, part moan, part cough. *Wa-uggh, wa-uggh.* In a moment, two cubs, a male and a female, bound from a saltbush thicket a hundred yards away. They leap on their mother, licking face and flanks, and she licks theirs.

"Oh, God, that's adorable," Leslie says.

It's not my custom to use words like "adorable," but that's what the scene is. I need to remind myself that if one of us were to get out of the Land Rover at this point, Her Leanness will quickly become something other than adorable.

Cubs in tow, the lioness commences to retrace her steps, and we again follow. The wary cubs stop to stare or hiss at us, but their mother keeps walking without a break.

Iain speculates that she'd stashed the cubs in the saltbush to go hunting or scouting, probably in the company of another lioness, because it would be difficult for a lone female to tackle a zebra. She's probably leading the cubs to the kill, if one's been made, or back to the pride.

It would be good if she leads us to the pride. If we can get an idea of where it is, we'll have an objective tomorrow when we will be on foot. I love walking in the wild, but I love even more walking with a purpose.

The lioness presses on with her journey, and then she and the cubs pull one of the vanishing acts that seem a Tsavo lion specialty. As swiftly as she first appeared, so do she and her young dissolve. Ten minutes pass, then Leslie calls out, "There they are!"

She points, and we see them, wading across the river. They stop on a sandbar in midstream. There the cubs gambol for a while, one mounting its forepaws on its mother's hindquarters and allowing her to pull it along as she looks for a spot to complete the crossing.

"All we need now is background music from *Born Free*," Iain remarks, but I think of Santiago's dream in *The Old Man and the Sea*, his dream of lions on the beach.

She plunges in and swims a deep, narrow channel, the cubs paddling after her. The three climb to the bank and then are swallowed by the saltbush. We are sorry to see the lioness go; for all her scruffy appearance, we've grown fond of her and her self-possessed air. Still, she looked awfully thin, and I say that I would feel better about her prospects if we'd seen her and the cubs reunited with their pride. I'd read that lionesses are sometimes evicted from prides, and when they are, their chances of survival are very low. Lions are social animals, after all, the only felines that are.

"Don't worry about her," Iain assures me. "She knows exactly what she's doing, she's in complete command of her situation."

*

The preprandial campfire discussion turns to film and literature, Iain presiding. He is an avid fan of both and can speak about both, intelligently, for hours. I'm not too up on movies, but Rob is, and serves to keep the conversation from becoming a monologue. A shift of gears to books brings Leslie and me in. The subject ranges from Don DeLillo to Salman Rushdie, with whom I'm familiar, to Martin Amis and several new Indian novelists, with whom I'm not. Iain's favorite book is Vikram Seth's *A Suitable Boy.* "A bit of a soap opera," says the safari guide turned critic, "but it's a damned well-written soap opera."

Kahiu's dinner—grilled eggplant, pumpkin soup, and bread pudding with cream—is, as usual, terrific. Mealtime chitchat returns to wildlife, specifically to *Panthera leo.* It continues as we adjourn back to the campfire, where, over coffee, Iain tells another bedtime story.

A Texas couple and their two sons were on safari with Tropical Ice. One midnight, Iain was awakened by the parents' screams: "Iain! They're here! They're coming in!" He tumbled out of bed, unzipped his tent flap, and saw a lioness walk right past him. Worse, he could hear other lions in the underbrush near camp—and the crunching of bones. Iain shouted to his clients to get on the floor of their tents and cover themselves with their mattresses. More lions appeared, playfully batting the guylines of the couple's tent, as if to tease the frightened occupants. Their two sons, scared witless but desperate to pee, filled their water bottles with urine. Iain, in the meantime, sought the help of his two armed Masai guards, who had managed to sleep through the commotion. As they approached the thicket in which Iain had heard the crunching noise, they were greeted by growls. The Masai did not live up to their reputation as fearless lion hunters; they fled in panic. It turned out that the lions were guarding their kill, which wasn't a person but a warthog. Iain attempted to drive them away by clapping his hands—a sound that usually frightens lions because no other animal makes it. It had no effect on those lions, who eventually just sauntered away.

The next day, the couple asked to leave the area. Iain agreed. Later, as he brought the Land Rover around, he saw what he termed "a horrifying sight." A lioness was sauntering alongside the woman's tent, which was open at one end. She was inside, packing. As calmly as he could, Iain told the woman to come out, but not to run, and get in the car. She had no sooner jumped in and shut the door than the lioness rounded the corner and walked into the tent. Had the woman still been inside, the lioness would have killed her. "Maybe not eaten her," Iain adds, reassuringly, "but definitely killed her because she would have tried to run."

The wind falls off as we retire for the night. What little breeze there is blows out of the south, and it's stifling inside the tent. I lie awake, my hand resting on my useless K-bar, and reflect on Iain's tale and on the theory, hypothesis, whatever it is, that the lions of Tsavo have an inherited tendency to hunt people. I need to get my mind onto something else. Much has been written about the eroticism of African safaris, and I consider a conjugal romp on the tent floor, but my fears rule that out. Eventually, I fall asleep.

At two in the morning, I wake out of a hideous nightmare probably induced by the anti-malaria drug I'm taking, Lariam. The list of its side effects, as long as a column in the Manhattan phone directory, covers a gamut of physical and psychological reactions, the most common are vivid, bizarre dreams. I cannot recall the details of mine, but its terror remains inside me. I hear something splashing in the river, then a loud rustling in the undergrowth. My 21st-century side tells me it's a hippo, but the puny hominid in me says it's a lion. Leslie's breathing becomes a lion, panting with hunger just outside our tent. Every crack of a branch, every little sound becomes the pad of a stalking cat. I picture him creeping up on the thin canvas that separates us from him, and I know that he isn't there out of curiosity or because he's smelled the food in the cook's tent or because he's winded a zebra herd beyond camp and is only passing through, but because he's scented us and we are what he's after. Deep into paranoid delusion now, I imagine the horror of what it's like to feel him bite down on my ankle or shoulder with his strong jaws and then drag me out and run off with me, wonderful, indispensable me, apple of my mother's eye, and me screaming and scratching and kicking and punching, all to no avail, until he releases his grip to free his jaws to crush my windpipe, snap my neck, or drive his tusks through my skull, and the last sensation I'll have is of his warm breath on my face.

Such are my waking nightmares. I'm not sure how, in the span of a few hours, I have gone from feeling sorry for a real lion to being in abject terror of an imaginary one. At two in the morning, the higher brain doesn't function as well as it does at two in the afternoon, and you start thinking with the older brain, that cess of primeval dreads.

*

Dangers imagined are always worse than dangers confronted. I am in high spirits this morning and have a good laugh at Rob's expense.

His tent is splattered with shit. Gobs of it stick to the roof and walls or run down in streaks, so that the canvas looks a little like a scatological Jackson Pollock. The hippo I heard last night was responsible, spraying feces all over his tent to mark it as his—or her—territory. Hippos do this, we are informed by Clive, by twirling their tails while they defecate. Literally a case of the shit hitting the fan.

The plan for the morning's hike is a no-brainer: walk upstream some ten miles to the Sobo Rocks, where Simon, the driver, will pick us up. I am actually looking forward to facing a lion on foot, if for no other reason than to conquer my fear. Still, in the event of such an encounter, I hope that Adan and Hassan will not imitate the behavior of the Masai in Iain's story. If they do, we won't have much in the way of self-defense—my trusty K-bar, Iain's Gurkha kris, a souvenir from a trek in the Himalaya, and Clive's Masai simi, backed up by a Masai war club. It's made of some sort of hardwood and is about as long as a baseball bat, with a slender handle and a knob at its business end. A nicely balanced weapon, and Clive says he could break a lion's spine with one blow from it. Of course, that would require the lion to stand passively and allow itself to be whacked across the back.

Lions, however, aren't the only dangerous game we might encounter. The saltbush forests easily conceal elephant, Cape buffalo, and the hippopotamus, which kills more people in Africa than any other animal. Since Tropical Ice started running safaris in 1979, Iain's guards have rarely had to fire over the heads of elephant and never shot a lion, but they have had to kill six hippos, which are very territorial and very aggressive. On one safari, a woman in his party was bitten by an angry hippo, losing half her buttock. A satellite-phone call brought an evacuation helicopter to her rescue; otherwise, she would have died from loss of blood.

With Adan on point and Hassan as rear guard, we wade the warm, silty Galana to the north side, Iain instructing us to stay close together so we sound not like seven average-size things but like one big thing—an elephant—to deter crocodiles. We see one of the reptiles, a nine- or ten-footer, a quarter of an hour after we've forded. Alarmed by our approach, it crawls quickly away, its plated tail sweeping behind. We continue upriver toward the Sobo Rocks, following game trails blazed by elephant and hippo. It is still cool enough to hike comfortably, an overcast, breezy morning, with a fan of pale sunlight piercing the thin clouds. The saltbush is dense enough to conceal a dozen elephants or buffalo, so we must be alert as we pass through. Now we are out on the scrubby plain north of the river galleries, now we are back in the saltbush. A gerenuk appears in the distance, a delicately built gazelle with a glossy hide and giraffelike neck. I rather wish I'd taken courses in evolutionary biology so I'd have some resources to draw on to figure out what nature has in mind creating such animals. Sometimes, being anthropogenic, I like to think that she's giving us a diverse and interesting world to live in, a notion that would elicit howls from evolutionists. Probably, nature has nothing in mind; like some retired craftsman tinkering in the workshop, she likes to mix that with this and see what she comes up with.

A few Cape buffalo watch us from about 200 yards away. Although they are aggressive only when surprised or wounded, we keep our eyes on them as they do theirs on us. The difference between encountering buffalo on foot and in a vehicle is like the difference between flying a commercial airliner and hang gliding. There is a tingling in the scalp, a quickening in the blood; not fear but an alertness. The bends go out of the Galana for a while; the river looks artificially straightened. A few zebra stand on a ridge, completely still, gazing at the river with what seems to be longing. They are dying to come down to drink, but are afraid that die is what they'll do; a croc or lion might be waiting for them at the riverbank, and so they stand frozen between the poles of fear and desire. A psychologist would call this an "approach-avoidance conflict." Iain terms it "the paradox of survival."

He stops, squints.

"Fringe-eared oryx."

The animal is close to 300 yards away, amid the zebra. I raise my binoculars and behold one of the most distinctive antelope in the world. A black stripe streaks horizontally along the lower flank, dividing white belly from brown hide. Its forelegs are banded in black; a black patch on the forehead almost touches another on the upper muzzle, contrasting with the white hairs on the lower muzzle. The ears stick straight out, tufted in black, and still more black stripes, one on each side of its face, a third extending under the chin and around the throat, provoke more wonder at nature's diversity, her whimsical artistry. A pair of horns as long as spears make a deep V above its head. With them, Iain says, an oryx can wound or kill an attacking lion.

Forgetting the mission for a moment, I begin a stalk, hoping to reach a bush roughly halfway between me and the oryx. From there, I should be able to get a decent photograph with the 300-millimeter lens. In the crosswind, I'm confident the oryx won't scent me. Walking very slowly in a low crouch, then crawling, it takes me a quarter of an hour to cover the distance. When I get to the bush and raise the camera, I see that I'm still too far away, and drop into a low, infantryman's crawl, the camera with its heavy, two-foot-long lens cradled in my elbows. After five minutes of this, I get into a sitting position, and rest both elbows on the insides of my spread knees, as you would a rifle, to steady the lens. A slight twitch would be all it would take to blur the picture. I frame the oryx and snap a photo, but

I doubt it will capture the sharp contrasts of the animal's fine markings. I start to crawl again, head raised to watch the oryx. It spots me, tenses for an instant, and trots off over a ridge.

We walk on, and the morning passes from cool to scorching in minutes. We take a break beside the river, where Adan, with his naked eye, spies a bull elephant almost a mile downstream. It's invisible to Leslie and me. We need binoculars, and even then strain to see it, with its reddened hide camouflaged against the steep, red riverbank. Much closer to us are a dozen hippos, dark heads showing above the water, the high, protruding eyes watching us. Hippos spend most of the day partly submerged to avoid overheating. I wish we could— the searing air is reminiscent of Arizona in July. Rob and I creep forward for photographs, Iain warning us to be careful. The hippos tolerate our photographing them for a while, but when we edge closer, a big bull lunges from the water with astonishing speed for so cumbersome a creature, his cavernous mouth open and bellowing. Only a warning, which we heed by moving on.

A fish eagle glides over the Galana. We have the whole immense wild to ourselves; most modern tourists are unwilling to walk miles in triple-digit temperatures and too timid to confront wild creatures on foot. What a difference to observe game on their own terms. To photograph them, we read the wind as the hunter does and practice stealth and keep our eyes peeled for the slightest motion. We stalk up close to a band of Cape buffalo and a small elephant herd and the experience is far more satisfying than driving up to them. Sweating, exercising caution and bushcraft, we earn the right to bag them on film.

It's like hunting, but it's not hunting. Even afoot, observing game is passive. The photographer is still in the audience, whereas the hunter is a full participant in the dance of predator and prey, and that's an experience of an altogether different quality. I've tried to explain this to friends who are nonhunters or anti-hunters, in futile attempts to get them to see why I hunt. My friend, novelist Jim Harrison, thinks I'm wasting my breath. When anyone asks him why he hunts, the question usually freighted with moral indignation, as if hunting were equivalent to, say, child molestation, Harrison responds, "I'm just less evolved than you are." It's his way of stating the old argument that the armed man is a predator, responding to a call that comes down to us from the Pleistocene, when hunting was the primary means by which man got his food. Jim and I in fact are meat-hunters, never killing anything we don't intend to consume. I think most modern Americans and Europeans no longer realize that the chicken, beef, veal, and pork they buy in perfectly trimmed, plastic-wrapped pieces were once living creatures. The hunter at least knows where his meat comes from and is grateful. Of course, there's more to it than that. Hunting grouse and woodcock in the Michigan and Vermont woods, I am more alert, more attuned to sound and movement than when I'm merely hiking. In hunting dangerous game, assuming it's done ethically, you enter an entirely different universe, much as Wayne Hosek did in his pursuit of the Man-eater of Mfuwe. On an Alaskan big-game hunt, my friend Alan Richie brought down a big male grizzly with one shot from his .300 Magnum. The bear sprang up and crashed off into a willow thicket. Had Alan's gun been a camera, we would have left and gone on to the next photo opportunity, but the hunter's ethics demand that you never leave a wounded animal to suffer unnecessarily. Besides, we were living off the land on that trip and we wanted the bear's meat—loin of grizzly bear is delicious, roasted over an open fire. We were virtually certain Alan had fired a killing shot, but virtual only counts in computer games;

we had to make sure. Dusk was falling. Way off in the distance, a wolf had begun to howl, and in the dim light, rifles just off our shoulders, we pushed into the willows, both of us quivering inside from a surge of adrenaline. If the bear had been wounded, its charge would be ferocious and fast, giving us each a microsecond to fire before the grizzly was on us. It lay ahead of us, brown fur rippling in the breeze. We tossed a few rocks at the bear, and when it didn't move, approached cautiously from behind it, then lay down our rifles and drew our skinning knives.

I recall that experience, walking the Galana, and the remark Iain made a few days before, that the old-time Africa guides wanted nothing to do with photographic safaris. I can understand why: Something essential and elemental is missing, a certain tension, a certain danger, a certain seriousness, if you will. There is no moment of truth. It's not quite the real thing. It's play.

Well, not quite...

We are on the last mile of the trek when we find pugmarks in the sand, leading straight along the shore toward a grove of doum palm a couple of hundred yards away. The tracks are deep and well defined, that is, recent. Iain and I fall into a discussion as to how recent. Clive, looking ahead with the naked eye, says very, because two lions are laid up under the palms. Clive points, and Iain and I raise our binoculars.

"It's a log," I say. "A big palm log."

Iain concurs.

"I am telling you, lions," Clive insists, peevishly. "Two bloody lions. One's maned, too."

Then Adan says, "Lions! One hundred percent!" and the log lifts its head.

My binoculars frame an atypical Tsavo lion, a Metro-Goldwyn-Mayer lion with a golden mane, lying in the shade with his companion and gazing straight back at us. With the palms overhead, the scene looks biblical.

Well, this is curious, a deepening of the Tsavo mystery. Is the lion an immigrant from the plains? Or do two different types of lion live side by side in Tsavo, maned and unmaned? We'll need photographs, but we're much too far.

The easterly wind favors us. We begin a stalk, heading up over the embankment to approach the lions from above, Rob and I with our cameras ready, Adan with his rifle at low port, prepared to shoot if necessary. Hassan's is braced on his shoulder, the muzzle pointing backward at the rest of us. Iain, directly behind him, pushes the rifle barrel aside. Hassan shifts the G3 to his crooked arms, holding it upside down as if he were cradling a baby, and saunters along like a man strolling in Hyde Park instead of in Tsavo with two big lions just ahead. A less than inspiring guard. I decide to grab his rifle if I have to.

We file along a game trail between the saltbush and the riverbank, closing the distance. The idea is to capture an image of a maned lion where there aren't supposed to be any, but something more is at work, at least inside myself, than documenting a feline anomaly: to photograph a lion up close and personal while on foot. What's the difference between a picture taken from a car and one taken on foot? I don't know, only that there seems to be a difference. Is it necessary? Is it stupid? What used to be called "manly courage" is considered atavistic, like a prehensile tailbone. The ancient Roman stoic Epictetus said: "Reflect that the chief source of all evils to man, and of baseness and cowardice, is not death, but the fear of death. Against this fear, then, I pray you, harden yourself; to this let all your reasonings, your exercises, your reading tend." Still true, I'd say. The point of life is not success in e-commerce or in any sort of commerce; it is to be brave; it is to master fear of death, which is the genesis of all fears. And one of the exercises by which you steel yourself to that fear is to confront something that could break your neck with a swipe of its paw.

None of us are trembling. We're apprehensive instead, in the old sense of the word. We apprehend, in a state of heightened aware-ness, our senses quickened. Coming abreast of the palm grove, Iain walks in a crouch, and we follow suit, trailing him and Hassan over the lip of the embankment to look down into the pool of shade beneath the trees. Rob and I raise our cameras.

The lions are gone. They must have fled at the sound of Adan's voice, though we never saw them move. We search under the palms, along the riverbank, into the saltbush, but cannot find their tracks. It's as though they've dematerialized. The ghosts of Tsavo.

*

Tsavo. Tsavo. In the language of the tribes who inhabited these regions, the name refers to massacres committed by Masai raiding parties in the distant past. The Masai were not curiosities then, but feared as the Apache and Iroquois were once feared in North America. Parties of roving warriors called *morani*, haughty and tall, nourished on the milk and blood of their cattle, ranged out of their Serengeti strongholds plumed in ostrich feathers, metal jewelry clattering on their wrists and ankles, spears banging against their buffalo-hide shields. They raided other tribes, sometimes for women, most times for cattle, the theft of which they considered reclamation of their property because they believed that God had given all the world's cattle to the Masai. With the exception of the Zulu, there was probably no tribe in Africa as warlike, fired as they were by an overweening pride and a total scorn for everyone else, including the pale Europeans whom they called *ilorida enjekat*— "those who confine their farts." The morani came to the thornbush flats where the Kamba and Waliangulu lived and killed them without quarter, and so the land came to be called Tsavo—"Place of Slaughter."

Masai raiders, slave caravans, man-eating lions—no wonder it was thought to be cursed. It looks cursed this morning as we trek downriver. It is a brighter morning than yesterday, and hotter. The dusty plains are empty, reaching to the horizon, where Sala Hill rises as abruptly as a pyramid from the desert. My shirt is soaked through, my eyeballs feel sunburned, but Hassan and Adan saunter along as I would on some fine spring day in New England. Adan tells me that on anti-poaching patrols he covers 25 miles a day. "To me, this isn't even walking," he boasts.

Elephant skulls appear, remnants left by poachers. They are as big as boulders and spur-winged plovers have built nests in the eye sockets. Piles of fresh elephant dung dot the trail, giving Iain an occasion to lecture again on pachyderm ecology. Hornbills, he says, pluck seeds and grasses from the dung and spread them over the savanna, thus regenerating growth.

The skull of a big buffalo lies above a lugga. Iain and Clive poke around, studying the area like homicide detectives.

"Probably an old bull, alone," concludes Iain. "The lions were down in the lugga, behind that big bush, two to three of them. They sprang at the buffalo from the side, just as he was about to come down the bank."

But that is all we see of lions. We slip off our boots in preparation to wade the Galana to the point where Simon will pick us up. As I slide down the bank, I discover, too late, that the clasp to my knife scabbard has been cut by thorn bushes. My K-bar falls out into the water. It's more than a mere knife to me—a souvenir of Vietnam, the only one I've got besides my pair of cracked, battered jungle boots. I search for it, pawing the muddy river bottom, but can't find it. Adan volunteers to find it for me. Poking with his bare feet for a minute or two, he says, "Ah!" bends down, and comes up with it. I thank him profusely, maybe too profusely, because when I ask if there's anything I can do for him, he replies, "Yes. Please buy a car for me. A Mercedes." I glance at him to see if he's having a bit of fun with the *mzungu* from America. He's not. Absolutely serious. I tell him a Mercedes is out of the question, so he switches to a Volkswagen. Informed that a Volkswagen is also out of the question, he asks if I will send him a new TV set, and promises to give me his address when we get back to camp. I refrain from asking if he prefers a Sony, an RCA, or some other brand.

Simon arrives in the Land Cruiser (it has replaced the ailing Land Rover; Tsavo is tough on trucks, too) and returns us to camp. On the drive back, he tells us that we need not have walked eight miles to find lions; they had found us. Only 45 minutes after we left on our walk, four males appeared on the north side of the river, almost directly across from camp. Simon thinks they have since moved off.

I nap after lunch, make some notes, and sit shirtless and shoeless in front of our tent, my baked brain a perfect tabula rasa. Iain approaches, walking fast over the Bermuda grass. Gesturing, he whispers to follow him to his tent and to be quiet. The four lions have reappeared.

With cameras and binoculars, we run on tiptoe and squat down. Across the river, between 200 and 300 yards down-current, two of the four crouch on the bank, drinking. Their hides so match the sand and beige rock that they seem to be made of the same stuff. I put the binoculars on them. They lack manes, and I would think they were females, but their size suggests otherwise. Thirst slaked, one turns and pads up the bank, displaying pendulous testicles. He disappears into a clump of doum palm; the second drinks a while longer, then joins his friend. A moment later, the first lion emerges to walk slowly into the saltbush behind the palms, the other following shortly afterward, and then a third—a band of nomadic males, hunting brothers, mature in size but still too young to challenge an old lion like Scarface for leadership of a pride.

"See how relaxed they are?" says Iain, softly. "They're not acting as if they're aware we're here. If they are, and they're this casual about it, we may have some major problems tonight."

Black-faced vervet monkeys hop from the trees nearby, scamper warily to the river's edge to drink. Are our primate brothers and sisters aware of what is on the other side? Maybe they're too small for a lion to bother with, I think out loud. Iain shakes his head, repeating that Tsavo lions will attack and eat anything they can catch. Encouraging.

Now the fourth lion shows up, just as I get out of my seat to fetch my field notes from my tent. Leonine eyesight is as keen as our own, and he catches the movement and stops, turning his head to face in our direction. I ease back down, carefully raise the binoculars, and have the unsettling impression that I'm staring into the lion's face, and he into mine, from a distance of, say, ten yards. Crouched low, the joints of his bent forelegs forming triangles, his shoulders a mound of muscle, sinews, and tendons twisting like aircraft cable under his skin, he is so still that he could be a carving. Like the others, he has no mane.

I ponder the two riddles—no one knows why Tsavo males lack manes because no one knows why other lions have them.

Considering how thoroughly Serengeti lions have been studied for the past 35 years, beginning with George Schaller's pioneering work in the 1960s, you would think the latter question would have been answered long ago. Another intriguing point of the Gnoske–Kerbis Peterhans hypothesis comes to mind. The two researchers believe they have identified a historical trend in man-eating, which can be traced geographically to environments like Tsavo's. If that's correct, then, yes, maneless lions could be more likely to prey on humans.

Which brings something else to mind, of a more personal, immediate nature.

"What did you mean, if they know we're here and are casual about it that we could be in for problems tonight?" I whisper to Iain.

"They won't attack, but they could come into camp."

He doesn't say what leads him to make so confident a prediction, and I don't ask.

We sit around the nightly campfire, entertained by Clive, who turns out to be a yarn-spinner and a terrific mimic of Australian accents and British brogues. Garbed in a striped *kikoy*, he tells funny folk tales from the south of England, where he was born, and although the humor in these antiquated stories that go back to the 18th century doesn't quite translate to a 21st-century mind, Clive's vocalizations keep us laughing.

Clive wraps up his act. Iain picks up the slack, talking rock groups with Rob, novels with Leslie and me. The author reviewed in this session is Gabriel Garcia Marquez. I contribute to the discussion by asserting that the opening line to *One Hundred Years of Solitude* is the finest in all of Western literature: "Many years later, as he faced the firing squad, Colonel Aureliano Buendia was to remember that distant afternoon when his father took him to discover ice."

In the middle of this erudite discussion, the lions begin to roar from across the river. It's a sound like no other, deep and resonant. *Waaugh-waaugh-unh-unh-unh.* "Your wit and brains don't impress us," it seems to say. "You're meat to us. Meat-meat-meat."

THE FINISH LINE for yesterday's walk is the jump-off point
for today's. Driving there, we see two of the male quartet on a
beach, quite a ways off, but they're soon gone. A crocodile suns
itself on a sandbar, gray-green, plated body glistening in the early
morning light. We begin trekking at eight, Adan at point, Iain
having relieved the lackadaisical Hassan. It's plain that Iain is
unimpressed with both our askaris. He pines for the ranger who
accompanied him on his epic march from Kilimanjaro to the sea,
a six-foot-four-inch Turkana named Mohammad, a switched-on
guy in whom Iain had absolute confidence. We walk another ten
miles, all the way to the eastern border of the park at Sala Gate,
seeing elephant and giraffe and carmine bee-eaters, a bird so gorgeous it stops your heart. We do not find the bachelor gang of four,
nor the lean lioness we spied three days ago. Frustrated, I decide
to postpone tomorrow's interview with Chap Kusimba, the Field
Museum anthropologist, and persuade Iain that we must make a

concentrated effort to find lions. We have less than three full days left in Tsavo.

*

On the first day of those three, we begin where the lioness crossed the Galana with her young, a broad bend a few miles downstream of Durusikale. Distinct pugmarks are printed in the fine sand near a stand of doum palm. The strong sundowners in Tsavo scour animal tracks pretty quickly, so the prints must have been made last night or early this morning. There are more on the sandbar, where the cubs cavorted with their mother, and on the opposite bank. One set of tracks lead us into the saltbush and to a lion's day-bed—a patch of flattened grass and dirt—but we lose them farther on, where the earth is hard as pavement and covered with foot-high, yellow grass.

"You can see why that dumb movie called them ghosts," Iain murmurs. "They're always in ambush mode. They stay hidden, come out to hunt and kill, then hide again. They are ghosts."

His commentary is borne out a little farther upriver, when we strike the track of the two males spotted from the car the previous day. Again we follow it, again we lose it. The lions could be anywhere or nowhere. As Adan pushes into the saltbush, his rifle at the ready, I compare Tsavo lions not to ghosts but to the Viet Cong: masters of concealment, of hit and run, showing themselves only when they choose. As Hosek did in Zambia, I'm beginning to appreciate what Colonel Patterson endured a century ago. It's an adventure for me to track these lions, but I would not want to be charged with the task of finding and killing them, and all the while see to the building of a railroad bridge.

We continue upriver, splitting up for a while, with Iain and Hassan tracking on the land side of the saltbush corridor, Clive,

Adan, Leslie, and me on the river side. (Rob is at park headquarters, photographing Kusimba, Andanje, and the park's collection of lion skulls.) The sand is almost white and crunches underfoot like snow on a sub-zero day. More lion tracks, vanishing on broad terraces of sandstone fissured so symmetrically they appeared to be man-made. Clive gives me a brief lecture on Tsavo geology and then, spotting a rock cairn seven feet high, on the Oromo people who wandered Tsavo hundreds of years ago, burying their dead in mounds like the one that rises up out of the saltbush and commiphora. Clive says he read about the Oromo in the library of the Royal Geographic Society, which he describes as a "great suppository of information."

I decide to leave it to Iain to correct the malapropism.

Joining up again, we go on. I feel oddly comfortable in these strange surroundings, as if they are not so strange, and wonder if it's a genetic memory, bequeathed by some upright ancestor who lived 10,000 generations ago.

Still no lions, then Adan finds another set of prints.

"These are very new," whispers Iain, pointing at one. "This is now."

A dry wind hisses through the acacia, the palm fronds rattle. A sand grouse, flushing five feet away, makes me flinch. Great predators can make their presence known even when they aren't seen or heard. When such monarchs are near, your senses heighten for the simple reason that your life may depend on it. I had experienced that keenness of perception every day in Vietnam, when the predator was a man with a rifle, and several times in Alaska, coming upon grizzly tracks, and once in Arizona, crossing the fresh prints of a cougar while I was quail hunting. But I've never experienced it as deeply as in these haunted thickets of Tsavo. There is something else as well. To walk unarmed in the lion's kingdom demands a submission not unlike the submission required of us in the presence of the divine, and it graces those who walk there with a humility that is not humiliation. I am acutely aware of being in a place where I, as a man, do not hold dominion, but must cede to a thing grander, stronger, and more adept than I.

Iain stops suddenly, wrinkles his nose, and asks, "Smell that?"

I shake my head. My sense of smell is the one that has not been heightened; I suffer from allergies. In fact, my nose has started to run. One of the things I'm allergic to is cats.

"A kill. There's something dead, rotting in there." Iain gestures at a thicket.

Then the wind eddies a bit, and I catch a stink a little like skunk, a little like week-old garbage.

Adan and Hassan push into the saltbush, while we who are unarmed wait in the open. When the two rangers emerge, they report they've found nothing except hyena and jackal tracks, indicating that the carcass, wherever it was, has been abandoned by the lions and is now the property of scavengers.

Iain grows reflective.

"I don't believe the man-eaters of Tsavo were man-eaters per se. Like all Tsavo lions, they were opportunists who would snatch, grab, and eat whatever came their way."

"Sure," Clive interjects. "Put 3,000 coolies out here, and of course the lions will go after them. They'd be bloody fools not to."

Iain, gazing upriver, continues his thought.

"If one of us, right now, tried to walk back to camp alone, the odds are he wouldn't make it. The lions would study you and see that you're alone, and they would take you."

We resume walking and no one is taken and the trek ends at the palm grove across from camp, where the four males had laired up. A lot of pugmarks, dark stains in the sand where the lions had urinated, but nothing more.

The next day is equally fruitless, as far as lions go, but we do see a black rhino, all by itself a quarter of a mile away. It's the first one Iain has seen in the wild in 15 years, and he is joyful.

Now it's our final full day in Tsavo (for this trip anyway), and we tramp to the saltbush where the lioness had stashed her cubs. Hoping to spot her once again, we make our way through, not talking, watching where we step, looking for tracks, then enter a grove of old doum palm.

"Make a perfect movie set, wouldn't it?" Clive says in an undertone. The trunks of the high trees are worn smooth where elephants have rubbed up against them, and the lanes between the trees are like shadowy halls, some blocked by flood-wrack from the rainy season: barricades of logs and fronds, behind which a dozen lions could be lurking, unseen. We expect to hear a low, menacing growl at any moment, an expectation that is not fulfilled until, making a circle, we come out of the trees and reenter the saltbush. The sound isn't a growl, however—more of a loud grunt or bellow.

It happens all at once. A cloud of dust rises from behind a thicket, Adan whips around, leveling his rifle, and Iain shouts, "Get behind me!" to Leslie and me. Just as we do, certain that we're about to be charged by a lion, an elephant appears not 20 yards to our right. It's a young female of some two or three tons, shaking her head angrily, her ears flared. She stomps and scuffs the earth, then starts toward us. Adan fires a shot over her head to scare her off. She stands her ground and trumpets, her ears thrown out again, dust rising from her feet, dust spewing from her hide as she tosses her great head back and forth. Iain yells to Adan in Swahili. He fires again, and for an instant I think he's shot her—some trick of light makes a puff of dust flying from her shoulder look like the impact of a bullet. In the next instant, as the female runs off, I realize that he'd put the second round over her head.

Iain lights into Adan, all in Swahili, but it's plain that the ranger is getting a royal dressing down. The close call has left me breathless. I'm grateful to Adan and can't understand why Iain is so angry.

"Rangers are supposed to know that you don't have to shoot at an elephant to scare it off," Iain explains. "That female was old enough, about 15, to have seen other elephants shot by poachers. You had to have been here in the '80s to appreciate it. Elephants are traumatized by the sound of gunfire. They're very intelligent animals, and it's not necessary to fire over their heads. A hand clap will do it, or just waving your arms. That's what Muhammad would have done. I've seen him do it. What we try to do on a foot safari is to observe without disturbing the animals and move on without them ever being aware that humans are around."

*

I am not yet out of Tsavo and I'm already nostalgic. Driving toward the Manyani Gate, I know I'm going to miss the soul-stretching expanses of its savannas and the elephant herds moving in the red dust and the brass-colored glint of the Galana and the late-afternoon African light that strikes my eye like a light it's seen long ago, in some previous life. After ten days of observing or seeking them, the lions of Tsavo seem more enigmatic than when I came. I have learned nothing except how little I know—which is generally the first step toward knowledge.

Before heading back to Nairobi, we make a pilgrimage to the "Man-Eaters' Den."

When Rob was photographing at park headquarters, Kusimba told him that the result of his team's excavation work had been a little disappointing. They never found the copper bracelets Patterson claimed to have seen, nor any human remains. Kusimba's conclusion is that his first assumption was right: The legendary cave never was a lion's den, nor any sort of den, but a Taita burial cave. He took Rob to it, and now Rob will show it to us. Entering the gate to Tsavo West, we drive less than a mile to an abandoned airstrip and park. Iain and Clive are as eager for a look as Leslie and I. So, with Rob in the lead, the two guides become the guided. After thrashing around for a while, we come to a ravine, one of many in the labyrinth of the Ngulia Hills. Rob shouts from up ahead, "Here it is!"

And there it is—a corridor between two big boulders leading beneath an overhang and into a cavern. A fig tree spreads its branches above, its roots clinging like tentacles to one side of the entrance.

"Well, I don't think it looks so fearsome," says Iain, recalling Patterson's description. I sense that his opinion of the colonel hasn't improved.

I agree that the cool, shady spot is almost idyllic. But we're not trying to build a bridge in the African wilderness and, at the same time, hunt down two clever cats that are using our workforce as fast food. To Patterson, with his memories of his worker's screams, of his servant's gruesome remains, of the tense, interminable nights waiting with his rifle, the cave would have appeared "fearsome." And given the ignorance about lion behavior that prevailed in his time, it was understandable why he mistook a burial cave for a man-eater's den. Imperial martinet or not, he did pretty damn well with what he had.

That said, I do find Patterson's characterization of his adversaries as brutes and outlaws objectionable. I recall our second to last day in Tsavo, after we finished the morning's hike. As we sat in camp, we watched a zebra herd warily come down the far bank of the Galana to drink. They had been waiting on the ledge above the river for a long time, suffering from "the paradox of survival." The animals were parched, but the whole herd stood still, gazing at the river with what seemed to us equal measures of longing and dread, until the desperation of their thirst overcame their fear of death. They did not rush down with abandon, but watered in orderly stages. A dozen or so animals would drink, while the others waited their turn and the stallions stood watch. Their heads bent, the ranks of their striped backs were a study in geometric beauty. If one group got greedy and took too long, the stallions would let out a series of loud, sharp brays. It was a strange, distressing sound, falling somewhere between a whinny and a bark.

Even a layman should not anthropomorphize, but to me, the stallions seemed to be saying, "You've had enough, get a move on, we don't have much time." In a way, I identified with them. They were lion prey, and out there, so was I; but that recognition did not offend my sense of human dignity. The offense was to my human pride. Nothing wrong with pride, except when it becomes excessive and denies others, whether men or beasts, the right to their pride and dignity. If I had been in Colonel Patterson's boots, I would have pursued the lions with as much determination—after all, his first responsibility was to finish the bridge and protect his workmen's lives—but I like to think I would have respected the lions and avoided regarding them as savage brutes violating some law of heaven.

I had learned little about Tsavo's lions, but I had learned something about myself. To realize that I shared something with the wary, anxious zebras was not degrading, but merely acknowledged my true place in nature where nature is wild, the stage on which the drama of predator and prey is played out.

INTERMISSION

A TRIP TO THE MUSEUM

THE MAN-EATERS WERE GONE, moved from Stanley Field Hall to an exhibit room off a side corridor, and the Masai morani had been banished to a basement storage room, where I pictured them frozen in eternal combat with two-fanged adversaries that no longer faced them. That image struck me as emblematic of modern Masai, confined to ever shrinking reserves, with no lions to fight, posing for photographs snapped by the pale those-who-confine-their-farts, their long-bladed spears now mere symbols, like the halberds carried by the beefeaters at the Tower of London. The only familiar exhibit remaining in the hall was the elephants, though they were dwarfed by the new attraction that had drawn swarms of visitors to the Field Museum on this splendid June morning: the re-created skeleton of a 42-foot Tyrannosaurus Rex named Sue. The lines extended from the turnstiles inside the hall, out through the doors, and down the steps into the street. Wearing a special badge that had allowed me to jump the queues, I waited for Tom Gnoske and gazed around, pleased that the grand structure hadn't lost its power to evoke wonder and that

I, just two days shy of my 59th birthday, hadn't lost a capacity for wonder. The museum had recently undergone an extensive refurbishment; it was better lighted than I remembered, and the newly scrubbed stone and marble gleamed like a Roman palace. The renovations were part of a huge public works project commissioned by Mayor Richard M. Daley, son of the sometimes famous, sometimes infamous Mayor Richard J. Daley, late boss of the late Chicago political machine. The museum, the Shedd Aquarium, and the Adler Planetarium now formed a campus joined by broad, tree-shaded walkways and surrounded by parks and flower gardens. Eastward, the slate green expanse of Lake Michigan provided an illusion of ocean. To the south were the McCormick Place Convention Center and Soldier Field, where the Bears continued to wage gladiatorial contests in rain, snow, and mud. A domed, climate-controlled stadium might be appropriate for Dallas or Houston, but not for the City of the Big Shoulders. To the north, the towers of the Loop and Michigan Boulevard rose into an unblemished sky, creating a skyline as spectacular as Manhattan's, and maybe more so because it was a less congested, less aggressive tyranny of brick and concrete.

In appearance and atmosphere, as well as geographically, it was all very far from Tsavo, yet a thread of shared history tied the great midwestern city to the sere and distant landscapes where Indian laborers had cried out, on those fearful nights in 1898, "Watch out, brother, the devil is coming!" As Julian Kerbis Peterhans had told me on the phone: "The story of the Tsavo lions is a Chicago story."

Pursuit of that story had brought me back to Chicago from my home in Connecticut, some four months after returning from Africa. Kerbis Peterhans and Gnoske were planning an expedition that would take them up the Tana River in eastern Kenya. From there, they would fly to Uganda and the Kyambura Gorge, then on to the Luangwa

Valley in Zambia, hunting ground for the man-eater killed by Wayne Hosek. The objective would be to do field surveys of lion populations, gathering sufficient evidence to document their thesis that there isn't one, but two species of lion in Africa, and one is a direct descendant of a lion that lived when woolly mammoths roamed the Earth.

Like the scientific expeditions of a bygone age, the one Gnoske and Kerbis Peterhans were proposing would be a red-blooded adventure with a purpose. Most adventures these days are Evel Knieval stunts (the first man to jump a motorcycle over the Snake River) in which someone overcomes artificial obstacles and braves manufactured dangers to achieve some pointless goal. A quest that intended to add to the sum of human knowledge interested me a great deal. I hoped to write about the two men as they took risks and endured hardships to make a new discovery, and had come to Chicago to meet them and discuss the chances of my joining them. But first I had to assure myself that they weren't pursuing a mythological beast, some sort of leonine yeti that existed in their imaginations. After all, the best minds in the business had been saying for decades that all African lions belonged to the same species; the only known subspecies was the rare Asiatic lion, of which roughly 300 survived in the fastness of the Gir Forest in northern India. Who were these two guys to say different?

Gnoske spotted me waiting at the information booth. Dressed in jeans and a faded blue shirt, he was a stocky, broad-faced man of about five feet ten, with wispy, light brown hair, a mustache, intense, gray-blue eyes, and a ready smile. Introductions, handshakes, and I recognized immediately that he was, like me, a native of Chicago's blue-collar neighborhoods. The accent gave him away—that broad, nasal "*a*'s," and the habit of turning "*o*'s"s into "*a*'s"s, so that the name of the city isn't pronounced the way Frank Sinatra sang it—"My kind of town, Chicawgo is"—but comes out the way Boss Daley used to say it—"Chicahga."

Gnoske escorted me past Sue, with her rib cage like the frame of a small ship, to an elevator that carried us to the third floor. That was where the museum's sausages got made, and it wasn't pretty: long corridors as dimly lit as mine galleries ran under exposed pipes past cubbyhole offices and research rooms and specimen lockers and preparation rooms smelling of mothballs and preservatives. There was something about the quasi-industrial atmosphere that appealed: Real work is done here, it said. If the marbled hall below was the showroom, this was the shop floor.

Gnoske's office, in the Bird Division, looked like a stage set for a period drama, except for a couple of computer terminals. Ergonomically correct chairs were absent. There were wooden desks of a kind I hadn't seen since grammar school, and they'd looked like antiques then; glassed-in bookcases filled with dusty volumes in the no-nonsense bindings of yesteryear; field trunks stenciled with the names of expeditions and the countries where they'd taken place; black-and-white photographs showing long-dead scientists and explorers in former terrae incognitae that can be reached today in 24 hours by commercial jet. One of the pictures showed Carl Ackeley standing beside the strung-up carcass of an 80-pound leopard. Ackeley, a renowned naturalist and taxidermist who'd collected and mounted many African animals for U.S. museums, had wounded the leopard slightly on an expedition in the late 1920s. At 80 pounds, the cat was only half full-grown size, but 80 pounds of injured, enraged leopard is not the same as 80 pounds of, say, golden retriever. It sprang on Ackeley, who managed to kill it with his bare hands, wrestling it onto its back and then crushing its ribs between his knees, puncturing its lung. A remarkable feat of self-preservation, considering that he wasn't a particularly powerful man. He took his licks, however. In the photo, Ackeley appears to be wearing a pair of white boxing gloves—after the fight, his hands looked like they'd had a brush with a chipper-shredder.

"Lucky he'd put a bullet in that cat," Gnoske remarked. "Slowed it down. Otherwise, I don't think Ackeley would have made it."

We segued from leopards to lions and to Gnoske's fascination—obsession would be a better word—with the latter.

It began only a few months after he was born in Andersonville, a mostly Swedish neighborhood on Chicago's mid-north side. Gnoske fell in love with a stuffed toy lion and would not go anywhere without it. For the next four years, he refused to talk to anyone except it and, now and then, his mother. The shy child was captivated by wild animals, especially lions and tigers, and watched *Mutual of Omaha's Wild Kingdom,* narrated by Marlin Perkins, every Sunday night before he started kindergarten.

Around that time, his father, to encourage his interest in the natural world, took him to the Field Museum. He toured the highlights—dinosaurs, the elephants, Bushmen, the 500-pound gorilla who had lived at the Lincoln Park Zoo. By that time—1969—the man-eaters of Tsavo had been moved from where I'd seen them 17 years earlier to a dim, mysterious exhibit hall devoted to large African animals. While walking through it, young Gnoske spotted the lions, whose maneless heads, lifelike eyes, and great size seized his attention. As he stared at them, his father told him the same story I'd heard from my father and that Hosek had heard from his. The tale terrified him, and he never forgot it.

At Gordon Technical High School, a Roman Catholic boys school on the north side, Gnoske was a running back on the football team and developed an interest in painting birds and mammals. He entered Chicago's Art Institute in 1984 on a partial scholarship, but dropped out after two years to study the anatomy of his subjects while working part-time in the Field Museum's zoology department. Two years later, he accepted a full-time position as a preparator in the bird division. In his spare time, he became a self-taught authority on big cats, reading everything he could on them in the museum's library, paying particular attention to historical accounts of lions, tigers, and leopards preying on human beings.

"I got to be really good at preparing birds," he said to me, there in his cluttered office. "Eventually, because curators have families and don't like to spend too much time in the field, I got to go on bird-collecting expeditions."

On one such foray in Uganda's Ruwenzori Mountains (Mountains of the Moon) in 1990, Gnoske took time off from his vocation to pursue his avocation. He traveled to Nairobi and hired a guide to take him to the Masai Mara, where he got his first good look at the classic lions of the African grasslands. Later that year, he again journeyed to the Ruwenzori, and there, in the mountains where the Nile begins, he made a couple of observations that would eventually send him off on his obsessive quest. The lions he spotted prowling the river and its tributary streams appeared to be traveling in much smaller prides than those he'd seen in the Masai Mara: one or two females with cubs instead of a harem. The males were maneless or had restricted manes. That would have been obvious to anyone, but another detail would have escaped notice. Gnoske's artist's eye, honed by his studies in anatomy, picked it up.

"The males had narrow faces and smaller heads than the pride males I'd seen in Kenya, who had heads like basketballs. I said to myself 'There's something different about them, without question.' I'm visual. Most scientists speak in terms of numbers, or in words, so I'm speaking a different language. I knew I would have to prove what I saw. I can't just say that one lion has a smaller head than the other. I would have to show it by taking a lot of measurements to prove that my eyes weren't fooling me."

He filed his perceptions in the back of his mind, returned to Chicago, and dug back into his research, looking for any reference to maneless lions in the literature. The pursuit took him backward in time from George Schaller's monumental study, *The Serengeti Lion,* published in 1972, to the annals of early African exploration. It was there that he came upon a few lines in an account of David Livingstone's journeys in 1849 into what is now Botswana. A few days after discovering Lake Ngami, the famed Scottish explorer and his companions shot two lions, one with worn teeth and blunt claws, the other with perfect teeth, and both, Livingstone wrote, "were destitute of a mane." In 1896, a Field Museum curator named Daniel Elliot brought down a maneless lion in Somalia and noted in his report that rarely were lions found in Somalia "with even a fairly long mane." Gnoske found another intriguing remark tucked away in a report of a 1913 expedition led by Edmund Heller, a zoologist who later became the museum's assistant curator of mammals. Heller, who'd done extensive fieldwork on the Athi and Serengeti Plains and was very familiar with *Panthera leo massaicus,* declared the discovery of a new subspecies of lion from near the source of the Nile. He called it *Panthera leo nyanzae,* and noted that it had a disproportionately small head compared with its body size. Eleven years later, another scientist, J. A. Allen, of New York's American Museum of Natural History, discovered another small-headed, big-bodied lion living along the upper reaches of the White Nile and named it *Panthera leo azandicus.*

Aware that taxonomists no longer recognized subspecific differences among African lions, the artist turned amateur zoologist was puzzled and curious. Were maneless lions more common than was generally believed? If so, why did they lack manes? Could Heller and Allen have been right after all?

Gnoske moved from his desk to a small table beside one of the glass-covered bookcases and pulled out several volumes from the shelves—Schaller's tome and old, leather-bound editions with dried-out pages yellowed at the edges. *Travel and Adventure in South-East Africa*, by Frederick Selous, the hunter and explorer who became the first British governor of Rhodesia, now Zimbabwe. Hollister's *East African Mammals*. R. Cummings's *A Hunter's Life*.

"Reading these old accounts and the observations I'd made in Africa, I felt that I had a discovery to make. My motivation was to prove that maneless lions weren't all that uncommon. I thought it was a widespread phenomenon, but I kept it to myself until I felt sure I'd observed a real pattern of maneless lions."

In the early 1990s, he made several trips to Uganda with Kerbis Peterhans, the only person in whom he'd confided. The two men had become friends in the 1980s when Kerbis Peterhans was doing doctoral research at the Museum.

I met Kerbis Peterhans after Gnoske and I adjourned to the Shedd Aquarium cafeteria for lunch, and remarked to myself that they made an odd pair, different in every way. Gnoske was a son of the proletariat, Kerbis Peterhans, as his double-barreled name suggests, of the upper class, raised on Chicago's gold coast, graduated from the exclusive Francis Parker prep school. Gnoske, the broad-shouldered ex-football player; Kerbis Peterhans, the lithely built tennis player. Gnoske, the art school dropout; Kerbis Peterhans, the professor of natural sciences at Roosevelt University, with degrees in biology and zoology and a doctorate from the University of Chicago in palaeoanthropology. Gnoske, 35 and single; Kerbis Peterhans married and 12 years older.

What they had in common was a fascination with big cats. Kerbis Peterhans's also arose early in life. He grew up across the street from the Lincoln Park Zoo, and there, in that most urban of environments, went to sleep to the same feline roars heard by children in remote African and Indian villages. His mother keeps a photograph of him in a childhood Halloween costume; he's dressed in a lion suit and a mop head dyed brown.

"My parents were divorced, and my mother was a professional, an architect," he said. "I was a latchkey kid, so after school I would hang out at the zoo. I befriended the zookeepers, who let me feed the smaller animals with them. There were no restrictions then, no concerns about litigation and safety. That experience got me interested in zoology."

And the story of the Tsavo man-eaters got him interested in cats that prey on people. His doctoral research focused on bones from early human fossil sites, which he analyzed to find out if our ancestors were normal fare for primitive felines. His conclusion—yes, they were. Bones of *Australopithecus* uncovered in South Africa indicated that they were to leopards as mice are to domestic cats. *Homo sapiens,* larger, stronger, and above all smart enough to think ahead and develop weapons, was more successful at avoiding big-cat grocery lists; nevertheless, early man remained on the menu. In fact, Kerbis Peterhans had written in his doctoral thesis that palaeoanthropologists owe a vote of thanks to the genus *Panthera:* Much of the fossil evidence of early human evolution consists of leftovers— human bones deposited by large feline predators.

"Lions and tigers eat people," he said as I munched a club sandwich and fries. "Primates are part of their diet and we are primates. Until the advent of firearms, we were prey. To my mind, the question isn't "Why did the Tsavo lions eat people?" but "Why don't all lions eat people?""

Ah, that dismal truth once again. The paragon of animals, cre-ator of epic poems, of the Pyramids and Taj Mahal, of the airplane, automobile, and microchip, is to *Panthera*'s eyes a slow- moving, vul-nerable biped. Easy meat.

Gnoske's ideas about maneless lions tantalized Kerbis-Peterhans. The preparator of birds could be on to something, and, possibly, that something had a bearing on his own work.

Their journeys to Uganda focused on modern predation of humans by lions, and they encountered instances of peculiar behavior. In one region in the southwest of the country, a mature male lion had invented his own version of Meals-On-Wheels: He had staked out a road fre-quented by bicyclists. The lion would hide in the long grass, wait for an unsuspecting rider to pedal by, pounce on him, drag him off back into the grass, and devour him on the spot. In Queen Elizabeth National Park, a healthy lioness showed a preference for drunks. Her method was to lurk in the shadows near a village pub, keeping an eye out for an inebriated patron to come staggering outside. When he did, she would stalk him, spring on him from behind, and carry him off for consumption. That certainly made a good case for temperance. At the time Gnoske and Kerbis Peterhans visited the village, 13 people had been claimed by the lioness, most of them frequenters of the pub. Nev-ertheless, the overindulgent continued to reel out of the establishment in the post-midnight hours, dinnertime for carnivores.

Actually, the lions' behavior might not have been all that bizarre, Kerbis Peterhans mentioned in an aside. When stalking four-footed prey, they look for abnormalities—limps, staggers, any sign of weak-ness or injury. It may have been that the "Meals-On-Wheels" lion regarded the labored movements of a cyclist pedaling on a rutted dirt road as not normal, whereas the lioness, like any big-city mugger, saw the stumbling drunks as easy marks.

For the next several years, Kerbis Peterhans and Gnoske commuted between Chicago and Africa. They rediscovered the false man-eaters' den in Tsavo and the apparently real den in the Kyambura Gorge. Their research also took them to museums in Europe, Africa, and North America to study the skins, skulls, and skeletons of modern and extinct lions, the purpose of which was to test the validity of Gnoske's visual impressions that certain lions had atypically small heads and big bodies.

"Tom has this great artist's eye," Kerbis Peterhans said. "He can look at a fossil skull in a London museum and then a recent skull in Nairobi and see that they're the same. Most people wouldn't notice that. But then you have to take careful measurements to confirm the impression."

There are few complete lion skeletons in the world's museums and they are hard to find. The two men had examined ten so far, and they said that what they found tended to support their hypothesis of two distinct types of lions living side by side in Africa.

It was show-and-tell time. We returned to Gnoske's office, where he produced two boxes and pulled a lion's skull from each and laid them side by side on his desk. The first was from a mature plains lion, and it was obviously larger than the second, which came from a mature "buffalo lion," the nickname the two researchers gave to the second type because it preys predominantly on buffalo. They used the term interchangeably with "Nile River lion," having observed the animal most often in river valleys, or near lakeshores—habitats where buffalo congregated.

The skull of the classic plains lion, said Gnoske, averages fifteen inches long by ten inches wide, and weighs five pounds dry; buffalo lion skulls average thirteen by eight inches and weigh three and a half pounds dry. There are other differences. The spheno-palatine foramen, an opening through which a nasal artery passes, is bigger in plains lions than in buffalo lions. The former also have a deeper sagittal crest, a kind of ridge atop the skull to which the upper jaw muscles attach, and a more developed pterygoid process of the lower mandible, to which the lower jaw muscles are fixed.

Moving lower in a lion's anatomy, a flange on the shoulder bones, called the deltoid ridge, is larger in buffalo lions, which, being anywhere from six inches to a foot taller, also have longer and stouter humeri.

Dizzied by the terminology, I asked, What does it all mean? Gnoske and Kerbis Peterhans took me through it, step by step.

The spheno-palative foramen: They didn't know why it was larger in plains lions, but speculated that it accommodates a larger nasal artery, which suggests that those lions have a keener sense of smell. Why? Again, no answer, but possibly because they live in large prides, that is, are more "social." They need a more acute sense of smell to better locate other lions. But that explanation, the two men stressed, was purest speculation.

The sagittal crest may be larger in pride lions to support more powerful jaw muscles. Ditto for the lower mandible. Plains lions require much stronger jaws than buffalo lions, not to kill prey (because they do little hunting) but to deliver decisive bites in battles with rivals for control of their prides. Their shorter stature and more compact build give them a lower center of gravity, making them harder to knock off their legs. A plains lion is a warrior, a buffalo lion a hunter. Despite its greater size, the latter would probably lose in a fight with the former. "It would be like a fight between a pit bull and a German shepherd," Gnoske said by way of illustration. "The pit bull would probably win. A German shepherd is a lot bigger, but a pit bull has a bigger head and stronger jaw muscles relative to its body size."

The deltoid ridge would be larger in the buffalo lion because, according to the Gnoske–Kerbis Peterhans scenario, they do most of the hunting—larger deltoid ridges support bigger deltoid muscles, which are necessary to bring down their huge prey. Allen Turner, an African naturalist, had theorized that the deltoid ridge in buffalo-killing specialists becomes even more pronounced over time due to the constant muscle stress of wrestling with the three-quarter-ton bovines.

Turning from the lion's skeletal structure to its exterior, the two researchers stated that plains males always develop luxuriant manes at maturity, whereas buffalo lions, which tend to live at lower elevations, grow variable manes, ranging from sparse crests, collars, and side whiskers to manes roughly half the size of their Serengeti cousins'. Abbreviated manes and tail tufts thicker than plains lions' are features that Asiatic and buffalo lions have in common. They also share a physical peculiarity with tigers—a belly fold: a thick, pendulous flap of skin on their bellies not found in lions on the savanna. Interestingly, the lions in cave paintings, in addition to having restricted manes, are also portrayed with belly folds. The pronounced deltoid ridge in buffalo lions bears some similarities to a flange found on the shoulder bones of extinct cats, like the saber-toothed cat and the prehistoric feline predator with the dire name of *Smilodon fatalis,* both of which were equipped to kill big prey. One possible explanation for such physical differences—and it was no more than a possibility, Gnoske emphasized—is that buffalo lions and the lions of India's Gir Forest may represent the "primitive condition" of the lion. That was another way of saying that they are a kind of missing link or living fossil, virtually unchanged from the lions painted on cave walls during the Stone Age.

Finally, there were differences in behavior and social structure. Lion society on the prey-rich savanna is matriarchal, with females in charge of hunting chores and the males in charge of controlling and defending large prides that are the leonine version of extended families. Along the riverbeds in what field zoologists call the "prey-depauperate" African scrublands, lion society is patriarchal and characterized by smaller prides, ranging from a single breeding pair with cubs to perhaps half a dozen animals—nuclear families. In Tsavo, for example, Gnoske and Kerbis Peterhans observed a solitary bull buffalo warding off repeated attacks by a single male lion for 45 minutes while a female with three adolescent cubs watched from a distance.

Assuming that there are marked differences between buffalo lions and the lions of the wide-open spaces, what accounts for them? Because the fossil and historical record is sketchy, Gnoske and Kerbis Peterhans can offer only an explanation that is partly factual, partly a scientific folktale.

The facts: Palaeontologists argue that the unmaned lions depicted in 30,000-year-old cave paintings were 25 percent bigger than modern lions. Gnoske and Kerbis Peterhans argue otherwise: The skeletons of extinct lions they'd studied in museums are virtually identical to those of buffalo or river lions.

Palaeontologists also assert that the genus *Panthera* arose millions of years ago in Central Asia. They preyed on wild oxen and cattle, the ancestors of domestic livestock. Environmental changes taking place over a vast span of time, between one million and two million years ago, caused the herds to begin migrating along river systems into western Asia, southern Europe, and eventually into Africa. The great predators followed them, so that, when the world entered historical times, Asiatic lions were established in what is today's Near East, Greece, the Balkans, and southern France, hence the numerous references to lions in the Bible and other ancient texts. In his *Histories,* Herodotus mentions that the lions of his era (the fifth century B.C.) preyed on the wild cattle and buffalo that roamed Greece and Turkey.

Gnoske and Kerbis Peterhans conjecture that the Jordan River depression, joining the Euphrates River to the Nile, created a corridor for primitive lions to invade Africa from Eurasia. Over time, these feline nomads, trailing herds of wild ungulates, established themselves along Africa's major river systems. During that era, they conjecture further, the social structure of the lion was in all likelihood no different from that of other cats in the genus *Panthera* (which includes leopards, jaguars, and tigers): It was a solitary animal, or, at most, lived in quite small family groups, just as leopards, jaguars, and tigers do today. In social terms, that was the primitive condition of the lion.

At some point in the past, perhaps drawn by the wealth of prey animals, some lion populations emigrated from the river valleys to the African savannas. But they were confronted by a problem: Yes, there was an abundance of prey on the grassland, and it was less dangerous to the predator than wild buffalo, but animals like wildebeest, zebra, and gazelle were also much faster and more nimble. Lions may have developed specialized traits to neutralize that advantage, taking to living in the large, cooperative hunting societies we call prides. Sexual roles changed as lion society underwent a kind of feminist revolution that made plains lions the only social animal among the big cats. Bands of sisters and aunts shared in caring for the young, but also became the primary hunters.

Any tourist who has spent time in an African national park, or any couch potato addicted to TV nature shows, has seen lionesses venturing out in disciplined hunting parties, executing pincer movements around a zebra or wildebeest herd or making "game drives" in which a couple of females set up an ambush position while three or four more chase prey animals into it. Why did females become the hunters? Killing buffalo requires brute strength and ferocity; seizing hard-to-catch prey on the savanna demands stealth and agility, attributes that lionesses possess to a greater degree than males. They are smaller and more nimble, and they don't have manes, which make males too obvious to plains prey and also slow them down when in hot pursuit.

So, with buffalo and other large prey like young elephant and hippo relegated to secondary items on the menu, masculine physical power was no longer so necessary. Having become semi-obsolete as a hunter, the grasslands male evolved into a formidable fighting machine. With females concentrated into tightly knit groups, he couldn't single out one breeding-age female and, so to speak, carry her off to live in isolated bliss. Marry one and you married her sisters as well, with her mother and aunts thrown into the bargain. Limited access to fertile lionesses caused competition for their attentions to become fierce, so adult males developed massive heads and jaw muscles, shorter, more compact bodies, and luxuriant manes. Meanwhile, back on the river systems, lions morphologically and behaviorally remained the same as they'd been in the Pleistocene era. The Man-eater of Mfuwe, whose stuffed replica was being ogled three floors below, was a classic of the breed: a solitary, maneless rogue with a small head relative to its enormous body.

And so the conversation briefly turned to the topic that had drawn me to Tsavo in the first place. If the two researchers accomplished nothing else, they hoped to soon solve the century-old mystery of what had caused Ghost and Darkness to become such ravenous consumers of human flesh. They were working on a study structured around several factors that lead to man-eating, factors they'd isolated during their work in Tsavo: the traditional one of injury, sickness, or old-age; decimation of "normal" prey; access to dead or dying human beings; a "social tradition" of man-eating; the role of habitat and vegetation; and livestock predation that causes conflict between carnivores and humans.

Flipping through my notes in Gnoske's office, I recalled the observation I'd made in Tsavo that seemed to refute one aspect of his and Kerbis Peterhans's hypothesis: that the big male, Scarface, appeared to be the leader of a large pride no different from the ones on the Serengeti. Was that an anomaly, and if so, how did they explain it? The question slipped my mind, because I was absorbed in sorting out the facts, theories, and assumptions I'd been scribbling down so feverishly. Also, I was more concerned about determining what significance all the theorizing would have for people outside professional circles. If the two men were able to prove that the buffalo lion was a distinct subspecies, what would the ramifications be? All right, such a discovery would not draw crowds to Times Square to cheer or hoot, but what about its effect in the scientific community? Once again, what did it all mean?

As if anticipating the question, Kerbis Peterhans had a ready answer.

"If this proves to be true, it will revolutionize ideas about the role of females in lion society. Beyond lions, it will revolutionize ideas about subspecies, which are now thought to be distinguished geographically. There has to be a significant geographic distance."

By way of example, he cited the African and Asian lion and two extinct subspecies, the Barbary lion, which lived in northwest Africa, and the Cape lion, native to South Africa.

"What we're saying is that because buffalo lions and pride lions live in the same general area, but look and behave differently, subspecies can be distinguished by morphology, behavior, and ecology." He paused and then made reference to the invisible elephant in the room. "People are going to look askance because of Tom's background," he said, meaning that other scientists were going to question Gnoske's lack of academic credentials. "That's why I've been extremely careful about gathering enough data and avoiding drawing the wrong assumptions from it." Another pause. "Two of the Field Museum's staff who have published in the most scientific journals don't have any formal training. Neither does [Richard] Leakey himself, yet he's called 'Dr. Leakey.' Tom has made so many remarkable observations that if only a few of them hold up, it will be an achievement."

One pat on the back deserved another in return, and Gnoske interrupted to say that his colleague, in addition to acting as a mentor, also helps him navigate in academic and social circles where he feels uncomfortable.

"I remember when we were in Kenya and we met the ambassador from South Africa. Julian got along with him very well, you know; with his social graces, he mingles very well in high society. We got an invitation from the ambassador to study lions in Kruger National Park."

That said, Gnoske added, with utmost serenity, that he felt confident enough in his ideas to publish right now and that the only thing restraining him was Kerbis Peterhans's insistence on further observations, more data, more measurements.

Which brought us, finally, to their future plans. Those would be divided into two phases.

First, they were going to complete their examinations of lion skulls and skeletons, concentrating on those in the American Museum of Natural History in New York and the British Museum, which also housed the skulls of 70 lions shot in Sudan and Ethiopia by Wilfred Thesiger. Now in his 90s, Thesiger, one of the few living figures from the heroic age of exploration, had written that several of the lions had no manes or restricted manes. In taking additional measurements, the two researchers hoped to prove that there are two body types of extant lions.

"There can be no overlap," Kerbis Peterhans stressed. "The differences have to be completely discrete."

If further study turned up significant overlap, then the hypothesis that buffalo lions are physically different and closer to extinct lions would be disproved. That would not, however, disprove that there are wide variations in behavior and social structure among African lions.

And so to the second phase: the combined expeditions to the Tana River in eastern Kenya, Uganda's Queen Elizabeth National Park, and the Luangwa Valley in Zambia. In all three places, Gnoske and Kerbis Peterhans intended to make additional observations of lion behavior, focusing on hunting practices, and to compile data on mane lengths. Their trips to Tsavo and studies they'd made of lions killed by hunters or game rangers had persuaded them that dense vegetation and the prevalence of thorn bushes did not explain how maneless lions get to be that way—plenty of thickly maned lions had been killed in forested country. They believed that mane length in lions with variable manes is controlled by climate and elevation. The Tana River, 600 miles long, would be ideal for testing the theory. With its sources on the slopes of 17,058-foot Mount Kenya, in the Aberdare Mountains, the Tana tumbles down through wooded foothills to stark, scrub-covered plains only a few hundred feet above sea level, then into equatorial rain forests before emptying into the Indian Ocean. If the assumption about elevation and climate was right, then lions found at the high, cold elevations should have thick manes, whereas those at lower, hotter elevations should have sparse manes. For at least half its length, the Tana, a verdant gallery in an arid landscape, also provides the type of riverine environment the hypothesis says is typical buffalo lion habitat. By observing if lions used their forelegs to bring down buffalo or other large game, Gnoske and Kerbis Peterhans could confirm if those carnivores had indeed developed massive bodies to tackle king-size prey. Conversely, the two men could study the carcass of a recent kill, examining it like forensic pathologists to determine how it had met its death. (I recalled Iain Allan's description of the two males he'd watched dispatching a buffalo on the Galana River. They'd used their brains as much as their brawn.)

The undertaking would be expensive as well as dangerous, the major danger being posed by our fellow *Homo sapiens,* not by lions. The danger would in fact contribute to the expense: Gangs of Somali shifta were active in the middle reaches of the Tana, and an expedition there would require adequate security in the form of armed KWS rangers, as many as seven or eight men, all of whom would have to be paid a per diem for up to six weeks. Gnoske and Kerbis-Peterhans were now scratching and scrambling for funding; they and their former boss, Dr. Bruce Patterson, had fallen into a serious disagreement regarding their research and they were now on their own. They promised to keep me abreast of their progress, and if the expedition looked like it was a go, I would of course be welcome to join it. I very much wanted to. While I wasn't ready to judge if their ideas were valid, I was persuaded that they were doing serious work that could lead to something interesting. Maybe these two Chicago boys were qualified to challenge the prevailing wisdom.

Well, for an armada of reasons, most having to do with money, the Tana River expedition never came off. The next time I returned to Tsavo it wasn't with Gnoske and Kerbis Peterhans, but with two scientists who disagreed with them on almost every point and thought the men from the Field Museum were chasing a chimera.

ACT TWO

CHASING THE CHIMERA

Thy bones are marrowless, thy blood is cold;
Thou hast no speculation in those eyes
Which thou dost glare with...

—Macbeth

May 16, 2001—Kanderi Camp, Tsavo East

I WAKE UP just before six, roused out of a nightmare by the sound of a camp attendant pouring hot water into the bucket outside my tent. The nightmare was one of those quasi-hallucinatory narratives induced by Lariam. In literary terms, Lariam dreams are pre- rather than postmodern, having a logical structure—beginning, middle, end. As soon as my eyes open, the story flees my mind. All I can remember is that I was locked in a spiritual battle with some vague satanic force, and that I won. Despite the triumph, a sense of an evil presence lingers as I splash smoke-scented water on my face, dress, and watch the morning stars vanish one by one.

The creepy-crawlies leave me as I eat breakfast in the mess tent with the rest of the cast: Dr. Craig Packer and his protégée Peyton West from the University of Minnesota; Ogeto Mwebi, a soft-spoken Kenyan who heads the osteology department at the National Museum of Kenya in Nairobi; zoologist Dennis King and

147

his companion, Sarah Hamilton; our safari outfitter, Verity Williams; and photographer Bob Caputo, who is no relation to me, as evidenced by the disparity in our stature: Close to six five, he's got me by nine or ten inches.

The meal is a rushed, dietetic affair—a slice of toast, a bowl of cereal, coffee. We need to get into the field before the day turns hot and sends the lions into hiding. We divide up into teams, with each assigned a destination, and drive out of our camp at the edges of the Kanderi swamp. Peyton and I are in the Land Rover that she and Craig brought up from Tanzania. We head west, toward a place called Ndololo, where we've been told a lion pride has taken up residence. The vehicle has seen hard use, and looks it. Peyton handles it skillfully and is at ease with the right-hand steering, which isn't surprising. She's spent the better part of the past few years piloting this battered box of steel and rubber around the Serengeti, seeking to discover why lions grow manes. She will be in Tsavo for the next 23 days investigating the question from the opposite angle: Why do the lions here not grow manes?

Beyond that, she and Craig will try to determine if Tsavo lions really are different by studying their behavior, and they're going to do that by subjecting them to a series of experiments using two life-size dummy lions that were employed for the same purpose in Tanzania. The dummies are Craig's innovation. They were made in Hong Kong, according to his specifications, and each lion can be coiffed with one of four imitation manes sewn in different lengths and colors. To make sure the colors were authentic, Craig had supplied the Hong Kong manufacturers with mane hairs taken from real lions. Thus, each dummy can assume one of four identities. Craig had dubbed them: Fabio (a long blond mane), Julio (long and black), Romeo (short and black), and Lothario (short and blond).

ROB HOWARD

A lioness yawns after feeding. She belongs to the harem of a
dominant male nicknamed Scarface, who rules a pride of 23
lions near the Aruba Dam in eastern Tsavo.

IMPERIAL WAR MUSEUM

EAST AFRICAN RAILWAYS

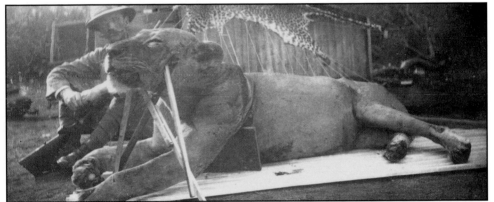

ABOVE, OPPOSITE: Toward the end of his military career and following his tenure in East Africa, British Army engineer John Henry Patterson served in World War I.

BELOW, OPPOSITE: A gang of Indian contract laborers take a break during the construction of the Uganda railway. Patterson documented that 28 of these men fell victim to the Man-eaters of Tsavo, but it is believed that the actual number of the lions' victims, including Africans, was as high as 135.

ABOVE: Patterson peers from behind the carcass of one of the two man-eaters nicknamed Ghost and Darkness. Tsavo males tend to be significantly taller and heavier than the average lion of the Serengeti Plains. It is thought that they develop greater bulk to tackle the predominant prey in Tsavo, the huge, fierce Cape buffalo.

ROBERT CAPUTO

ABOVE: Colonel John Henry Patterson (seated) supervised the construction of the Tsavo River railroad bridge in 1898 and 1899. Progress was slowed, and at one point stopped altogether, by two man-eating lions. Patterson, an experienced tiger hunter when he served in India, needed nearly nine months to track down and kill the marauding pair.

BELOW, OPPOSITE: Dr. Craig Packer and his graduate student Peyton West devised an ingenious method to test the behavior of lions in the wild under controlled circumstances. They created two dummy lions who, with manes of varying lengths and different colors, could assume four different identities.

ROBERT CAPUTO

ROBERT CAPUTO

OPPOSITE: In the semiarid thornbush scrub of East Africa, prey
animals such as this hapless zebra are scarce. This lioness and
her cubs are enjoying what is a rare treat in the harsh environment of Tsavo.

ABOVE: These male lions may be play-fighting, or this may be a real
battle between the ruler of a pride and his youthful challenger.
Some researchers think lions sport a mane to warn off rivals.
But what happens in places like Tsavo, where they don't always
have manes?

RIGHT: Iain Allan is one of the most experienced safari guides in Kenya. Here he scans for game during our trip to Tsavo in February 2000. Allan says he loves Tsavo because "it's raw and primitive and doesn't tolerate fools or forgive mistakes."

BELOW: Allan and his business partner, Clive Ward, relax at a campfire on the Galana River. The two men, skilled mountaineers and rock climbers who have scaled peaks all over the world, specialize in leading trekking parties to the summit of Kilimanjaro. They also conduct walking safaris in areas of Tsavo closed to most visitors.

ROB HOWARD

ROB HOWARD

The two scientists have come equipped with an arsenal of other tools: a FLIR, an infrared camera that measures body heat and converts the measurements to digital images, to test levels of heat stress; GPS, to mark locations of prides; night vision scopes; and tape recordings of various animal calls, to summon lions from their lairs.

I'd heard Craig Packer's name frequently during my research; he's considered the world's foremost expert on the Serengeti lion, an heir to George Schaller. After contacting him at the University of Minnesota, I learned that Tsavo had intrigued him for some time. His friend, documentary filmmaker Simon Trevor, had been urging him to go there to study its unusual lions. It seemed to me that we had mutual interests, and we discussed teaming up. Following several conversations, by phone and e-mail, Packer worked up a plan for a three-week expedition. Meanwhile, I sought funding. Thus, the project came to fruition, with a lot of help from Gnoske and Kerbis Peterhans, who generously "loaned" their Tsavo research permit to Craig and Peyton.

Our agendas mesh, with some differences in nuance. Peyton is here to round out her research, so that, when she returns to Minneapolis next month, she will be able to begin writing her dissertation and eventually become Dr. Peyton West. Craig is here to advise her and to get a firsthand look at Tsavo and its lions. And I am here hoping that their work will shed some light on the Tsavo mystery.

Although I've told her that I saw several maneless or restricted-mane lions 16 months ago, Peyton remains agnostic on the subject. "Frankly, I think it's bull," she told me last night as we sat by the campfire. She hastened to explain that she didn't think I was lying or hallucinating, but that she believes bald male lions are adolescents mistaken for adults by amateur observers like me. That's Craig's opinion as well. I was no one to argue—Craig has studied lions in the Serengeti and Kruger National Park in South Africa for a quarter of a century—but I argued anyway, pointing out that the lions I'd observed had been too big to be teenagers and had dropped testicles—a sign of maturity. I was given to understand that he and Peyton would withhold judgment until they'd seen for themselves.

A few yards ahead, francolin alarmed by the Land Rover's approach scuttle along both sides of the road, the males wearing bright yellow bibs. They remain earthbound until we almost run them over; then they flush in a panic of brownish wings. Off in the distance, the checkered periscope of a giraffe's neck rises out of *nyika* wilderness, nyika being the general term for the thorny scrublands of East Africa.

Of all the questions currently confronting America and the world, why some lions have manes and others don't doesn't rank very high on the list. I am haunted by a conversation I had three nights ago in Nairobi with two friends, Wayne Long and his wife, Marianne Fitzgerald. I'd met them a little under a year ago, shortly after interviewing Gnoske and Kerbis Peterhans, while I was doing a story on the United Nations airlift to aid the victims of the endless civil war in southern Sudan. Marianne, an Englishwoman who has lived in Kenya for years, is deeply committed to doing good works; she started a nongovernmental organization to bring food and medical care to Sudanese refugees in Kenya, as well as to drought-stricken Kenyans themselves.

Renewing acquaintance at dinner, I told her and Wayne about what had brought me back to Africa, describing Gnoske and Kerbis Peterhans's theory and the upcoming expedition to Tsavo with Packer and West. Marianne, who'd just finished telling me that four employees of her organization, Samburu tribesmen, had been killed recently in ambush by Turkana bandits—looked at me with a mixture of incredulity and bitterness.

"That's the difference between the West and here. In the West, you have time to do things like observe lions and measure their skulls. Here, everyone is just trying to survive, day to day. It's a little like ancient Athens. They had slaves to do the dirty work so Plato and Aristotle and that lot could sit and think."

Something of an overstatement, I supposed, but her remark awakened memories of the things I'd seen in southern Sudan—boys with legs blown off by land mines, a mission church blasted by a Sudanese air force cluster bomb, a mother who had walked through the bush for six days to bring her child, feverish with malaria, to the nearest clinic. I recalled that and the *Newsweek* cover I spotted in a newsstand in London's Heathrow Airport as I was returning home. It showed a blond, porky American boy, his lips smeared with the icing of the cake he was stuffing into his mouth. Above his photo was the headline "Are We Too Fat?" That wasn't an irrelevant question such as, "Why do lions have manes?" It was obscene when you placed it beside the emaciated wraiths wandering southern Sudan. Tsavo and the Serengeti are what tourists—and writers and scientists—want to see of Africa, but the real Africa is millions upon millions of people suffering through dismal poverty, AIDS, malaria, drought, famine, utterly corrupt regimes, overcrowded cities, intractable civil wars.

I need to keep them in mind. This vast national park bears less resemblance to the Africa Africans have to live with than Yellowstone does to the Ventura Freeway at rush hour.

And yet I cannot be insensible to its harsh beauty. Under cumulus clouds sailing on a strong southerly wind, the land is greener than the first time I saw it; this is the season of the long rains, though they've been late and are sparser than normal, and the acacia are throwing forth pale yellow blossoms. Near Ndololo, we spot tracks in the road and climb out for a closer look, discovering that they've been made by hyena. A Kenya Wildlife Service ranger sees us and orders us to get back inside, telling us that there are nine lions nearby.

"I saw them just a little while ago, making quite a drama with some elephant," he says, and when we inform him that we are on a lion research expedition, he leads us to them. Peyton calls Craig and Bob on the radio—they're not far behind—and soon they join us and the ranger at a dried-up water hole, where the lions—ten altogether, females, subadults, and cubs—are gnawing on the remnants of a Cape buffalo that's been dead for some time. The stench is revolting. Its huge rib cage, blackened with dry blood, resembles the tarred ribs of a small boat, and maggots spill by the hundreds from the thick hide, which one lioness is tearing at with single-minded purpose. Peyton breaks out a sketchpad and draws the number and pattern of spots on the lioness's muzzles. Each lion possesses a unique number and pattern of muzzle spots—it's a kind of leonine fingerprint. Peyton's glance bounces quickly from the pad to the lions and back; her hand's movements are hurried, like a sidewalk portrait artist with a queue of impatient customers.

She is a slender, fair-skinned, blue-eyed blonde, 32 years old, and she came to the sciences by a circuitous route. After graduating from Yale with a degree in English, she went to work as a buyer for a New York City jewelry store and found herself working in a windowless room, sending expensive baubles to outlets around the country. Not for her.

She quit and migrated to San Francisco, where she did editorial work for a literary magazine. She didn't take to that either, but while volunteering at the San Francisco Zoo, she found that she was interested in wildlife. Although she'd never shone in her science courses, Peyton entertained the notion of becoming a field biologist or zoologist. The idea took root and sent her back to Yale, where she enrolled in science courses while working part-time in the university's micro-biology lab and at zoos in Connecticut. After two years of classes, she'd found her calling—animal behavior—and began applying to the best schools in the country in that field.

Eventually, Craig Packer accepted her as one of his students at the University of Minnesota, where he held the position of McKnight Distinguished Professor in the Department of Ecology, Evolution, and Behavior—a weighty title matched by his reputation. Peyton will always remember when she met him the first time.

"I'd heard he was a hypochondriac who would run out of the room if a sick person was around. I had a cough and a temperature of 102°, so I put a cough drop in my mouth before going into his office. When I opened my mouth to introduce myself, the cough drop got stuck in my throat. I couldn't swallow it, so I spit it up and it popped right into Craig's lap."

Despite her contaminating him, Craig took Peyton into his graduate program, and she was soon in Africa, trying to figure out why lions have manes.

The male or males who control this pride are nowhere to be seen, which may be just as well. The ranger informs us that a big male lion from around here attacked a minivan full of tourists recently. They had caught the lion in flagrante delicto, copulating with a lioness, and persuaded the driver to move closer. The lion rushed the van with a roar and smashed two windows with his forepaws before the terrified driver could put the van into gear and speed away. Considering the circumstances, the big fellow's reaction was understandable, indeed admirable, but the attack added its little bit to the image of Tsavo lions as bad actors. After all, the "tourist" lions in the Masai Mara don't object to being photographed while trysting. Perhaps the oglers in the van hadn't read the latest edition of the *Rough Guide to Kenya,* which warns visitors to remember, "Tsavo's lions have a reputation for ferocity."

Finished sketching, Peyton estimates the lions' ages by noting the color of their noses. Leonine noses darken as they age, from pure pink in infancy to pure black at eight years old. Peyton's guess is that all these adult lionesses are under eight, except for one with the atrophied chest muscles and rounded teeth that indicate old age. None of the lions look in very good shape; their ribs are prominent, their hides matted with burrs, and one, walking with an unsteady gait, appears to have an injured hip. She and three others amble to the water hole to drink from a shallow puddle in the middle. They are watched by sacred ibises in priestly vestments of black and white. The crippled lioness ventures a little too far and sinks up to her middle joints in red muck, struggles her way out, and hobbles off to rest in the shade of a bush decorated with white blossoms. Peyton drags the heavy FLIR from the back of the Land Rover onto the front seat, plugs it in, and trains it on the lioness to locate her injury. Injuries give off more heat. She lets me have a look, and I'm presented with a digitized image of a lion in a pastiche of colors: reds, yellows, blues, greens, and blacks, yellow being the hottest, black the coolest. The whirring camera disturbs the lioness briefly, but she soon goes back to snoozing, while the others continue to gnaw at the maggot-infested ruins of the buffalo.

"I've never seen lions feeding on such disgusting stuff," Craig says, his and Bob's vehicle pulled alongside ours.

I mention Iain's observation that Tsavo lions are blue-collar cats who work hard for a living and take what they can get.

Craig nods. "Yeah, a harsh environment, difficult prey..." He leaves the remark unfinished.

We proceed on to park headquarters, a cluster of low, white-washed bungalows near the Voi Gate, where we rendezvous with Dennis King. We ask the assistant warden for permission to conduct call-ups and to go off road (off-road driving is prohibited in Tsavo). We also sound him out about relaxing the park's practice of discouraging radio-collaring and darting. King is an odd but familiar figure in Tsavo, which he's wandered for the past four years in a knocked-up Land Rover with a flip-up wooden sign on its roof that reads "Research." The sign is supposed to tell minivan drivers that King is on official business and not to follow him when he journeys cross-country; however, it's not clear exactly what he's researching. The KWS had given him permission to study Tsavo lions, since so little is known about them, but without backing from a university, museum, or international wildlife organization, he's on his own, scratching by on what he calls "private grant money," most of which appears currently to be coming from his girlfriend, Sarah. Consequently, King hasn't added too many bricks to the unfinished edifice of knowledge about Tsavo lions. He's teamed up with us to benefit from Craig's and Peyton's expertise. We've teamed up with him because he said he can lead us to lion prides, saving us a lot of time, but he's already proved a little fuzzy on that score. He caused Craig's and Peyton's eyebrows to rise by declaring that he doesn't think there is such a thing as a lion pride, anywhere; it's just a word scientists use to describe groups of lions that come together, break apart, and come together again, like random atoms. A novel notion, to say the least.

Verity, the safari outfitter, has warned that he can be a difficult, prickly character, and although we haven't seen evidence of that yet, a certain resentfulness sometimes shines through in his faded blue eyes, as if we are interlopers on his turf. He's another of those deracinated Englishmen I've run into over the years, like Clive Ward; but where Clive is cheerful and informative, Dennis is sullen and close-mouthed, offering, when asked a question, cryptic remarks or enigmatic smiles through his sandy, gray-streaked beard. But he can be candid in expressing his opinions. Last night at the campfire, I outlined Gnoske and Kerbis Peterhans's hypothesis and asked what he thought of it. "It's complete bullshit," he replied. That appears to be Craig and Peyton's shared view as well, but they express it more politely, if for no other reason than that they're in Tsavo on the Field Museum's research permit. That's one of the reasons Ogeto Mwebi has joined us—he's part of the museum's team.

The hope is that Dennis's familiarity with park authorities will smooth the way, but the assistant warden, a man who listens patiently and says little, is noncommittal about off-road driving, more or less telling us that we are not to do it if tourist vehicles are anywhere near, lest the drivers get the idea that they can do it too. He's adamant about not allowing radio collars or darting, despite Craig's arguments that he's anesthetized more than a hundred lions over four generations in the Serengeti without harmful effect.

"It's the bunny-huggers, it's the Daphne factor," Dennis mutters outside, after the meeting.

This is an unkind reference to Daphne Sheldrick, wife of David Sheldrick, the founding warden of Tsavo East. She wields a great deal of influence over how the park is managed. She wants to keep it as wild as possible. Although she is fondest of elephants, its lions rank high in her esteem, precisely because they're nasty. In *The Shadow of Kilimanjaro,* she tells Rick Ridgeway that "when you see a Tsavo lion, you see a real lion. It is not going to sit there with its legs in the air waiting to be photographed. It will probably want to eat you, because it is a lion that's had to earn its keep."

Daphne's philosophy is that radio collars and darts could eventually sandpaper the lions' rough edges. I wish to learn all I can about them, but not at that price. I would not want to see some future Tsavo male tolerate people photographing him while he mates, but to come at them, roaring and raging. It isn't necessary for us to know everything about everything. Maybe some things are best left cloaked in the mists of myth and mystery. So as Dennis and Craig grumble about "heartstring pullers with constituencies to raise money," I give three silent cheers for Daphne Sheldrick, though I know she would despise me because I hunt and approve of hunting, so long as it's done right. I would reply to her that hunters, real hunters, love the wild as much as she.

While Bob and I have lunch at camp, Craig and Peyton look at Dennis's photographs. One is of a lion with a full, black mane, a "problem animal," i.e., a cattle killer, that had been relocated to the park. Two of that lion's possible sons, Dennis says, have short, abbreviated manes. At any rate, Dennis confirms that maned lions can be found in the park (like the beauty I saw under the palms near Sobo Rocks), but he doesn't know if they're imports or natives. This leads to a round of speculation, Craig and Peyton venturing that our story could evolve in one of two ways. If maned and unmaned lions are part of the same indigenous population, then the maneless variety would represent a "morph" of the species, and that would be stunning because it would be the first documented case of morphing among mammals. Highly, highly unlikely, Craig says. And so to the second possibility: If fully maned lions in Tsavo are imports and native males are maneless, due to adaptation to the heat or some other environmental factor, it would represent what Craig terms "an interesting example of variation within a species." Which is to say (though neither he nor Peyton says it) Gnoske and Kerbis Peterhans may not be completely off base.

Our two scientists, however, remain infidels when it comes to manelessness, convinced that the bald or crew-cut males we're all seeing are youthful nomads, waiting to grow up so they can take over a pride. Once again, I bring up Scarface, saying that I'll lead them to the place near the Aruba dam where I'd seen him. Good luck, Dennis chimes in. His name for that same lion was "Orion," and he'd observed him and his pride (or group, as Dennis would prefer to say) for a long time. Four months ago, they vanished, never to be seen again. He has no idea why. Another Tsavo mystery.

Nevertheless, we set off, on the chance that Scarface, a.k.a Orion, will reappear. We wander all over the area, circling the lake, from which open-billed storks rise in swarms thick as locusts, and then over the plains to the swamp, and see giraffes and elephants and gazelles and that's all. A long drive toward Voi also nets us nothing except a real African moment when the sun dips below the Taita Hills, casting blades of light that kindle a golden fire across the dun-colored grasslands below and glint off the horns of Cape buffalos crossing the road in front of us while elephants trumpet in the distance.

May 18

PEYTON LAUGHS. "He looks so retarded," she says of the male lion who lies under a tree a short distance north of Aruba lake. I've come to feel a bit proprietary about Tsavo lions, and silently bristle at her remark, as if she's insulted a dear friend. The trouble is, he does look retarded, his eyes slitted, his tongue hanging out as he pants in the heat, his hide peppered with burrs, which also mat a short, scruffy mane that looks like it's been trimmed by a barber with a bad case of amphetamine nerves. A lioness dozes under a shrub nearby. Beside the male is a partially devoured buffalo carcass, its eyes pecked out by vultures, its legs, stiff as posts, splayed out, its bloody body cavity abuzz with flies and aswarm with maggots, and the whole thing stinking in the south wind like a gigantic overripe Limburger. Bob, in the other vehicle, gets on the radio and suggests I write a sequel to Colonel Patterson's book and call it *The Maggot-Eaters of Tsavo*. Again, I feel personally offended. My Tsavo lions, creatures of terrifying legend, are becoming objects of ridicule.

On the other hand, the fellow in front of us qualifies as maneless; the color of his nose indicates adulthood, but Peyton wants proof positive and imitates a hyena whoop in an attempt to make the lion get up so she can have a look at his testicles. He doesn't buy her mimicry and remains stationary, his long tufted tail whisking at flies. We wait.

Burr Boy, as Peyton has christened the male, at last gets up to snack on the buffalo. He methodically gnaws on the shoulder, ripping at the red, glistening meat, and then, in an impressive show of strength, bites down on a joint and drags the 800-pound carcass several yards to a more advantageous position. On the radio, Craig asks, "What do his balls look like?" Though Burr Boy is only 15 yards away, Peyton raises the binoculars for a close look. "Uh, large and pendulous," she replies. There is an interval of silence, and then Craig says, "Well, this is what we came to see," meaning an adult male with a restricted mane. I feel vindicated, but get the impression that this lone example isn't enough to convert the two scientists. Back and forth on the radio, they discuss mane growth, while I reflect on yesterday's "Packer Lecture." That's what Bob and I call Craig's daily disquisitions on biology, evolution, and animal behavior. They're concise and clear, even brilliant. They must be if I understand them, although I forget them if I don't play the good pupil and take notes; but that's my fault, not Craig's. I took notes on yesterday's tutorial, which began with Craig's declaration that Darwin has his vote as the Man of the Millennium.

Darwin's law of natural selection states that raw self-interest rules the natural world. Altruism is less known there than on the floor of the commodities exchange. On the face of it, lion society appears to negate this principle. Lions are cooperative. Females hunt in coordination, form creches of sisters and aunts, and help to raise one another's young. If there is more than one male in the pride, the dominant one gets the girls, but the others pitch in to defend the pride against outside threats. Years of study have persuaded Craig that when a cubless lioness helps raise her sisters' progeny, she is not just being nice; if young with similar genes survive, then indirectly, her genes survive as well. The same goes for males. They are not like soldiers in wartime, nobly putting their lives on the line for some ideal or cause, but to make sure that those with shared genes live on. In sum, cooperative lion behavior is consistent with Darwin's law of natural selection; lions act together and in support of one another, yet self-interest—the survival of the pride's gene pool—is the reason why.

Professor Packer then proceeded to Part Two, the title of which, "The Peacock's Tail," sounded like a Sherlock Holmes mystery. Certain species develop traits that at first glance appear to be liabilities, and in some senses are. The male peacock's long, cumbersome tail makes it more vulnerable to predators, but it's useful in attracting females. A peacock with an exceptionally long, flamboyant tail gets more chances to mate and pass on his genes, compensating for the shorter life span it will probably have because of its vulnerability to predators. The male lion's mane falls into the category of an ornament that's both a liability and an advantage. Although no one is yet sure what a fully developed mane costs a lion, Peyton and Craig are sure that its primary purpose is to attract females, its secondary purpose to cause rival males to pause and reflect before challenging its owner. Why does a luxuriant mane set lioness hearts aflutter? One beguiling theory holds that females of certain species, and female lions are one, have a built-in aesthetic sense, preferring males who display one trait over those who don't have it, or in whom it's less developed. But aesthetics cannot tell the whole story, leading to two possible explanations for the rest of the tale. The trait, in this case a mane, signals good genes, or it's a sign that the particular male, although he may or may not have superior genes, is healthy and well-fed, that is, a good provider and protector with whom it will be advantageous for the female to mate.

Peyton's experiments in the Serengeti (which will be repeated here in Tsavo) indicate that lionesses prefer dark manes to light (blonds don't have more fun) and that challenging males are most intimidated by long, black manes, least by short, light ones. To test the good-gene idea, Peyton has collected hair samples from Serengeti lions to be assayed for testosterone levels.

So we come to Burr Boy in Tsavo, an adult without much of a mane but with a girlfriend. Does the heat in Tsavo, whose elevation is considerably lower than the Serengeti's, cause the mane's liabilities to outweigh its advantages? Peyton breaks the infrared camera out of its metal case and trains it on Burr Boy. After a few minutes, she hands it to me. Burr Boy appears in a mottle of bright colors. The readings show a dramatic temperature difference between his upper and lower parts, 3°C, roughly 5.5°F. That suggests, Peyton says—doesn't prove but suggests—that he's stressed by the heat and must work harder to keep his underparts cool.

Burr Boy, finished with his snack, lies down again, slobbering, his chin whiskers scarlet with blood. Melinda, as the lioness has been dubbed, ambles over to the carcass, but forsakes the juicy shoulder meat for some reason and instead concentrates on gnawing off an ear. It's tough, and in her frustration, she chomps down and drags the carcass several feet, another display of leonine power: Melinda appears to weigh about 250 pounds, the size of your average NFL linebacker, but let's see one of them pull 800 pounds with his teeth. She finally succeeds in severing the ear, samples it, and spits it out before returning to her rest.

A pair of jackals appear and approach cautiously from down-wind. Melinda senses them regardless and sits up, her head thrust forward, her bright, brassy eyes focused on the scavengers. The concentration in a lion's eyes can be unnerving sometimes. The jackals take the cue and pause. That's not good enough for the lioness. With a coughing grunt, she springs from the shrub and sprints toward them, dust flying from her hind paws. The jackals turn and run off, though they don't go too far. Melinda resumes her nap, while to the west, where the sun resembles a scarlet, neon eye glaring from atop the Chyulu Hills, a troop of baboons file across the savanna, its grass bent in the hissing wind. I feel that I've been returned to the time of Earth's adolescence: The two great predators sleep alongside their prey's gory carcass, the patient jackals waiting and baboons on the march across the windy plain.

May 19

WE ARE AWAKE before dawn, the Southern Cross shining brilliantly in a sky as black as when we'd gone to bed. Another quickie breakfast gulped by lantern light, and Craig and I are off in the Land Cruiser I'm renting from Verity Williams. The dusty road leading out of camp appears as a trail of white ash in the headlights, a pair of hyena eyes glow back at us from the underbrush crowding the roadside. We head east. The new day suggests itself on the horizon and arrives in an eruption of light as we turn south, heading for the bleak Ndara Plains. Except for his green bush hat, Craig looks like he's dressed for a day of beachcombing: T-shirt, shorts, sandals. His 50 years have tarnished his jet-black beard with gray, but he has a high-pitched, boyish laugh and a sense of humor that can sometimes slice like a scalpel; you don't realize you've been cut till you see the blood. The lanky Texan, born in Fort Worth, long ago abandoned his drawl for the neutral accents of the Midwest as he forsook pre-med at Stanford (his father is a doctor) to major in biology. Working for Jane Goodall, the famed primatologist, in Tanzania's Gombe National Forest, hooked him on studying wildlife. Graduate school at the University of Sussex in England brought him in contact with John Maynard Smith, the evolutionary biologist, and that became Craig's specialty. In 1978, following a spell studying Japanese monkeys, he returned to Tanzania on invitation from old friends in Gombe to take over the Serengeti Lion Project, the research effort Schaller started in 1966.

"At first I was wary," he tells me, his dark eyes flitting from the road to the landscape and back. "I'd been studying primates, creatures with active, intelligent minds. That's not lions. I thought that lions would be boring. They are boring to study. Sometimes I think the only thing more boring than studying lions is being a lion."

Nevertheless, he got into it, discovering that those who had gone before had determined what lions do, but not why.

"That was Schaller. He got the basic parameters of what they do. I went after why. Schaller is a what man, I'm a why man."

We drive on. The Ndara Plains reach away, a disconsolate expanse that in its dusty, red flatness reminds me of the Australian outback, where I once spent ten weeks on assignment. Craig brings up Dennis, who, alternately defensive and arrogant, is beginning to annoy him and Peyton. His lack of professionalism is another irritant. Craig and Peyton have given him a stack of the data sheets they use in Tanzania because he has none of his own; ditto for the pre-printed cards with lions' faces on them that aid in identifying individual animals. After four years in Tsavo, Dennis knows the locations of only a few prides and has only a vague idea how many lions are in each. In fact, he stubbornly refuses to accept prides as a concept, let alone a reality. An observant tourist could accumulate as much information as Dennis has, and in less time. To cap things off, he has begun to criticize Craig and Peyton for the way they're going about their business, objecting to their excursions off-road, to the experiments they plan to conduct with the dummy lions.

Although I consider myself merely a chronicler of this expedition and both scientists its leaders, in certain matters, mostly having to do with personal relations, it appears that I'm in charge, by default, not because I'm some D-League Eisenhower with a talent for managing complicated personalities. Some of the expenses are my responsibility; so is making sure that things run smoothly and that everyone gets along. I don't want some Conradian scene of white people tearing at one another's throats in the heart of darkness, but I'll admit that Dennis is beginning to annoy me, too. I've given him $200 to cover his gas and other expenses and offered him and Sarah free access to our mess, and they've displayed such hearty appetites that Peyton was once left with a nearly empty plate. I was galled the other night when Dennis declined Bob's offer of a shot from his bottle of blended scotch, expressing a preference for my single malt. "Macallan?" he said, grinning. "Now you're talking." A bit cheeky, no? Strange, how people thrown together in these circumstances can get on one another's nerves, and petty irritations grow into major inflammations. I think of Conrad's *An Outpost of Progress,* which carries things to the extreme: A trader isolated in the jungle ends up murdering his partner in an argument over a spoonful of sugar.

No one is going to take an ax to Dennis, nor he to anyone else, but in the interests of maintaining a happy ship, I do a little psychologizing, pointing out that Dennis is probably "bushed," a term that covers the atrophy of social skills that results when you are quarantined too long from human society. Of course, Dennis may prefer his quarantine. Craig and I wonder if he's out here not to do science but simply to be out here, away from people, using "research" as a means to justify himself. We doubt he's eager to make new discoveries that will be published in scholarly journals and bring him renown. He's like a hermit prospector whose aim is not to find gold but to look for it.

Miles and miles of bloody Africa. Except for a small herd of impala, the only signs of sentient life in the nyika are the francolin and sand grouse that flush constantly from the roadside scrub. My pointer, Sage, would be in heaven here, though I don't suppose she'd be in this heaven more than half an hour before some ravenous carnivore sent her to the one in the sky. We go east again, then at a junction marked by a rock cairn south once more, pass a dry water hole pitted by buffalo hoofs and the great circular pads of elephants, and round a bend. Craig stomps on the brakes. Fifty feet away, three male lions lie by the road, two on one side, one on the other, all three almost as bald as females. Craig squints through the binoculars, noting the color of their noses, which are more black than pink. Around six years old, they are young adults, but adults.

"This is wonderful!" Craig exclaims. "This is what we came to see! They really are maneless!"

I do not feel vindicated. I feel, rather, the warm gratification of the missionary to whom the heathen declares, "I renounce my native gods and accept Jesus Christ as my Lord and savior."

Pole, pole—slowly—we proceed. The lions rise with lazy grace and amble off into the commiphora, and we follow a discreet distance behind. Two are stout lads, over 350, I guess, while the third, possibly younger, is at least 50 pounds lighter. Yet he sports the most hair, a furry, ocher bib and side whiskers. They lie down for a while, then the largest of the three gets up again and affectionately butts his mates, who rise and follow his leisurely stroll to the shade of a wide-spreading shrub. There they flop down once more. We watch them sleep, and soon, lion observing being the electric spectator sport it is, fall asleep ourselves. Five males from two different species, dozing in the middle of nowhere. We wake up at eleven o'clock and see that the lions haven't moved; they lie as still as three golden puddles in the sunlight.

Driving the quarter mile back to the road, Craig has me tie ribbons of toilet paper to the shrub branches to mark the way in—we'll be returning late this afternoon.

"Dennis would probably object to this desecration," he says.

Once out to the road, we note two tall acacia on the east side for landmarks, then set the odometer to measure the distance to the junction. This dead-reckoning navigation points to how little is known about Tsavo lions. On the Serengeti, the locations of lion prides are almost like street addresses, and Craig knows the population of each one and their family history, going back to their great-grandparents.

When we come back in a three-vehicle convoy, Peyton and Ogeto in one, Craig and I in another, and Bob in his Land Cruiser, a 600-millimeter lens mounted on a bracket on the door, we follow the toilet paper streamers and find the lions in the same spot. Peyton looks at them and joins the congregation of believers. It's four o'clock, the magic hour, and the light is superb for photographing, although there isn't much to take pictures of. The trio are studies in immobility and do not live up to the portrait Daphne Sheldrick painted for Rick Ridgeway. Flat on their backs, legs spread in shameless poses, we practically have to tap them with the bumpers to make them move so Bob can get photos and Peyton images with the infra-red camera. I wonder how lions maintain their muscular strength; if a human being were as inactive as a lion, he or she would soon be as toned as bowl of pudding.

The three need names. Peyton presides, dubbing the largest Baby Huey, the second Meathead (because his dropped lower jaw gives him a stupid expression), and the third Fur Boy, because he has the most mane hair. Meanwhile, I become the beneficiary of another Packer Lecture, but I have trouble following his train of thought. Something about red pandas being closer to raccoons genetically, giant pandas closer to bears. Eventually, he comes to the three lions, though I'm not clear about the connection between them and pandas, giant or otherwise.

"We may have here a lion adapted to its environment," he declares. "Asian lions also have short manes."

I bring up Gnoske and Kerbis Peterhans. They say that the Tsavo lion and the Asian lion have a common ancestor; the abbreviated mane, therefore, is an ancestral trait.

"No, no," Craig responds. "It makes more sense to say that these are African lions who've adapted to a hotter climate."

And why does that make more sense?

"Because the other animals I've seen in Tsavo, like jackals and gazelles, look different than the ones I've seen on the Serengeti. They have shorter hair. So it's simplest to say that these short manes are not ancestral but an adaptation."

When she's finished thermal imaging, Peyton decides to run an experiment developed in the Serengeti: A recording of a female lion's roar is played to two or more males, to see if the lion with the thicker or thickest mane is the first to respond, the first to get to the female. Peyton's previous work has shown that such is almost always the case, indicating a correlation between a luxuriant mane and masculine vigor. Neither she nor Craig, however, expects the same results today; Fur Boy may have the most hair, but he is also the smallest and is probably six months to a year younger than his buddies.

While Craig, Bob, and I remain in place, she and Ogeto drive off about a hundred yards, where Peyton—rather bravely, I think—gets out of the Land Rover and mounts a speaker on the roof. She climbs back in and inserts a cassette into a tape recorder. A deep, throaty grunt followed by a roar echoes through the growing dusk. Instantly, all three males go from torpid to alert, Meathead raising his head, followed by Baby Huey; but to everyone's surprise, Fur Boy is the first to spring to his feet, and he looks intently in the direction of the roar, which comes again, a scary sound, even though I know it's only a recording. Fur Boy sets off at a determined walk, while the other two stand side by side, some distance behind; then they start forward and catch up. Fur Boy picks up the pace and, striding briskly, easily wins the race to the Land Rover. The poor guy, expecting to find an amorous lioness, finds only a vehicle occupied by a female of the wrong species. "Where are you, girl?" he seems to be asking as, a little confused, he paces around, sniffing the air. He makes an arresting sight, "pussy footing" through the short grass by raising a forepaw, holding it in midair for a moment before slowly setting it down without a sound, his oval pupils dilated in the waning light. Craig giggles.

"He thinks we're hiding the female. He's going to liberate this lioness. Rapunzel, Rapunzel, let down your long tail. Or lift it up."

Finally, Fur Boy gives up. As we leave, all three lions lie down alongside the road, exactly as Craig and I found them in the morning.

They'd behaved in the same way Serengeti lions would have in similar circumstances—a small indication that Tsavo lions may not be as different as Gnoske and Kerbis Peterhans believe they are. Craig and Peyton are pleased with the success of the experiment.

"That's the thing about our science," he tells me as we return to camp in darkness. "We can make things happen. It would have taken years, observing things as they happen naturally, to see what we did tonight in minutes."

May 20

GALDESSA CAMP is a safari camp for the diamonds-and-Ferrari set on the banks of the Galana River. Its large, airy, thatch-roof *bandas*, domiciles of rustic elegance with showers and flush toilets, sprawl along the river's south bank for a quarter of a mile, linked by well-marked paths through the saltbush, the paths converging on a dining hall as big as a restaurant, splendidly furnished with cushioned chairs and tables built of native hardwoods, and decorated with buffalo horns and skulls that give the place the atmosphere of some heathen temple dedicated to animal worship.

Meals are served on china, wine poured into stemware, and no plastic, thank you. There is also a bar and a lounge, where people who can afford the rates—$600 (U.S.) per day—can drink their gins and listen to leopards and lions roar and elephants blare. Entering these swish surroundings, Peyton and I feel as residents of Bedford-Stuyvesant would on a drive through Greenwich, Connecticut. Our digs on the Kanderi swamp are comfortable enough, and Verity's company, Ker and Downey, is one of the most experienced in Kenya—they outfitted Hemingway's last safari. But because we're on a tight budget, we can't afford anywhere near the full Ker and Downey treatment and must put up with certain inconveniences such as open-air latrines and tents with zippers that don't work properly (which has caused me some anxiety, recalling Iain's warnings to keep a tent zipped up in lion country).

Brown-haired, brown-eyed, with a clean-shaven face that looks younger than his 43 years, Marcus Russell greets us, accompanied by his four-year-old son, Blade, a kid so cute you want to steal him, and Marcus's right-hand man and chief tracker, Saitoti, a six-foot-two-inch Masai who is got up in full Masai regalia—robe, cloak, bead necklaces, copper bracelets—and has muscles that look like mooring lines. Marcus manages Galdessa Camp. He is one of the twin sons of Bill Russell, a noted Tsavo warden, and has spent his entire life in the bush, serving for a while as an intelligence scout for Leakey's anti-poaching units. We've been told he's a font of Tsavo lore, which is why we've come to meet him. We plan to do some surveys in this neck of the woods, and Marcus knows it intimately.

"There's plenty of maned lions here in Tsavo," he says in his Anglo-Kenyan accent as we sit down in the dining room. "Plenty. I've seen 'em, photographed 'em, here. Look."

Out comes a photo album showing lions with black, blond, even auburn manes. Although none would meet Serengeti standards, they're fuller than anything I've seen this time out. Could these have been problem animals translocated to the park?

"Never heard of a problem lion being dropped here. Problem leopards, yeah, but don't know of any problem lions. Problem lions are shot, poisoned on the ranches near the park."

So both types exist side by side?

"You'll see prides with three resident males and two will be maned and one not. Got four males behind camp, all maneless, and we've got two with big blond manes." Marcus's hands gesture with Mediterranean extravagance, and he speaks so rapidly, with such compulsiveness, that I wonder if he sugars his breakfast cereal with cocaine. "Maned lion seen in camp recently. Go back to the records in the man-eaters of Tsavo days, go back to when I was a kid, maned and unmaned lions and females seen to mate with both. But I've seen more maneless than maned. I'd say it's a 60-40 split. Why maneless? I don't know. Heat? Maybe, but other hot places have got maned lions. Wait-a-bit thorns? Other places have thorns and maned lions. I've talked to Masai herdsmen from west of Tsavo West and they've told me they've got maneless lions there. Ask Saitoti..." He breaks off, fires the question in Masai, and Saitoti answers. "There you have it, yeah? Unmaned lions. I'll tell you what. These Tsavo lions are different. It's genetics, you ask me. There's a genetic difference."

Peyton begs to differ.

"How'd you explain it, then?"

"There are a lot of factors that could explain..."

"Nah, it's genetics," Marcus interrupts, the words coming like machine-gun bullets. "They're bigger. There's a pride of 16 lions on the Hatulo Bisani, lot of buffalo there, and they follow the buffalo. Three males in the pride, two blond-maned, but the brigadier is a bloody great black-maned lion. Biggest bloody lion I've ever seen, and I've seen millions. I was raised in Tsavo. He stood this high." Marcus leaps to his feet, holding his hand a few inches above his waist. "And he had the bulk to go with it, oh, he had it all. Sixteen. Him, the other two adult males, seven cubs, six lionesses. Yesterday, saw two other females on the Hatulo Bisani. Don't think they were from his pride. Farther away, down by Buffalo Wallows. Feeding on a dead buff, scrawny, lethargic, both in a bad nick. Bad nick. See, lions here have a much tougher life, and therefore you get a tougher lion. They're more aggressive here. Not too long ago, I was walking along the river"—his hand flings at the Galana, glittering through the ranks of bordering doum palm—"Lioness on the other side roars at me. Next thing, she jumps into the bloody river, trying to get at me. Another time, I was driving along with two clients, couple of pretty ladies like you, Peyton, when the Land Rover stalled right near a couple of lions. I got out and walked in front of the Land Rover and clapped my hands—lions don't like that sound, and they'll usually run off—clapped my hands and said, 'All right, run along, now.' I was showing off, yeah? Well, those lions turned around and came right at me and didn't I get back in quick. What you don't want to do is get near a Tsavo lion when he's mating. Did that once, and he attacked the Land Rover. Bit the tires."

There is a lull in the verbal barrage, then Marcus launches into another, an impassioned condemnation of the way the vast cattle ranches surrounding Tsavo (some are as big as a million acres) are managed. Not making any money, with beef prices down. Sold to Arabs, who hire Somalis to look after their livestock. Somalis! This close to Tsavo! Talk about letting the fox into the henhouse! Already been some instances of elephant poaching north of the Galana. Bloody Somalis put out poisoned baits to kill lions that wander out of the park. Kill anything else that eats them. Hyena. Vultures. That's why you don't see a lot of vultures in Tsavo. Poisoned.

Whatever the merits of his theories about Tsavo lions, he is obviously an ardent conservationist, and he outlines an ambitious scheme to buy one of the ranches and build houses on it on large acreages and put them up for sale. It will be a privately owned game reserve, anyone with the money will be able to own his piece of an African paradise, and there'll be rangers and guides...

In the midst of this narrative, Blade snuggles up to Peyton, who takes immediately to the charming little boy with the mop of sandy brown hair.

"Now, don't bother the pretty lady," Marcus admonishes.

Peyton replies that she doesn't mind, she loves children, and Marcus says he can see that and then, with a searching look at the blond scientist, volunteers that he and Blade's mum are split up. Peyton says nothing, composes her expression into one of studied indifference, and Marcus resumes describing his plans. When, finally, he's done, we mention that we hope to study the lions inhabiting the Galana corridor. With another look at Peyton, he invites us to stay at the camp. It's the off season, and the camp will be closed for another couple of weeks, so we can stay on his invitation at a super-bargain rate, $50 (U.S.) per person per day.

"Looks to me like Marcus is sweet on you," I remark as we drive away, down the Hatulo Bisani road to look for the big, dark-maned lion.

Peyton offers a slightly rueful smile.

"I've run into all kinds of guys like him. Random dudes with big plans and ideas that won't go anywhere."

I ask what she makes of Marcus's commentaries. If maned and unmaned lions coexist and even interbreed in Tsavo, then why would some be crowned with hair and others not?

She shrugs. It's hard to assess the accuracy of the stories you hear about Tsavo; the legends have encrusted into fact. Peyton's task is to peel away the mythological layers to get at some core of scientifically verifiable truth. She waxes philosophical for a moment, wondering aloud about the price we pay for knowledge; sometimes it comes at the cost of wonder, of mystery.

Elephants graze in the Hatulo Bisani, scores of them, cropping the bright green sedge with their trunks, showering themselves with water drawn from the stream wending through the middle of the riverbed. Buffalo wallow while yellow-billed storks roost in the trees and egrets seek sign of fish or crab, long necks extended or coiled into an S that straightens suddenly as a head darts forward, a beak captures prey. The sky darkens and a light rain falls, dimpling the stream. The remains of the buffalo upon which the two mangy lionesses had been feeding lies on a slab of rock, the ribs like barrel staves, the hide rent into twisted rags, and the stench strong even from a distance. In a while, the clouds part and race on the south wind across the green rim of the Taita Hills, with the sun slicing through in glimmering planes. There is a sort of symbiosis in wild Africa between stunning beauty and violent death. The primeval grandeur of its landscapes would be diminished if they were not scene for daily struggles of life and death, daily dramas of pursuit and flight; but the grandeur somehow elevates all the hunting and killing, which would seem like so much ugly slaughter in a more mundane setting.

May 21

I LEARNED A HYENA was in camp late last night. It broke into the cook's tent and made off with a box of scouring pads, so it will have very clean insides if it eats them. We had another visitor at around four this morning, a leopard. I heard its rasping, two-toned roar while I was taking a leak, and that sound caused me to finish up in a hurry and get back into my tent, where I lay listening to the roars diminish as the unseen cat moved on.

In Dennis's Land Rover, I am bouncing down an elephant path that leads almost as straight as a surveyed road through the scrub. The sunrise bookends yesterday's sunset, so spectacular that we all take pictures of it, even Bob, for whom sunsets are the cliché of all clichés. Eastward, strato-cirrus arranged in layers, in wisps and sweeping curtains, change color by the minute, and when the sun bursts through, Dennis and I are blinded through our sunglasses. Craig was with him yesterday, and I guess it wasn't an altogether pleasant experience. He said he wasn't going to partner up with Dennis again, so I've volunteered, once again in the interest of keeping a happy ship. One on one, he's more likeable than in a crowd (and I think a crowd to him is any more than three people), but he's still a bit of a difficult character who appears to be difficult for the sake of it. I take out my notebook and ask his age, a routine journalistic question. With a sly smile peeking through his graying beard, he replies, "Depends on which reincarnation you're talking about."

"Oh, come off it, Dennis."

"My birth records were lost during the First World War."

I concede, and having won that little skirmish, he volunteers that he was conceived in Scotland, where his soldier father was training for a diversionary operation for the D-day landing. I do some simple math and calculate that he's around 57.

Further interrogation yields a sketchy biography. He describes himself as a loner who got interested in wildlife in his childhood, somewhere in England. His parents didn't require him to be home at night, so he stayed out, tracking badgers until midnight.

"The parents of other kids, who did have curfews, wouldn't let them go out with me."

He smiles again, as if to savor the memory of those solitary boyhood expeditions.

A three-year hitch with the British army in the last outposts of the fading Empire was followed by night school at University College in London, where he gained a bachelor's degree in zoology. Afterward, he was employed by the government nature conservancy, managing grouse habitat in Scotland. Restlessness drove him to Canada, where he spent 17 years wandering in British Columbia and the Canadian Arctic, studying bears, and became a Canadian citizen. In 1994, he went off to Australia, and three years later applied for Australian citizenship before returning to the United Kingdom for a visit.

"I'm a professional emigrator," he says. "In 1997, I was on my way back to Australia to fulfill a residency requirement, and I happened to be passing through Africa and I wanted to see it without being a tourist. I asked Kenya Wildlife Service officials if there was any work that needed doing, and they told me that very little was known about Tsavo lions. That struck me as a glaring void in knowledge, and it needed to be filled if you wanted species like it to be here in the future. I got an overview, submitted a report to KWS, and they gave me permission to do research. I went back to Australia, got my citizenship, and then returned to Tsavo. I love Africa. The people are so gracious and warm."

I think of Marianne Fitzgerald's employees, murdered by bandits, and the cruelties I saw or learned about in southern Sudan, but decide it's best not to dispute Dennis's assertion.

As we continue east toward Aruba, a small herd of Thompson's gazelles appears on the horizon. A few animals are "spronging," leaping with all four feet off the ground. It used to be thought that gazelles did this to warn their herd-mates that danger was near, but subsequent research has turned that explanation into a sweet illusion. Darwinian selfishness wins again. Gazelle sprong not because they're looking out for their fellow gazelle but to show an approaching predator that they're in prime condition and will be very difficult to catch, thus turning its attention toward other animals in the herd. Truth is beauty and beauty truth? Not always, Mr. Keats.

We swing down into a grassy bowl near Aruba Lake. A male oryx stands in the distance, tormented by flies, its ears beating the air like duck wings, its tail switching. I am once again captivated by the artistry of this animal's markings, the black blaze on its nose, the black garters, the black stripe, like the racing stripe on a car, streaking along its buckskin flanks. A lone buffalo bull crosses our path. By now, I have seen more than 2,000 in Tsavo, and this one is the biggest yet, a Land Cruiser with horns, five and a half feet tall at its muscle-bunched shoulder, mud black, hoofs as big around as bread plates and sharp as mattocks. He pauses to give us a baleful glare, as if he's contemplating whether to charge the strange, square, noisy thing lumbering through his pasture. I can't imagine any lion, or any number of lions, capable of taking him on, but I guess they would if they were hungry enough. I bring up the theory that Tsavo lions are more likely to turn man-eater because they're more likely to be injured, preying on buffalo.

"One of the things that mitigates against wise management of wildlife is mythology," Dennis responds. "But people don't want to give up on the mythology. One myth is of the rogue beast, the cattle-killer, the man-eater. I am so sick of this man-eater business. Colonel Patterson made a helluva lot of money off that book of his, and so have a lot of writers since." (I'm not sure if this remark is directed at me.) "Lions in Tsavo aren't more likely to turn to people for food than lions anywhere else."

We skirt the Aruba water hole, its shores stalked by purple herons and sacred ibises, and find Burr Boy and Melinda, still noshing on the buffalo carcass, which is by now so rotten that vultures would reject it. We observe for a few moments, and then get a surprise. Baby Huey rises out of the grass, followed by Meathead and Fur Boy. They are a good 10 to 12 miles from where I first saw them on the Ndara Plains. That isn't the surprising part—lions can travel much greater distances in a single day—but, rather, that they and Burr Boy appear to form a masculine coalition that may have taken over from Orion, alias Scarface. Big and tough as he was, he could not have prevailed against this gang. But where is his pride? Was Melinda one of the young lionesses I had seen 16 months ago?

We return to camp and report our find, discovering that Peyton had come upon the five lions just before us. She reports that she observed Melinda "wasping" in front of the three younger males. Wasping is phonetic for "walks sinuously past," the flirtatious walk females adopt when they're in heat. Meathead responded, Peyton tells us, but it appeared that Burr Boy had prior claim. With a roar and a charge, he ended Meathead's romantic fantasies.

As far as a takeover goes, Craig says that a coup d'état in lion society "raises all kinds of hell." Scarface's pride may have broken up. The adult lionesses and their subadult progeny may have gone off to stake out a new territory. With sufficient numbers, they could get buffalo, as females sometimes do on the Serengeti, where six to eight lionesses will gang up to hunt big prey. But I wonder about another, darker possibility: If Scarface was the primary breadwinner, the entire pride, or most of it, may have perished after losing him.

May 23

I AM WRITING this a little after midnight, by a headlamp's light. I fell asleep around ten and woke up an hour ago, after another Lariam-mare. As usual, it left me with a residue of free-floating dread. I waited for it to pass, as it normally does within a few minutes, but it hasn't yet. It seems to have taken up lodging in my brain or nervous system or both, bringing on a mild vertigo, a prickling sensation up and down my arms, and a hyper-alertness I haven't experienced since I was in Vietnam listening in the vaultlike black of jungle nights for a rustle, a crack of a branch, the soft, metallic snick of a rifle bolt easing a round into the chamber. I feel as if I am going to lose my grip on reality at any moment. This anxiety that has no reason breeds an anxiety that I'm going nuts, so I write in this journal to discipline my mind. I am a kind of drill sergeant, whipping a mob of disordered thoughts into shape. I record yesterday's experiment...

Late in the afternoon, Craig and Peyton loaded the dummy lions on the trailer and drove them to Aruba, where Bob had spotted Melinda with another lioness earlier in the day. The males were not in sight. A pair of isolated females provided an ideal setup for Peyton to test one of her hypotheses. Turning hairdresser, she trimmed one dummy's mane to look like a typical Tsavo male's, and coiffed the other in the flowing mane of a traditional Serengeti lion. The point was to see which the females preferred. Her expectation, based on the work she'd done in Tanzania, was that the lionesses would go for the one with the more extravagant hairstyle.

A stiff wind was blowing when we arrived at Aruba. Melinda and her friend were still there, bedded down in the thornbushes. While my car, with Dennis and Ogeto aboard, stayed near the females to keep an eye on them, the two scientists unloaded the dummies some 200 yards downwind so the lionesses wouldn't be distracted by human scent, and then positioned them facing the lionesses and about 20 feet apart. Bob mounted a remote-controlled camera on a tripod between the two decoys. The loudspeaker was bolted to the Land Rover's roof and hooked up to the tape recorder, which would play a recording of a dying wildebeest to get the lionesses' attention. Once they were up and moving toward the sound, they would see what appeared to them to be two strange males guarding a kill. And we would see which the girls attached themselves to. If they followed the Serengeti script, it would be another indicator that one of a mane's purposes is to attract females, even females accustomed to the bald males of their home range.

When everything was ready, we moved all three vehicles well behind the make-believe lions. The wildebeest moaned, a truly doleful sound that seemed to express the misery of death like nothing I'd ever heard. After five minutes, Melinda rose to her feet, followed by her friend. The two cautiously padded toward the mournful groans.

They made an arresting picture, muscles in sinuous play; it was as if they were flowing through the grass. Then they spotted the two dummies, a contrived illusion, a scientist's magic trick, and stopped. They were wary; females usually are when confronted by strange males, Craig whispered over the radio. This pair was especially shy. A few steps forward and stop. Forward again, stop again. Fifteen minutes passed and still they didn't move. When they did, at last, it was only to slip away and hunker down under a bush. Craig counseled patience; it could take them an hour to overcome their caution. We would give them until dark, but when darkness came, the lionesses hadn't stirred and the experiment was called off. It had failed, no one knew why.

"Well, it looks like Tsavo remains a mystery within a riddle wrapped in an enigma," Craig quipped, paraphrasing Winston Churchill's commentary on Russia.

Peyton didn't take things quite so philosophically. It was her experiment and it hadn't worked out and she was upset, although science is largely a record of a thousand failures before one success. Back at camp, she didn't finish supper and went to bed early. I was afraid she'd overheard a a none-too-diplomatic remark Dennis had made to me: "What are you proving with these dummies? All that was proved tonight is that Tsavo females don't like boys."

Queasy dread has not been overcome. I have heard that acute anxiety can be a side effect of Larium. Whether the demons are pharmaceutical or not, I read from the Psalms to excorcise them. The first—"And he shall be like a tree planted by the rivers of water, that bringeth forth his fruit in season; his leaf also shall not wither; and whatsoever he doeth shall prosper"—the 95th—"O come let us sing unto the Lord; let us make a joyful noise to the rock of our salvation"— and the 118th—"I called upon the Lord in distress; the Lord answered me, and set me in a large place. The Lord is at my side; I will not fear…"

Those ancient and beautiful words help some, but not enough. I walk outside to look at the heavens, and the southern stars are a wonder. I recognize some constellations from my own hemisphere, Orion and Canis Major and Ursa Major, but most of the others are unknown, and that's fine. I don't need to know their names; their beauty is sufficient unto the day. In my mind's eye, I draw lines from the pointer stars of the Southern Cross and from the "false cross" above, and mark where they intersect—that's true south. The Dipper lies low on the horizon, and its pointers aim at Polaris, in Ursa Minor, also lower on the horizon than it is at home. True north. I turn, aligning myself between the two poles and extend my arms at right angles to my body. True east. True west. Thus I try to center myself, as the Lakota and Cheyenne and Ojibwa did when they turned to face the Four Sacred Directions. It might seem a little odd, mixing a shot of the Bible with a jigger of Native American religion, but when you are out in the African bush, 300 miles from the nearest doctor or hospital, and feel like you're losing your mind, it's not a bad cocktail. I walk around a bit to shake off my nervousness, and am startled for a millisecond when I practically bump into the two dummy lions. At night, they look all too real.

Paul Simon sings in the ear of my mind:

Joseph's face was black as night,
The pale yellow moon shone in his eyes.
His path was marked by the stars of the Southern Hemisphere,
And he walked his days under African skies.

At the fire pit, embers glow faintly. A waterbuck snorts out in the Kanderi swamp. Far off, an elephant screams. What on Earth am I doing here? I think of Marianne. A little like ancient Athens...slaves to do the dirty work so Plato and Aristotle and that lot could sit and think. Eight days ago, Bob and I were driven to Tsavo from Nairobi by Verity's driver, a short, stocky Kikuyu named Sammy. We stopped at the roadside and pitched into the cooler for sandwiches and a beer. A villager appeared, quite literally appeared out of nothing, like some wretched genie summoned from wherever genies spend their time. His belly was sunken, his glassy eyes haunted by hunger, his clothes ragged and filthy. He didn't beg, didn't speak a word, just stood there, his very presence a reproach. I couldn't eat. I gave him my sandwich, an act of charity akin to giving aspirin to someone racked by deep bone pain. So what if some lions have manes and others don't? Who cares why they do what they do? Isn't this expedition pointless? Considering the conditions in this country, and in most of black Africa, doesn't inquiring into all these fine points of animal behavior represent a form of decadence?

His path was marked by the stars of the Southern Hemisphere,
And he walked his days under African skies.

Under these African skies at two in the morning, it is best to be candid with myself, since such candor cannot hurt anyone. I yearn for the poet's, the songwriter's response to the natural world. I'm a little weary of the empirical approach, all these infrared cameras and skull measurements and data sheets. Data. Data. Data. Art and science, that hoary chestnut of a conflict. Candidly speaking, Phil to Phil, some part of me resists Craig and Peyton and Gnoske and Kerbis Peterhans and their theories and hypotheses, tests and experiments. I long for the company of a naturalist like John Muir, for whom the petal of each mountain flower was "a window through which we may see the Creator."

I believe that to be true, but I also believe that the theory of evolution is right, which is something of a tricky juggling act, because if you follow Darwinism to its logical conclusion, then you have to believe life on Earth isn't here because God intended it to be, or that it's evolved as it has because that's how he planned it. It could just as easily have gone some other way or never come into being in the first place. It's one vast accident, in so many words. Extending that thought from the animate to the inanimate, I have to conclude that all this around and above me, these stars of the Southern Hemisphere, is likewise accidental, unguided by a divine intelligence, without purpose. Yet we call it creation and creation implies a creator. We don't look at, say, a 747 and assume that 200,000 individual moving parts just chanced to come together to form a machine that takes off, lands, and flies at 500 miles an hour. In Craig Packer's own book, *Into Africa,* he states: "Zebras are bulk feeders, preferring mature grasses. Wildebeest seek any green grass. By mowing down the longer grasses, the two larger species create fresh swards of the short green grass preferred by the Thomson's gazelle.... What are the advantages of migration?...The short grasses of the volcanic plains are much richer in protein, calcium, and phosphorous than the tall grasses of the northern woodlands. Mineral levels in the northern grasses are so low that nonmigratory grazers would suffer reduced fertility from phosphorous deficiency. Browsers can obtain ample minerals from tree leaves, but grazers must migrate south as soon as the rains permit."

In the margins, I have scrawled, "The design of it!" A design implies a designer. That's what John Muir saw in the blossoms of the high Sierra.

Astrophysicists, cosmologists, biologists, bioengineers, doctors, and cutting-edge medical researchers are the Aztec priests of our secularized civilization, speaking to us from atop the temples of science, leading us on to a future in which we shall all be liberated from our comforting illusions and submit to the reign of a ruthless rationalism. Maybe we'll be better off, considering that one of those illusions, religious belief, has been and continues to be the source of so much bloodshed and misery. Nevertheless, I fear we'll suffer from a spiritual impoverishment in that brave new world.

It's in the field of bioengineering that the high priests join hands with the ministers of globalization. Private companies with shares traded on the computerized floors of the world's stock exchanges will extract stem cells from human embryos, will manipulate our genes and recombine our DNA, and all for the best of reasons: to cure diseases, save lives, repair defects in our natural makeup, give us children who will be superior in every way. Surely, Mr. and Mrs. Jones, you'll want your child to have a genetic head start, things are so competitive these days, it will be well worth the investment.... Such miracles will not come cheap and will be bestowed on those who can afford them; the miracle makers will have to show a profit to the cyber-traders and shareholders. I don't imagine the woman I met in southern Sudan, the one who had to walk six days under African skies to get her sick child to a clinic, will benefit. Darwinian economics won't permit it.

Just two months ago, I addressed the student body of the high school I graduated from in 1959: Fenwick, a Catholic prep school in Oak Park, Illinois. I told the young women in their dark skirts and uniform jackets, the young men in their blazers and ties that the great challenge that will confront their generation will be the one hurled by the bio-technocrats of our wired world. Someday, I said, in your lifetime, perhaps even in mine, a band of lab-coated geniuses, impatient with moral questions, are going to clone a human being.

Humankind will then possess a power commensurate to the har-nessing of the atom, and what will we do with it? This is going to happen, I told the students.

No matter how many laws and regulations are passed prohibit-ing reproductive cloning, no matter how many objections are raised by priests and ministers and ethicists, it's going to happen, and the bio-techs will get on television and in the soothing tones of practiced media-speak tell us that it's a good thing that will bring the greatest good to the greatest number. It's going to happen because the high priests of science are riding high these days, as are the cyber-capital-ists, and they obey one commandment, not ten: If it can be done, it should be done, especially if there's money in it. And once it's done, you will be faced with ethical, political, and even metaphysical ques-tions no one has faced before. If any man or woman can run off a Xerox of himself or herself, can we say that the facsimile possesses an immortal soul? Can we say that he or she is a sacred, unique indi-vidual, endowed by the Creator with certain inalienable rights? But can we say that if we are the creators? Can we say that when a clone, by definition, is not a unique individual? Human beings are fickle; values change with circumstances. What if, someday, it's decided that we who gave the clone life now withdraw its rights to equal treat-ment under the law?

Sometimes the post-industrial world's rush into the future strikes me as mindless. It's like Everest. We're going there because it's there. In my more paranoid moments, and I'm certainly in one now, stand-ing here under African skies, the cold stars' light in my eyes (the pale yellow moon has set, Paul), I think science is in a hurry to get there because it sees, glimmering on the temporal horizon, the final triumph over its old adversary, faith. There's another hoary chestnut of a conflict. They've been at war ever since the church persecuted Galileo for stating that the Earth was not the center of creation. Cosmologists have reported, with a certain bleak glee, that the universe will expand forever, becoming an immense, cold, dark void in which protons will be separated by distances equal to those separating galaxies today; in other words, the universe is pointless, spinning toward oblivion.

Contemporary research into the brain has found that our emotions, from love to rage, are the product of specific electrochemical reactions in the cranial soup, our capacity to think and reason not a reflection of the divine in our natures but functions of brain centers that can be observed with fast MRIs and PET scans. The hard-wired circuitry in the frontal lobe is the only path to knowledge. There is no room in this view of life for such fuzzy concepts as a poet's inspiration much less a prophet's divine revelation. We're almost there, the future, and we'll be there when man at last creates man out of his own skin, the soulless, identical copy, coming off the sterile assembly lines of Embryo, Inc., with genes that can be jiggered into whatever configuration may be desired. The paragon of animals will be shown to be mere matter, and science will do what logicians say is impossible, proving a negative: God is not the author of human life or any life. God provably does not exist. Sometimes, in these paranoid moments, I imagine myself beside Ted Kaczynski, there in the solitude of his madness and his Montana cabin, helping him make bombs to hurl against a future I want no part of.

What am I doing here, thinking these thoughts under African skies? I am a novelist by calling; my fundamental reaction to the natural world comes from the belly, which somehow communicates to the spirit. Nothing rational about it. I can feel myself slipping away from information and data and the empirical method toward a romantic primitivism. I long to be a savage, "suckled in a creed outworn," who stands in ignorant awe of creation and sees in the bursting volcano not geologic and thermal forces unleashed but the wrath of some malevolent deity; who dances to the shaman's drum and listens to mythic tales grunted round the tribal fire and has no way to reproduce except by fucking.

I return to my tent and write down these jangled musings, not to make sense of them, but to get them out of my system. The pharmaceutical demons still prod me, but not as sharply as an hour ago. I lie down, and having tried the Psalms and Lakota centering, I browse through Seneca's letters to Lucilius and Marcus Aurelius's *Meditations*. The headlamp goes off, and I doze, to be roused only an hour later by the sound of water poured into the bucket outside, the glow of the kerosene lamp the man has lit for me. In that brief hour of untroubled sleep, I have made friends once again with Craig and Peyton, Gnoske, Kerbis Peterhans, and Darwin, though not with the bioentrepreneurs. It's impossible for me to see human beings as anything other than creatures who exist to find out, to seek, to add to the great edifice of knowledge, brick by brick, even if, as we used to say in Vietnam, it don't mean nuthin', don't mean a thing. Still, I'm so tired I cannot get off my cot; then I recall the words Marcus Aurelius spoke to me just a little while ago: "When Thou risest reluctantly in the morning, let this thought be present: I am rising to do the work of a human being."

And that also answers the question, What am I doing here, under African skies?

*

The morning comes cool and overcast, with promise of rain. With Sammy at the wheel, we head north out of camp. A striped hyena comes down the road, bounding with its weird, hopping gait. An hour later we stand atop Mudanda Rock, looking down at the water hole, where baboons convene, and out toward a vista that reaches all the way to the Yatta Escarpment. Mudanda itself is a kind of miniature version of Ayers Rock in Australia, a reddish beige uplift perhaps half a mile long, a hundred yards wide, and a hundred feet high at its highest, slanting down to 75 or 50 at its north end. We walk along it, looking for lion sign, Craig expounding on Gnoske and Kerbis Peterhans's ideas. He says he's seen nothing so far to indicate that Tsavo lions are direct descendants of prehistoric cave lions. For that matter, there is no evidence he knows of showing that primitive lions lived in caves. *Panthera leo spelaea* is called *spelaea* because its image was found on cave walls, painted by cave men. (*Homo sapiens spelaea?*)

Likewise, he says no to classifying buffalo lions as a unique breed. All lions hunt buffalo, he declares. On the Serengeti, buffalo are the main cause of death among lions. Yes, females form packs to hunt the great beasts when wildebeest and zebra are not abundant, but the job falls most often to males. He recalls one time when he observed a lioness studying a buffalo herd. After some time, she turned and gave a scolding grunt to the two pride males lounging in the shade. Time to get off your butts and bring home some bacon, she was saying, and the pair got up and commenced their stalk. (This, however, doesn't deny that Tsavo lions are buffalo specialists.)

No also to the assertion that Tsavo lions live in small prides. My own observations during both a dry and wet season confirm that. There was Scarface's pride of 23, and so far on this trip, we've pegged 2 more prides—the Ndololo, with at least 11, and the Voi pride, another 11—and if we can take Marcus at his word, the Hatulo Bisani pride numbers 16.

Craig does concede on two points. One is skull formation and skeletal dimensions. "They might be on to something interesting there," he says, admitting that he isn't well versed in matters morphological. The other is climate and elevation as the determining factors in mane growth. The Serengeti is considerably higher than Tsavo, so males there can grow big manes without paying too high a price in heat stress. Down here, besides Peyton's thermal images, we've seen lions panting from heat, lying with their forepaws up on branches to aid circulation, or in shallow depressions pawed out of the ground to get at the cooler earth beneath. Yet there could be variations in Tsavo itself; the higher altitudes atop the Yatta Plateau or the Taita Hills could support greater numbers of maned males. (Tom Gnoske is in fact going to return to Tsavo soon to test that theory by running a transect from the Taita Hills, down along the Tsavo River to the Galana, then along the Galana into the low plains. It will be a scaled-back version of the aborted Tana River expedition.)

We head back to get ready for this afternoon's experiment. Bob has called on the radio to report that one of our quartet, Burr Boy, has separated himself from his mates at Aruba. This will give Peyton a chance to test her ideas on how a solitary male reacts to mane length in rival males. On the return drive, we spot a remarkable bird, the pintail whydah. Its forked tail, twice as long as its body, moves up and down in flight with a sinuous motion reminiscent of a dolphin's swimming. A perfect example, says Craig, of a male ornament. The male whydah displays its tail only during breeding season, to attract females. What does it signify? Better genes, better health? Something else that appeals to the female's sense of aesthetics?

Marcus Russell, Blade, and Saitoti pay us a call at lunchtime. Marcus is once again voluble, a nonstop talker. After delivering another speech about Somali herdsmen poisoning lions, he tells us that he once maintained a camp where ours now is, but abandoned it because lions began to stalk his clients. Maybe he's trying to persuade us to set up permanently at Galdessa. We firm up a date to visit his camp, and then Craig and Peyton go to prepare the dummies for their next performance.

Just before we're due to leave, I get into a brief but civil argument with Dennis, who doesn't think the experiment should be performed and expects me to put a stop to it. I've no intention of doing anything of the sort and tell him so. Since we're feeding him and Sarah, paying their expenses, and giving him material that will benefit his own work, he could be a little more gracious, or at least less prickly and obstructive.

The dummies have been re-adorned as Lothario (short and blond) and Fabio (long and blond). Peyton had run this experiment seven times in Tanzania, and every time the real lion approached Lothario first, leading her to conclude that a lion sees a prominent mane as a sign of strength, a short one as a sign of weakness.

We set up alongside Aruba lake, in the splendid light of a late East African afternoon, with a strong wind blowing. A hen plover and two chicks, each hardly bigger than a locust, peck grass seed at the shore. A sacred ibis flies low over the water, a winged spear of black and white, while a pair of hippopotamuses wallow, one giving a cavernous yawn— it looks as if you could park a Volkswagen in its jaws. In the far distance, an elephant herd files at a stately pace toward the water hole. The idyllic scene is shattered when Peyton switches on her call of hyenas on a kill. It sounds like hell's own choir accompanied by a madhouse glee club: a demoniacal medley of groans, cackles, giggles, howls, and shrieks. As unpleasant as it is to human ears, the racket hyenas make when devouring prey is an irresistible summons to lions, telling them that there is food to be had, ready to eat. No stalking, running, springing, wrestling. Just drive the hyenas off and take the meat for yourself.

The ghastly chorus wails for a few minutes. Burr Boy's head appears above the berm of the Aruba dam. He starts forward boldly, but instead of finding a pack of hyenas and a more or less free meal, he sees what look like two invading males. His manner changes instantly. He approaches with utmost care, amber eyes riveted on his adversaries. A few steps, then stop and stare for three or four minutes, a few steps more, then stop and stare again, nostrils twitching to pick up a scent. Another advance. He licks his lips, signaling that he's nervous. He crouches and creeps on, a mesmerizing sight, all that tawny muscle moving in tawny light, but I am not too impressed with leonine intelligence. I've seen ducks smart enough to recognize decoys from the real thing. In the Land Rover with Peyton, I whisper that even a lion ought to have figured out by now that the two creatures in front of him, scentless, motionless, and silent, are fakes.

She points out that a confrontation with a rival male or males is the biggest event in a lion's life; he can't afford to be anything but extremely cautious, the consequences of rash action being so catastrophic: eviction from his pride, serious injury, even death.

"If you were in a dark alley and some guy pointed an authentic-looking toy pistol at you and said, 'Give me your wallet,' what would you do, even if you suspected the gun was fake?"

My hubris comes down a notch, one notch more, when I recall that slivered second last night when the dummies fooled me.

Burr Boy is belly to the ground now, facing his adversaries. He remains motionless for 20 minutes, until dusk falls, and then pads forward ten more feet, pauses, creeps closer, pauses again, and creeps still closer, to within five yards of Lothario. He appears to have chosen the short-maned dummy to confront first, and that's confirmed a moment later as he circles around Lothario to approach from the flank. Facing another male eyeball to eyeball is sure to provoke a fight, and Burr Boy wants to avoid that if he can.

The experiment will be complete if he sniffs Lothario, but just as he's about to, his nose barely three feet away, he's attacked by a horde of gnats that so distracts him he trots off a distance and rolls in the dirt, snapping his jaws, swatting with his paws, flicking his tail. It's good enough for Peyton and Craig. Burr Boy obviously wanted no part of Fabio. Peyton's disappointment with the last experiment has been overcome; she's quietly thrilled. Eight times in a row, the last time here in Tsavo, a lone male lion approached the dummy with the sparser mane first, calculating that it was the lesser of two evils. In two out of three situations, Tsavo lions have acted exactly as Serengeti lions would; insofar as behavior goes, the arrow is pointing toward a similarity, rather than a difference, between the two.

May 24

THE CAMPFIRE DANCES its welcome. Showered, changed into a fresh shirt, I sit beside it sipping a scotch, very happy that Peyton and I are not now slabs of road-burger or pâté in a lion's belly. Today, we came close enough to becoming one or the other. I should have known better than to complain that lion research was often as excit-ing as putting up drywall. Hours and hours of boredom punctuated by moments of sheer boredom, waiting for the indolent beasts to do something. This morning, I learned that the work can be otherwise.

While our band of seekers fanned out for distant realms—Craig to the Ndara Plains with Ogeto, Bob to Aruba, Dennis and Sarah off to have a look at the Voi pride—Peyton and I stuck close to home, going in search of the Ndololo pride. Following a lightly used track that paralleled the Voi riverbed, Peyton looked for a spot where we could see for a distance, but there weren't many such vantage points, the country a maze of brush and tamarind groves and thickets of the white-flowering shrub called *Maeva triphilia*. Finding a fairly good location, with a view of about a hundred yards right and left, she parked and climbed up on the roof. I handed the speaker to her, then she connected the wires, coiled around a spool in back, and got back in and put a cassette in the tape recorder. Once again, the hideous chorus of hyenas on a kill echoed across the landscape. We sat and sipped coffee from our thermos and glassed with binoculars. The noise got on my nerves. Every now and then the pack's screeches and cackles paused, allowing one hyena to do a solo that sounded like the bellowing of a deranged cow. A hornbill lofted from a branch, and I wished I could hear its sweet, sad call. As I peered intently to the left side of the road, Peyton watched the right.

"Ohhhhhh shit!" she shouted. "Holy shit!"

In almost the same instant came the trumpet blasts of elephants. My head snapped round to see nine of them charging us from out of the scrub: three calves and two adolescents behind a phalanx of four matriarchs, coming on at a stiff-legged run, throwing up dust, ears flapping like barn doors in a gale, tusks glinting in the early light. Evidently, the racket had got on their nerves as well. They were a hundred yards away at most, a distance they halved in about two seconds, which was when the lead matriarch ceased trumpeting and lowered her head to let us know that the threat displays were over. This was the real thing. She came straight for us with a terrible sin-gleness of purpose. Her tusks could easily pierce the Land Rover's thin aluminum skin, and with a little help from her friends, maybe without it, she could overturn the vehicle and stomp on it until it looked like a flattened beer can and we looked like—well, I didn't care to think about that. With admirable sangfroid, Peyton switched off the tape recorder and started the engine. We took off as fast as the road would allow, meaning not very fast, certainly not fast

enough to suit the matriarch. We hadn't gone far before she, followed by the rest, thundered through our parking spot. Eight of the
elephants carried on, but the old girl, with astonishing agility, turned
abruptly and chased us down the road. She was not about to let a
good tantrum go to waste.

Peyton stepped on the gas. The matriarch continued in hot pursuit. Finally, satisfied that we'd been well and properly seen off, she
halted, and with a parting scream and a final toss of her great head,
turned back to rejoin the others. The herd shambled off, now as calm
as they'd been enraged—a beautiful and magisterial procession against
an eastern sky going from bright orange to peach to primrose.

After a silence, Peyton said, "I'm really scared of elephants. I've
gotten to know lions so well that I don't feel frightened of them.
Maybe it's a false sense of security, I don't know, but I'm irrationally
scared of elephants."

I assured her that in the moment just passed, her fears had been
perfectly reasonable.

We composed ourselves and doubled back to see if the hyena call
had stirred any lions out of hiding. I doubted we would see a one;
if the call had drawn them in, they would have been scared off by the
elephant charge.

"Stop!" I yelled.

There, 40, 50 yards away on the riverbank, posed as if for a family portrait, was the Ndololo pride, 11 altogether, but once again,
all females, cubs, and subadults. Peyton turned off-road and eased
toward them. We recognized the old female and the lioness with
the injured hip. They were not "tourist" lions, and before Peyton
could identify the others, they nervously stole away across the dry
riverbed. It was steep-sided, 20 to 30 feet deep. Looking for a drift
so we could cross and follow them, we drove slowly along the near

side, the Land Rover lurching into and out of hidden potholes. We spotted another lioness, who was pregnant, and followed at a discreet distance.

"Look! The males!"

Peyton pointed ahead. They lay in the grass, two of them, both maned—sparsely, but maned nonetheless—the one black, the other blond. The lioness vanished into the brush beside the riverbed in classic Tsavo fashion—she was there and then not there—but the males stayed put for a while, allowing Peyton to count their muzzle spots and make note of their ear notches (another point of identification). Then they rose and padded away, and both were by far the best-looking males we'd seen so far, fully mature and in prime condition, with sleek, tawny gray coats, deep chests, shoulders striated with muscle. Four hundred fifty pounds, each of them. We trailed them, bumping over deadfalls concealed in the grass, and found them resettled nearby; but they moved again, crossing the Voi to dissolve into the deep scrub beyond. We found a drift and crossed the riverbed, the Land Rover in low-range four-wheel drive and canted at a 45° angle, climbing the bank on the far side.

The black-maned lion had found a cozy bed in the shade. Peyton focused her still camera and imitated a hyena's whoop to get him to raise his head. It was then that I recalled the ranger's story about the big male who'd attacked the minibus; the pregnant female must have been the lioness he'd been mating with, and recalling that black-maned lions tended to be dominant, I figured the culprit was the one in front of us. I hoped he didn't object to having his picture taken. Another whoop, but the lion didn't cooperate. Just then, two juvenile elephants appeared, browsing under a tamarind tree only yards away, on my side of the vehicle.

"Guess what's going to happen in a few seconds," I whispered.

Sure enough, Mom hove into view, probably one of the matriarchs who'd come at us like Hannibal's cavalry. It was simply amazing and unsettling how something so big could show up so quickly, with barely a sound. She cast an ominous stare in our direction, flapped her ears and shook her head, and we didn't need a translator to interpret her body language. Off-road, in close country, there would be no escaping a charge now. Peyton put the car in gear and we left. The lion also wanted no part of the matriarch. As he vanished into the undergrowth, we saw, through a corridor in the ranks of *Maeva triphilia,* eight lionesses and cubs file past, like cars crossing an intersection. Then they disappeared. The entire pride had become invisible, cloaked in the thick greenery. We pressed on for another quarter of a mile. Apparently, Peyton meant it when she said she wasn't afraid of lions. I was. The vegetation was so thick that branches screeched against the windows. The lions could have been anywhere from three feet to a mile away, but if the testy male was hiding in one of those thickets and decided to repeat his perform-ance with the minibus, one of us would get a paw in the face before we saw it coming. I was all for calling it quits, but didn't want to interfere in Peyton's research and kept my anxieties to myself.

We entered a lovely, shady grove of tamarind, trunks rust red and polished from elephants rubbing up against them. We'd both drunk too much coffee. Peyton got out to pee and asked me to keep a lookout for lions. When she was finished, she did the same for me, but fear overcame shame and shyness and I stood pissing right beside my door. It was now past nine and already hot, and Peyton decided it was time to call it a morning. Wonderful, I thought, but didn't say it.

Ten minutes of slow, cautious driving (there were pits in the ground two and three feet deep) brought us back to the drift. As we started down, the right wheel banged into a ridge of dried mud, hard as curbstone. Peyton's foot was jarred off the clutch, killing the engine. She turned the key to restart it. Not even a click. Another turn and still nothing. It was like we were in a motorless car.

"Ohhhh, shit," Peyton said. That was becoming the watchword of the day.

We tried the lights. They didn't work. Peyton turned on the radio to tell our companions about our predicament, assuming the VHF could reach them. No matter. The radio didn't work.

"That bump must've knocked a battery cable loose," she speculated.

We had a stalled car on a steep incline deep in the bush, with a herd of temperamental elephants and a pride of 14 lions close by. I didn't relish climbing out to check the battery, but relished much less the idea of walking over four miles back to camp.

"Okay, pop the hood hatch and I'll have a look," I said.

"It's under your seat."

We got out and pulled off the seat. Everything had been direct-wired to the battery—the GPS, the electronic altimeter, and the radio, along with several other gizmos, and I looked down at a linguini of wires. After detaching them and the cables, we cleaned the battery posts and reattached everything and again tried to start the car. The silence told us that a long, hot, dangerous hike was probably in our immediate future. Wishing to avoid that with all my heart, I looked down the riverbank, which formed a ramp some 60 to 75 feet long to the riverbed. I made a suggestion: While I dug out the ridge blocking the right wheel, Peyton would stay in the driver's seat, keeping a lookout for lions, elephants, or any other dangerous wildlife. I would then push the Land Rover, and, as it rolled downhill, she would try to jump-start the engine.

I untied the shovel from the roof rack, took a long, careful look around, and got to work. Ten minutes and a gallon of sweat later, we were ready to try. I got behind the vehicle and pushed with all my strength. The Land Rover wouldn't budge. More shovel work followed, with Peyton lending a hand by chopping at the ridge with the jack handle (although I would have preferred she stick to her sentry duties). I tried once more, really putting my shoulder to it. How heavy was a Land Rover anyway? It was as if I were trying to push a semitrailer.

"Parking brake off?" I called.

She said it was, and then suggested that she get out and help me push. I pointed out that if the vehicle ran away on us, we would lose our only chance to get it started again; so I pushed a third time and maybe got two inches of forward motion out of it. Peyton joined me, stating that the incline didn't look too steep; if we left both doors open, we could jump in as the car rolled gently down, and then she would try the jump start. She could not have weighed more than 115 or 120 pounds, but she was stronger than she looked, because, with her shoving on the right side and me on the left, the stubborn thing started to roll. We'd misjudged the degree of incline, however. The Land Rover sped toward the river bottom, both of us dashing after it. I made quite the hero of myself by tripping and falling when my sandal wedged into an exposed tree root. Just as I hit dirt, I heard Peyton hoot like a cowgirl and glimpsed her leaping onto the running board and swinging herself inside. The vehicle bounced into the riverbed. A lovely puff of oily smoke burst from the tailpipe, and I heard the still lovelier rattle of a running diesel.

"You are quite the young lady," I said when I got back in.

"Major bush girl." She flexed a bicep, then graciously added, "But it was a team effort," then let out a laugh. "That was just totally awesome!"

There is nothing so stimulating as to be shot at without effect, Winston Churchill had written while covering the Boer War. Tsavo had just shot at us without effect, and Peyton was stimulated. I wasn't—deeply relieved, rather. I guess that's one of the differences between being 32 and 59.

May 25

BABY HUEY HAS somehow won Melinda over from Burr Boy. The pair are mating on the berm of the Aruba dam. Lion mating is lascivious, quick, and savage, each copulation lasting but a few seconds and ending with jaw-snapping snarls from the female. Male lions have a barb on their penis, which is thought to stimulate ovulation but which apparently hurts the lioness. Baby Huey dismounts and lies down beside her. The loving couple stare out into space for a while, then Melinda crouches, her tail raised, and Baby Huey mounts her again, with swift thrusts. She grunts and snarls once more and tries to bite him, but he leaps away at the last second. This is to human love as ripping out a wildebeest's windpipe is to fine dining. As the couple rest from their reproductive labors, Meathead, some hundred yards away, is engaged in a drama with four buffalo bulls, guardians of a herd 200 strong. The bulls are not pleased to have five lions so near (Burr Boy and Fur Boy are also in the vicinity), and advance on Meathead at a slow, deliberate pace. Instead of slinking away, the lion stands his ground and gives the buffalo what for with two rumbling roars. The bulls halt, as if surprised by his temerity. A Mexican standoff ensues, the golden lion bravely—or stupidly—confronting four sets of massive horns backed up by a total of, say, 5,000 or 6,000 pounds of muscle and bone. After a minute of silent staring, Meathead advances on the bulls and roars again, as if to tell them that he meant what he said the first time. The buffalos turn and trot off, but seem to think there's something wrong with that picture, and turn again to once more plod toward the lion. Finally, he backs off, though he doesn't flee—merely makes a graceful retreat. What else from the king of beasts?

While this goes on, Baby Huey and Melinda have at it again. They could not care less about the buffalo, driven by a sexual imperative that leaves no room for distraction. You could say that when lions make love, they don't take calls.

Off to the right, Fur Boy leaps at Burr Boy, cuffing him. Burr Boy ambles away, and the younger lion chases him, making as if to bite him.

"He's play fighting," says Craig as we observe. "I would have thought he's too old for that."

Burr Boy certainly is, wants no part of Fur Boy's antics, and swats at him angrily.

Watching this, Craig begins to spin a hypothesis, which can be considered nothing more than a scientist's yarn.

Tsavo, he says, is a lot like Kruger in South Africa, a harsh, penurious environment. Lions in Kruger take far longer to grow up than do lions in the Serengeti. They attain full body size at the same rate, but males spend several years in nomadic bachelorhood, killing and eating buffalo, before they're ready to assume leadership of a pride.

On the Serengeti, where food is plentiful and the climate more temperate, the bachelor period is much shorter.

Conditions in Tsavo, he goes on, are even tougher than in Kruger. It's a hardscrabble place. Possibly, Tsavo males take even longer to grow up, and aren't growing manes even though they've attained the physiques of mature lions. In other words, superannuated adolescents. The maned males we've seen or heard about very possibly didn't sprout them until they were well on in years, and then the hot climate probably limited their growth.

"It could be that conditions here are such that they won't allow lions to express what's in them genetically until they're older."

The other possibility is the more exciting: Tsavo lions really are genetically different, though not, Craig hastens to add, so different as to constitute a distinct subspecies. The best way to resolve that would be to capture male cubs from Tsavo, Kruger, and the Serengeti, then raise them in captivity under identical conditions. If all grew manes at roughly the same rate, that would indicate that tough environments account for manelessness; if not, then we would have evidence suggesting genetic variation.

I listen out of one ear, reluctant to allow the theorizing to detract from the magic of the scene: the fish eagle soaring on the thermals above Aruba lake, the two lions mating, the young lion cavorting with his older brother or friend, the fifth staring down the bull buffalo, the herd milling behind them out on the savanna in the morning sun.

A short drive northward brings us to the second female, whom we call Granny because she's old, her teeth rounded down to nubbins. She's resting in thornbush shade after gnawing at an eland, its gutted, bloated, fly-covered carcass nearby.

"Know what's needed in Tsavo?" Craig asks rhetorically. "A two- to three-year study. We define the lion by its mane, but here they don't have them, but there are a lot of things of interest besides manes. Human-animal conflict on the park borders, the whole basic ecology of Tsavo. A lion census too. What they eat, what their ranges are. No one knows any of that for sure."

But Gnoske and Kerbis Peterhans had already tried that, and park regulations prohibited them from completing their work.

May 28

CLOUDS LYING LOW on the eastern rim of the world part to form what looks like the door to a furnace, or perhaps the mouth of a huge cauldron, filled with molten gold: the biblical refiner's fire.

With Sammy at the wheel, Ogeto and I search for the Aruba pride, if six lions can be called a pride, but find no sign of them. From the branch of a leafless tree, a pale chanting goshawk surveys the plains for prey. We wander northward, following buffalo signs, in the hopes the lions have been trailing the herd. It's all MMBA again, Ogeto and I passing the time with small talk. He's 37, a warm, quiet, thoughtful man who is never happier than when picking up old bones. Buffalo bones, lion skulls, femurs of gazelle. Though his English is excellent, it's hard to understand what he's saying, his voice is so subdued. I constantly have to cock an ear, like some half-deaf geezer, and ask, "What's that again?"

I am delighted to have captured wonderful shots of a lilac-breasted roller yesterday—the gorgeous bird was very cooperative, remaining still while I got close enough with my 105-millimeter lens. Dennis and Sarah have left, which delights me further. Yesterday, learning from Verity that our food bill was rising because so much was being consumed, I had to cut off their mess privileges. Later, I caught Dennis asking Sammy to go into the town of Voi to fill up his jerry cans with gas and informed him that Sammy was my driver and not his servant. Finally, Dennis apparently got into another disagreement with Peyton and Craig about another experiment involving the dummy lions—he objects because it involves too much off-road driving, which he seems to think is his right alone. Whatever happened, Peyton was upset, furious actually. She takes her work very seriously, and, by her lights, Dennis is not only obstructive, but a dilettante, playing at science. I empathized. She feels toward him what I feel whenever I'm forced into contact with phony wanna-be writers who have a great story to tell, if only they could find the time, and would I please look at what they've done so far and offer some advice? It was my task to serve the eviction papers, but I hadn't spoken more than two or three words before Sarah took the cue and volunteered that they leave. I have begun to like her, a Scottish schoolteacher who quit to join Dennis in Africa, perhaps because she loved him, perhaps to put some adventure in her life, perhaps for both reasons, and I would not have been unhappy if she stayed. But where Dennis went, she went. The camp is a much happier place now, the oppressive cloud of mutual resentment lifted.

Returning there, I call Leslie on the satellite phone. I left home more than two weeks ago, and though I'm an experienced nomad, accustomed to loneliness (at last count, I've lived, worked, traveled, and fought and covered wars in 48 countries on 4 continents), I miss her terribly; miss her face with morning light on it, and little domestic chores like making coffee and feeding Sage and our cat, Ditto: all the joys of the hearth.

I'm old enough to remember wall phones, with their wooden boxes and brass bells and black Bakelite mouthpieces and earpieces: back in the late 1940s, we had them in the cabins we rented in northern Wisconsin, where my machinist father serviced canning factories. We were on a party line, with each party assigned a specific ring. Ours, if I remember right, was two shorts and a long.

Being able to call Connecticut from the African wilds therefore strikes me as close to miraculous. It's also expensive, sat-phone rates running about $8 a minute. The conversation is consequently brief, and the news from home isn't good. My 85-year-old mother, suffering from vascular dementia for the past two years, was hospitalized two days ago with internal bleeding; stomach cancer has been diagnosed. Dementia's symptoms are almost identical to those of Alzheimer's: a slow, relentless destruction of the victim's personality. It's death by inches, death on the installment plan; everything that makes my mother who she is has been vanishing week by week, but her heart and lungs and kidneys and liver have not quit. She's a living shell of herself, outside of time, lost in some inner world of childhood memories but unable to recall what happened five minutes ago and, sometimes, to recognize familiar faces, confusing me with one of her deceased brothers. Once she thought I was her father. The only saving grace is that she's unaware of what's happening to her. Her condition is hardest on my father, my sister, and me. Knowing that there isn't a damn thing we can do to arrest, much less reverse, it, I've been praying that she die without suffering. Now, it seems that simple request won't be granted. Stomach cancer, from what I know of it, is an agonizing death.

Leslie assures me that the doctors will keep her out of pain, which is to say they'll pump her full of drugs that will doubtless thicken the fog in her mind, making it impenetrable. No, there's no need for me to rush home, Leslie says. The cancer isn't going to be treated; at this stage, there would be no point to chemotherapy, radiation, operations. My mother is back home, under the care of the home health worker who's been living with her and my father for more than a year. I am grateful that she isn't in a nursing home; still, a shroud of gloom drops over me when I hang up. Now, I silently pray that my mother will die before the cancer gets to her.

For some reason, a scene from my early childhood springs up from whatever vault it's been buried in. It's the summer of 1945, and we are living in one of those Wisconsin cabins, near a town called Chetek, on the Minnesota border. My father is off making his rounds of the canneries. My mother takes me in one hand and my two-year-old sister in the other for a short walk to a nearby general store to buy me a toy train. She's wearing beige shorts and her chestnut hair is long and wavy, in the style of the 1940s. She looks utterly beautiful (and she was) as we walk a dirt road along a northern lake ringed by tall pine trees. That's all I remember besides the train, its cars, caboose, and engine carved out of wood and painted in vivid primary colors. My mother would have been 30 years old then, younger than Peyton is now. Thirty. That somehow seems impossible, as that time when the war with Germany was won and the war with Japan still was on, when swing bands played on the radio and we lived in a cabin in the woods without indoor plumbing and with a crank-up wall phone, two shorts and a long ring, seems so distant that I can't believe I lived in it.

My thoughts inevitably turn to my own age—I will be 60 in two weeks, 60—and to my mortality. I was lucky to have come to terms with death in my early 20s—"Any day aboveground is a good day,"

we used to say in Vietnam—but the prospect of dying young and violently possesses a certain romanticism that mitigates its horror, and
there is always the hope that you'll dodge the bullet and go on, which
makes confronting that sort of death altogether different from facing
old age and inevitable extinction.

Last year, I became friends with a bush pilot, Heather Stewart,
who flies a single-engine Cessna solo into southern Sudan four to five
days a week, delivering food and medicine to victims of the civil war.
Heather doesn't give a thought to her age; sometimes, it seems as
if she doesn't even know she's a 60-year-old grandmother. It's para-
doxical that here in Africa, where so many are dying daily in its terrible wars or from an army of diseases conquered long ago in the West,
where prey animals fall to the fangs and claws of predators and the
foul odor of rotting carcasses is borne on the wind, that I too have lost
awareness of my age and haven't dwelled on thoughts of death. In fact,
I've felt younger than I do at home. Peyton seems like my contemporary rather than a woman who could be my daughter. I mentioned
this to her the other day, and she commented that Africa is so dangerous that no one thinks about getting old or dying of old age. "Out
here," she said, "everyone's the same age. You could go at any second."

This morning, while I was out with Ogeto, she and Craig spotted
the pair of Ndololo males again and tracked them a long way before losing them in the Kanderi swamp, within a mile of camp. The striking
lions didn't deserve the kind of charmingly condescending nicknames
we'd given to the Aruba band (there was something juvenile and goofy
about them), so we decided to call the black-maned lion Othello, the
blond one Prince Hal. Peyton wanted to run another experiment with
the dummies by dressing one with a long, dark wig, the other with a
blond. Her work in Tanzania, involving two tests with differently col-
ored manes, had given her strong hints that when threatened by

invaders with dark and light manes, male lions choose to attack the latter. Two days ago, out at Aruba, she and Craig tried the experiment on Burr Boy and company, and they followed the Serengeti script, reinforcing her assumption that a black mane is a sign of strength, light of weakness. Othello and Prince Hal will provide ideal subjects to test the theory one more time in Tsavo, if we can call them up. They've shown themselves to be more wary, more "wild," and less tolerant of human presence than other lions.

Two hours before dusk, we set off into the Kanderi, Craig and Peyton in their Land Rover, Bob and Ogeto in another vehicle, I in the third driven by Sammy. Fabio and Julio are placed in the usual way, side by side, with 20-odd feet separating them. We park twice as far from them as we normally do to avoid alarming Othello and Prince Hal. A female lion's roar blasts through the speaker. We wait. One the third try, the two males materialize; it's as though the recording were an incantation, summoning up spirits. The lions stalk up from behind us in total silence, necks as big around as medium-size tree trunks, backs curved gracefully, thigh and shoulder muscles rippling beneath glossy, gray-brown coats. Spotting Fabio and Julio, they slant well off to the side. Their eyes are studies in concentration. Using every bit of cover and concealment they can find—the most highly trained Army rangers could not have matched them— they slip through the brush without a rustle, disappearing, reappearing, disappearing again. Every movement is sure and purposeful. The word that springs to mind is "professionals." These two are the experienced masters of their pride and territory, and they inspire only awe and admiration.

They circle around to creep toward the invaders, Othello leading the way, Prince Hal a body length behind. Othello crouches in the tall grass, while his comrade stands upright in the dying light, facing the interlopers. Prince Hal hunkers down, and Othello moves forward a pace or two before crouching again. Prince Hal follows suit. Creep, look, crouch, creep. The whole swamp is still, as if every creature in it is watching to see what the lions will do. Suddenly, Othello lets out a roar, a roar you can feel vibrating in the air. It's not a single sound, but a succession of sounds, a throaty cough, then a rising, resonant roar, followed by a series of grunts in diminuendo. *Wauugh-aaraRRRAR-UNH UNH unh-unh-unh.* As his falls off, Prince Hal gives his—*Wauugh- aaraRRRAR-UNH UNH unh-unh-unh*— and Othello advances slowly. This is OUR TERRITORY—OURS ours-ours-ours. Both lions get down and remain motionless. Ten minutes pass, twenty. Daylight dies, the stars and a quarter moon come out. By their light we see Othello rise up to roar again; then, trailed by Prince Hal, he trots around to Fabio's flank and gives the dummy a good sniff. The actions declare that he and his pride-mate consider the light-haired Fabio the weaker of their two adversaries. Before they tear the dummies to bits, Craig instructs us to switch on our headlights and engines.

The sudden noise and glare startle Othello and Prince Hal and send them running into the long elephant grass. We then park our vehicles nose to tail, forming a barricade so Craig and Peyton can load Fabio and Julio back into the trailer, out of the real lions' sight.

That done, we retrace the path back to camp, headlights picking out our tire tracks. Peyton and Craig are elated, she especially. Now she has a fourth instance of males avoiding the darker-maned dummy. As for me, I have one more example showing that Tsavo and Serengeti lions, behaviorally, are more alike than otherwise, but I'm not thinking about that. I'm thinking, rather, about Craig's statement that a two- to three-year study will be needed to draw Tsavo lions out of the shadows of legend into the light of scientific knowledge. I'm not entirely sure that will be a good thing. I must be one of those people Dennis King doesn't care for, reluctant to surrender the myth.

Verity Williams has returned from Nairobi to supervise the staff for tomorrow's move to a new campsite in Tsavo West, where Peyton will continue her work. Craig will be returning to Tanzania to tie up some loose ends at the Serengeti Research Project. I will miss his quick wit and the Packer Lecture Series (a recent one, close to my heart, provided an excellent secular, scientific argument against human cloning). While the cook prepares dinner and the rest of the staff begin packing things up, we head for the showers.

From the stall just behind my tent, Bob calls out he's finishing up. I wrap a towel around my waist and step outside.

Wauugh-aaraRRRAR-UNH UNH unh-unh-unh.

The roar blasts from a shadowy thicket not 20 yards directly in front of me, and before I have a chance to feel anything, I make a standing broad jump backward into my tent, do up the zipper, and seize my knife.

Wauugh-aaraRRRAR-UNH UNH unh-unh-unh.

The lion is off to the left now, a little farther way. The other answers him, *Wauugh-aaraRRRAR-UNH UNH unh-unh-unh,* from a greater distance. Othello and Price Hal must have followed us back to camp.

"Bob!" yells Caputo-the-Short to Caputo-the-Tall.

"I hear 'em!" Bob shouts from his tent, close to mine.

I feel as ridiculous as I'm frightened, standing naked with a knife in my hand. If one of those monsters charges through the canvas, I'd better hope the impact drives the blade into my heart. I feel more ridiculous hearing the clatter of plates as someone sets the table in the mess, while Verity calmly issues instructions in Swahili to her people.

"Verity!" I call. "Lion in camp!"

"Yes, yes, we heard them," she replies, as if I'm speaking about raccoons knocking over a trash can in the backyard. I recall that this redoubtable woman grew up with lions, on a colonial sisal plantation in Tanzania. The big cats used to come down from a hill behind her parents' house and walk right past it, roaring so loudly that they rattled the windows. Usually, Verity had told me, they were on their way to the compound where the plantation workers lived; à la the man-eaters of Tsavo, they found the village to be a source of quick and easy meals.

"They're off," Verity assures me, and, yes, the next roar sounds muffled, farther away. "Get on with your shower. Dinner soon."

And I step outside once again, trusting that Othello and Prince Hal don't have dinner plans of their own, or if they do, that we're not on the list of tonight's specials.

May 29

I'M WRITING THIS in the shade of a tall *salvadora pasca,* better known as the African toothbrush tree. The tents have been struck, Verity's staff are piling them and the other camp equipment onto and into the Land Cruisers and Land Rovers. Craig has left for Tanzania, Peyton and the others are up at Galdessa for two or three days, and I will be off to Nairobi General Hospital as soon as Verity has seen to the move. She will drive me.

I want to say that I passed out last night at dinner, but apparently I did more than merely pass out. I recall sitting down under the mess fly and taking a sip of wine. It was no more than that, but I suddenly felt as if I'd chugged an entire bottle. The ground seemed to pitch one side to the other, like a small boat in a heavy beam sea. Then I entered a beautiful, peaceful room, painted the most soothing yellow, with high Palladian windows all around, through which shone a light of ineffable purity, a radiance such as I'd never seen.

There were presences in the room. I can't describe them in any other way, for I couldn't see their faces; but I knew they were all my relatives and friends, dead as well as living, and all were bidding me, "Welcome, welcome." They weren't speaking aloud, but communicating telepathically, as it were, and those presences and their greeting and that astonishing light filled me with a bliss deeper and more complete than the serene joy that would come over me when I was wounded and the nurse would shoot me up with morphine. Students of the paranormal will recognize this as what's come to be known as an NDE, a near-death experience.

"Phil! Phil!"

I opened my eyes and saw Peyton, kneeling beside me, her hand on my wrist.

"He's got a pulse," she said. "I can feel his pulse. Phil! Thank God you're all right!"

Someone had his hands on my chest, or his arms around me, I was too dazed to figure out which. It was Bob, and I heard him say that my heart was beating again.

I raised my head, and there were Verity, Craig, and Ogeto, sitting in the same places as when I'd last seen them, faces half lit by the kerosene lanterns. My companions told me what happened. I had raised a fork to eat my salad when one arm shot up reflexively and I keeled over. Bob, thinking I'd choked on something, rushed to seize me around the chest and perform a Heimlich maneuver, while Peyton grabbed my wrist and cried out that I'd lost my pulse. Bob pressed a hand to my chest and, finding no heartbeat, jerked me hard several times. He was about to administer CPR when I came to.

"How long was I..." I began in a groggy voice, hesitating because I wanted to say "gone." "How long was I out?"

Half a minute to a minute, they said.

Half a minute to a minute? I felt that I'd been in that radiant room for a long time, hours, maybe days.

It was a windy night, but warm; yet I felt chilled, the way you do when you're in shock. But the weirdest thing was the depression that settled over me. I was disappointed to be back among the living. I wanted to return to the yellow room where I'd been so impossibly happy. My real-life friends, much as I liked them, were poor substitutes for those faceless beings, calling out their benevolent salutation in a language that wasn't language. They weren't uttering the word "welcome," but filling me with the essence of the thing itself. Welcome welcome.

Shivering, I could not shake the feeling of letdown for a full quarter of an hour. Everything seemed so dull and pallid and imperfect compared with the yellow room. Finally, comprehending that I had come close to passing through that luminous space into some other state of being, or possibly nonbeing, I became frightened. The blackout, if that's what it was, had come on so quickly, with so little warning. It could happen again, and the next time....

Obviously, something was dreadfully wrong, and there I was in Tsavo, and the nearest hospital way up in Nairobi.

Craig was at that moment on the sat phone to Nairobi, talking to the flying doctor service. I heard him describe my symptoms, then utter a series of yesses and noes, and then the words, "Yeah, he's taking Lariam."

After hanging up, Craig told me that the service thought I was suffering from Lariam toxicity but didn't think I warranted an evacuation by air. The closest airstrip, at any rate, was at Manyani, 30 miles away by dirt road. I was to get plenty of rest, and if I wasn't any worse by morning get myself to Nairobi General by road straightaway. During the night, someone should keep an eye on me.

Peyton volunteered, which pleased me a great deal. Sick men turn into little boys, and they want a woman next to them. Her cot was moved into my tent for the night. Shivering from unnatural chills and scared of dying, I lay with my shirt on, the sleeves rolled down, under a wool blanket, and I was still cold. I couldn't sleep, convinced that if I closed my eyes I would never open them again. Peyton offered to read me to sleep, but her book was a murder mystery, and I didn't think it would do me any good. Soon, she was breathing deeply in a sleep that continued to elude me. I stared at the black ceiling, pondering metaphysical questions. In my bicameral mind, voices on the right side of the aisle argue that the yellow room had been the waiting room to heaven, if not heaven itself. I'd been given a glimpse of the after-life. The representatives on the left shout, No! That glorious, bliss-ful state was the product of endorphins rushed into my brain by a system in shock, beyond it lying only oblivion. Perhaps, these voices cried, mankind's belief in life after death, persisting through the ages despite lack of evidence, began when some Cro-Magnon survived an NDE and reported that there is something that lies beyond this exis-tence. There was one way to resolve that dispute, but that was an expedition I wasn't ready to make.

Finally, around three, I passed into unconsciousness, woke up in a fairly cheerful frame of mind, thanked everyone for being so switched on, and got a laugh at breakfast when I said to Peyton, "Thanks for sleeping with me—literally."

May 31—Galdessa Camp, Tsavo East

DR. MAURO SAIO, an Italian physician who specializes in tropical diseases at Nairobi General, diagnosed Lariam toxicity. He gave
me a month's supply of Valium to combat the anxiety reactions
caused by the drug and a prescription for Malarone, an anti-malaria
medication with less severe side effects. It has to be taken once a day,
however, compared with the once-weekly dosages of Lariam, which,
I learned from Saio, has a half-life of 21 days. Having made three long
trips to Africa in less than a year and a half, it's possible that the drug
had accumulated in my system, hence, the acute reaction this time
around. Saio regaled me with horror stories about patients he'd treated
with Lariam poisoning (he's much opposed to the drug, effective
though it is in preventing malaria), to which Verity added several
equally terrifying accounts about clients who'd suffered paranoid
delusions and suicidal impulses from taking Lariam. It would require
at least four months for the drug to pass out of my system, Saio had

forecast, so the effect of his and Verity's tales was to heighten the anxiety the Valium was supposed to combat. If I didn't drop dead again, I might suddenly turn into a raving lunatic.

Anyhow, pronounced fit for duty, I flew back to Tsavo yesterday in a single-engine Cessna piloted by a white Kenyan named Tom. As Tom was just getting back into flying after a 13-year layoff and did reassuring things like touch each switch on the instrument panel while moving his lips, apparently memorizing what each switch did, I popped an extra Valium for good measure. Still, flying was preferable to driving; not only quicker, but less dangerous. The move to the new campsite on the 29th took longer than expected, so Verity and I weren't able to get on the road till late afternoon and made most of the trip at night. Kenyan truck drivers are maintenance averse and their big rigs break down frequently. The Nairobi-Mombasa highway lacking a shoulder, the drivers simply park their disabled trucks on the road. Naturally, they don't put out flares or reflectorized warning signs, so on at least a dozen occasions, as we came over a hill or around a curve, 20 tons of stalled 18-wheeler would materialize only yards in front of us, which made me feel pretty much like the lookouts on the *Titanic* when they saw the iceberg loom out of the fog.

As accustomed to African road hazards as she is to lions in camp, Verity would deftly pilot the Land Rover into the opposing lane at the last possible second, then deftly back, dodging, again at the last possible second, the trucks bearing down on us at 50 miles an hour. How ironic, I thought, that I should escape being trampled by elephants and mauled by lions and survive a drug-induced NDE only to be killed in a head-on collision.

On the flight back, Tom had some trouble finding certain landmarks and had to break out his map to locate the Manyani airstrip. Dying in a plane crash in the bush, I guessed, would have a little more flair than a highway accident—Finch-Hatton did it, and Hemingway almost did it on his last safari—but when we landed and I spied Sammy waiting at the airstrip with the Land Cruiser, I practically ran into his short, round arms.

He brought me here, where I rejoined Bob, Ogeto, and Peyton. I was very glad to see them and they to see me. Marcus Russell had installed Peyton in the banda next to his, but I gathered that he'd been a perfect gentleman. My companions had not seen any lions during my absence. The country is densely wooded with doum palms, saltbush, and thorn thickets, and the lions in these parts are far more shy and secretive than even those of the Ndololo pride. One of Marcus's staff escorted me to my banda, but the camp's resident elephant, unimaginatively called Tusker, stood right in front of it, browsing on tree limbs. I was informed that Tusker isn't tame and would charge if I got too close, so I had to wait till he finished his snack before moving in. Very cushy, with its indoor shower and toilet, the comfortable bed with mosquito net, the veranda on which I whiled away the afternoon, looking out at the sun-brightened Galana, the palms and tamarinds moving in the wind, and the Yatta Escarpment, rising on the far side of the river like a huge, long tidal wave of earth and rock that is ever poised to come crashing down.

In the evening, before dinner, we tried calling up the big lion Marcus had mentioned before. Setting up at the Ashoka water hole, on the Hatulo Bisani, Peyton played the hyena medley. A clear sky and a half moon gave us light to see by, and it was aided by her night vision scope, which presented the landscape bathed in an eerie, greenish glow. No luck. A lone jackal was all that showed up.

A feast of curried chicken and roast potatoes followed in the mess, where we were joined by Marcus, young Blade, and the commander of the local KWS ranger unit, a beefy lieutenant named

Oliver. Blade cuddled up to Peyton again, happy to see her. So was Marcus, who could not have concealed that he was a bit ga-ga over her even if he tried.

Post-dinner conversation, however, was not romantic. Asked by Marcus if she'd come to any conclusions yet, Peyton related her ideas and Craig's about why Tsavo lions are maneless or short-maned. Marcus and Oliver bought none of it and told her why they thought she was wrong. Peyton told them why she thought they were. The poor woman sounded as if she were defending her Ph.D. thesis before a board of skeptical faculty. I thought she got the better of the argument, but the two bush naturalists did have a point or two.

"I've seen Tsavo males without a hair of mane who looked in a perfect nick," said Marcus, his tongue again on full automatic. "Seen 'em take down buffalo and even small elephant, and you don't do that if you're sick or under stress. I think it's something else, and you know what that is. They're genetically different."

Oliver leaned back in his chair, his dark face burnished in the flicker of kerosene lamps, the shadows deepening the furrows in his broad forehead. A hippo's call, part bellow, part honk, came from the river, and, from somewhere across it, the sawlike roar of a prowling leopard.

"I was raised in the Taita Hills, and I recall what my grandfather told me when I was a boy," Oliver said in a profound tone of voice. A hyena whooped close by. " 'When you are in the bush, don't worry too much about lions with manes—they will leave you alone. But the lions without manes are very dangerous. They will attack. Be careful of them.' "

The atmospherics—the sounds of wild beasts, the buffalo horns hanging above the mantlepiece, the skulls with gaping eye sockets on varnished pedestals, the lamplight on Oliver's face and the way he spoke the words "The lions without manes are very dangerous. They will attack. Be careful of them"—conspired to banish everything I'd learned observing Peyton's experiments. Just when I was ready to accept that Tsavo lions are not a breed apart, the chimera returned.

June 1

Venus blazes above the escarpment. We heard lions east of camp at four this morning, and now, at half past five, we're looking for them, Ogeto, Peyton, and I, following the Galana downstream, toward the twilight shimmering on the horizon. We stop, try a call-up, which fails, and continue on as the river turns from black to pearl to golden brown in the sunrise. We then turn south to a place called Punda Milia, where Marcus saw a pride a few days ago. An old track takes us alongside a lugga that has pools of water in it, and good graze above it; but no herd animals are seen, nor lions, and we head back to Galdessa.

After breakfast, Peyton and Ogeto decide to move on to the new campsite in Tsavo West, but I elect to remain in Galdessa for the rest of today and tomorrow morning. In my imagination, the chimera has taken the form of the lion Marcus keeps talking about, the black-maned monarch of the Hatulo Bisani pride, and I want to see him.

That's all. I don't expect to learn anything new, just to set eyes on him and photograph him, if I can.

I pass the heat of afternoon with Saitoti, who teaches me to throw a lion spear. Ever since early colonial days, Europeans, particularly the British, have carried on a love affair with the tall warriors and lion-killers of the Serengeti plains, and that's led to a lot of romantic noble savage nonsense, including absurd legends that they are descended from the Lost Tribes of Israel. The obsession with all things Masai has come to be called Masai-itis, and Marcus Russell may have a touch of it. The young *moran* came to him a couple of years ago, after he wandered out of Masai-land near the Tanzanian border to look for work. He found it at the Tsavo Hotel in Voi, where he swept floors and learned to wait on tables. Masai lack the obsequiousness required for service-industry employment. Russell visits the hotel fairly often. When Saitoti learned that the white man operated a bush camp, he begged him to hire him.

"He told me," Marcus said, " 'You're a bush man and so am I. I want to be with you. I can't stand living in town.' So I took him on."

Marcus assigned him as a camp askari with two other Masai, Muyandet and Lumuwju, their role to guard guests from wild animals at night. When Blade is visiting, Saitoti serves as a kind of nanny cum-Scoutmaster, taking the boy fishing, teaching him tracking and other bushcraft. There is something almost comic-book retro about that picture—the young white boy with his faithful Masai companion—but both Blade and Saitoti seem happy with the arrangement.

I catch a mild case of Masai-itis myself as Saitoti, in his robe and beads and long, tightly braided hair, hefts his spear to demonstrate how it's thrown. Cocking his sinewy right arm at the elbow, hand palm up on the spear's balance point, holding his left arm out in front, his left foot a little forward of the right, he is instantly transformed from a merely colorful figure into what a Masai moran is—an efficient killing machine, rather like a lion itself. Verity told me that lions are terrified by the sight of a long-limbed Masai, striding across the savanna with a spear. She recalled on one safari seeing two lionesses abort a zebra stalk when two morani appeared on a ridge a mile away.

Saitoti now takes half a step forward and casts the spear at the target, a bush about 15 yards distant. For him, that's short range: A skilled Masai can toss a spear three to four times as far. Obviously, the farther away you can stick a lion, the better.

The missile arcs and stabs into the ground at the base of the bush, the shaft quivering. Now it's my turn. I'm a little surprised by the spear's weight. Five and a half feet in length, its business end consists of a yard-long steel blade about two inches wide, with two narrower blades ridged along both sides. It's fitted by means of a metal cup into the hardwood shaft, which is roughly the thickness of a bat handle. At the other end is a long steel spike that balances the weapon and can be used in practice to avoid dulling the blade. I might point out that this spear is not the kind you'll find in a Nairobi "native arts and crafts" shop, but the genuine article that's been used in real combat with lions. The blade is razor sharp and there are teeth marks on it and the shaft, from the snaps wounded simba have taken at it. As I've mentioned before, Masai are prohibited from hunting lion, but the regulation is honored as much in the breach as in the observance. Craig told me that he once came upon three morani shortly after they'd killed one of his radio-collared lionesses in the Serengeti. They claimed she was a cattle killer, but Craig suspected they'd done it for other reasons: In Masai-land, a warrior who's killed a lion is something like a rock star in the West; women throw themselves at him. One hopes that the trio were rewarded by Masai groupies, because the lioness put up quite a fight and made them pay a price; when Craig saw them, they looked as if they'd been close dancing with a power mower.

Presenting, I'm sure, a considerably less lethal and graceful figure than Saitoti, I raise the spear as he's shown me, palm facing up, the back end slightly higher than the front. My main concern is to not make a fool of myself. I take a half step forward and make the toss. The spear sails level, then drops like a head-shot duck and skids pathetically along the ground before sliding to an ignominious stop a yard short of the bush. If it were a lion, I would now resemble a plate of *ropa vieja*. Saitoti picks it up, mutters something in either Masai or Swahili that can't be flattering, and gives me another demonstration. Although I don't understand a word he's saying, I see what I did wrong: I failed to raise my throwing arm just before making the cast.

My second try is a little more like it, and on the fourth attempt, the spear makes a fine arc and buries itself in the earth, the spiked end waving like an antenna in the wind. Saitoti smiles and clasps my hand in congratulations, and I feel like a Little Leaguer with his first base hit.

"Not bad. Now try that with a real lion in front of you."

It's Marcus, coming up from his banda. Time to go look for the big male with the black mane.

Our first stop is the ranger's camp, a collection of mud-walled huts near the river. It could be a guerrilla fighter's base camp, what with the rifle-toting rangers in their camouflage uniforms and the olive-drab truck parked outside. Inside one of the huts, the boys are cooking up a stew. Marcus attempts to persuade Lieutenant Oliver to allow me to accompany his men on a foot patrol the next morning. I'm tired of being cooped up in vehicles all day, eager for "foot-knowledge"—the intimacy with a place that can be acquired only by walking in it. Oliver isn't keen on the idea. He makes various excuses why it will be difficult. Finally, pressed by Marcus and me, he confesses the real reason, which is that I lack written authorization from KWS headquarters in Nairobi to accompany a patrol on foot. If anything were to happen to me, Oliver would have to answer for it.

He's adamant, so we thank him for his time, and with Blade and Saitoti in the backseat of Marcus's Land Rover we take off for the Hatulo Bisani, passing a female impala with two young. Along the way, Marcus teaches Blade and me some basic bushcraft, pointing out the tunnels Cape buffalo burrow into in the thickets of African toothbrush trees. He also shows me (apparently Blade already knows this) how to make a toothbrush from one: You break off a twig, strip the leaves, chew on the tip until you fray it into a brush, and then scrub your teeth. He has ten times the eye I do for spotting game and identifying tracks from a moving car. He spies three-day-old lion prints where I see only indistinct marks on the ground, and then the pugmarks of a big lion made sometime this morning. We follow them on foot for a while, Marcus pointing out that a lion's front paw is always bigger than the hind, and then lose them amid the rocks of a lugga. No matter, he says, it wasn't the black-maned male. That one would leave tracks like dessert plates—Marcus thinks he could go 500 pounds.

All the rest of the afternoon we search. The Hatulo Bisani teems with elephant, one dragging a deformed hind leg, probably an injury that healed improperly. The elephants could be the reason why no lions are around. Heading back at dusk, Marcus really astonishes me when he picks out a male kudu and a harem of five females, half hidden in the scrub 200 yards away. I don't see a thing until we draw much closer and the male bounds away with powerful lunges, his white-streaked flanks flashing through the shadows.

Nightfall brings visitors to Galdessa (the name is the Walian-gulu word for baboon, but "Galdessa Camp" sounds more welcoming than "Baboon Camp"). First, a hippo bashes through the saltbush, laughing and snorting. Later, two elephants pay a call and decide to stay. A hyena announces his presence with a whoop, followed by a leopard, whose ditonal roar raises gooseflesh on my back and arms. Although a leopard is the smallest of the big cats in Asia and Africa—the males weigh about as much as an average-size man—they are incredibly fast and far more limber than lions and tigers, able to use their hind paws, much as a domestic cat does, to disembowel their prey. The dewclaws on their back legs are employed for that purpose.

Because so much wildlife of the dangerous kind is present and the scrub in camp so thick, Saitoti and Lumuwju, spears in hand, appear at my banda to escort me to the mess for dinner. It's a walk of some 200 yards, and as I go down the dark path behind the two askaris, their raised spear points catching moonlight, I can feel in an almost tactile way Africa tightening its grip on me. My life in sub-urban Connecticut is, well, suburban Connecticut. Called to the table from my studio behind the house, I cross a hundred feet of backyard prowled by, at worst, a skunk or raccoon. Here, the ordinary act of going to dinner becomes extraordinary, requiring spear-toting Masai guards and carrying the risk of being charged, stomped, or mauled, and I am giddy with the excitement of it. The thrill is somewhat undermined by the memory of a tale Craig told me a couple of weeks ago about two couples who were on safari in South Africa, staying at a luxury camp like Galdessa. After dinner, one of the women left the mess to go the bathroom. When she failed to return after perhaps 15 minutes, the others and their guide went looking for her. They found her eviscerated corpse lying beside the swimming pool. She'd been jumped by two lionesses barely 50 yards from the mess, and no one ever heard a sound because none was made, either by the lions (which never roar when they spring) or by their victim, her neck snapped before she could scream.

Marcus and I dine with four human visitors, two young Englishwomen and two young Englishmen who teach school in a village near Tsavo for an Anglican missionary organization. They're taking a weekend holiday to see something of wild Africa. The girls, with their creamy complexions and healthy, British-milkmaid bodies, are attractive, and all four, devoutly religious, are refreshing in their youthful idealism. In a conversation about moral values, the women mention the importance of maintaining chastity before marriage. Marcus can't resist playing the wild bushman and treats them to his own libertine opinions about love and sex, which he generously seasons with profanity. His audience is hip enough to see through the act and is more amused than shocked.

June 2

LAST NIGHT, WE again heard lions roaring near camp. Marcus thinks they're trailing a big buffalo herd that grazes in the Hatulo Bisani, so we set off for it once more. I have only this morning to see the giant with the black mane, and I'm not optimistic. A male kudu, maybe the one we saw yesterday, bolts across the road in front of us, while down in the riverbed, spoonbills of purest white step gingerly through the grass on pink legs, sweeping their bills back and forth. A yellow-billed stork stands poised, unafraid of the elephants cooling themselves in river mud all around him. Overhead, a pair of bold drongoes, no bigger than sparrows, strafe a harrier hawk ten times their size to keep it away from their nested chicks. We come upon the buffalo, hundreds of them, resembling at a distance a field of enormous black boulders. Two big bulls stand sentry duty on our side of the riverbed. As we approach, they run off, Marcus heading off-road to follow on the chance that the lion is waiting in ambush. We jostle through thornbush and toothbrush, and then Marcus says, "Uh-oh, there's the brigadier," and we see a gigantic bull lurking in acacia shade. He's at least the size of the one I saw with Dennis near Aruba, possibly bigger. In fact, he looks like a hippo with horns.

"When you're hunting buff, that is what you look for," Marcus instructs both Blade and me. "A couple of them run off and you follow and you don't see the brigadier hiding in the scrub until he charges out and hammers you."

Literally hammers you, from what I've read in Capstick. Hammers you with his horns and with his plate-size hooves until you resemble something that's been repeatedly run over by a road grader.

We hunt for two more hours, and my pessimism is not disappointed. The big lion will have to remain in my imagination. Sammy is in camp, waiting to take me to Tsavo West. I pay the tab, say goodbye to Marcus, Blade, and Saitoti, hoping to see them again but suspecting I won't, and leave.

June 3—Chyulu Camp, Tsavo West

Iᴛ's ANOTHER COUNTRY here, more hilly than Tsavo East, and cooler because it's higher, and greener because the hills, the Chyulu and Taita and Ngulia, make weather and the weather brings rain. Clouds swirl on the crests, creating the illusion that those ancient vol-canoes are still active, and the trees are thick on the slopes and great gneiss outcrops rise up through the trees and change color in the dawn, from coppery red to gold. The grass in the valleys and the reeds in the marshes show bright green, the acacia darker green, and baobab with bare gray trunks shaped like bottles stand here and there, throwing out stubby, leafless branches. The backs of buffalo hump out of the reeds below, and Peyton, Ogeto, and I scan with binoculars for lion but see none. Standing up through the roof hatches, it feels almost chilly enough for a sweater, an article of apparel I don't associate with Tsavo.

Yesterday, my two companions and Bob came upon three thin lionesses and four cubs near where we now are, above a broad round depression called Rhino Valley (a tourist-friendly name if I ever heard one). Peyton's quest is to find the males to see if they have manes, and if they do, to image them with the infrared camera. We turn east, crossing a plain, while Bob, in his own car behind us, goes west, then south, paralleling the Ngulia Range.

At 7:30 a.m., he calls on the radio. He's found a male and it is maned. No accidental discovery, either. Bob used a little bushcraft by following buffalo spoor and the pugmarks of a lion tracking the herd. We rendezvous with him and see the light-maned lion lying on his belly in thick scrub a few yards off the road, facing a crowded minibus with lordly indifference. Today is Kenya's independence day and the park is full of tourists. The minibus partly blocks our view, making it impossible for Peyton to use the infrared. We have to settle for playing tourist ourselves and take pictures and watch. The lion's mane is ragged, typical, Peyton says, of manes that have been ripped up by thorns and underbrush; but it's fuller than the ones we've seen in Tsavo East, suggesting that maybe mane growth is affected by climate and altitude. Another male, black-maned, rises up out of a bush nearby, and then, having made himself visible, instantly becomes invisible again, slipping off into the scrub. The first lion, agitated by all the attention, follows him. Now you see 'em, now you don't. This was the area where Colonel Patterson hunted the man-eaters, and one look at the tall grass and tangled thickets renews my appreciation of how tough that must have been.

We push on, Bob southward, we eastward, and the road climbs between two hills, offering a vista of savanna and hills that practically sings. Water holes glitter below, the Kitani River shines through its bordering trees. We head down and follow the Kitani—Peyton and Ogeto had learned from a ranger that a pride of 11 live along it—but we don't see them, nor much game of any sort. Two female eland, largest of all African antelope, big as Brahma cows, a handful of impala, a giraffe.

We return to camp for a noontime brunch. Afterward, because Tsavo West is its own jurisdiction, Peyton and Ogeto go to head-quarters to seek the warden's permission to do call-ups. Restless and underexercised, I take a walk from camp to the Chyulu Gate, which is only half a mile down the road. That doesn't mean it's predator free. I don't walk as I do in the defanged woods of Connecticut and Westchester County, running Sage to keep her in shape for bird season. There, I'm usually lost in thought, musing on something I'm writing, random ideas flitting through my head; here, alone and afoot in a land little changed from Pleistocene, I am instantly alert for the slightest movement, the faintest sound. It isn't nerve-racking—stim-ulating, rather, as different from those tame woodland strolls as sleep from waking. I don't want things to get too stimulating, however. On the return leg, remembering Verity's comment about lions and the Masai, I pick up a long stick and carry it above my shoulder, par-allel to the ground. A discerning lion would notice that my stocky profile bears no resemblance to a Masai's, but it might make him think twice.

I have a visitor in my tent—a locust that comes straight out of the plagues of Egypt. It's at least as big as a hummingbird and sits on the floor, still as a piece of wood, its bristling hind legs poised for takeoff.

Picking up Peter Matthiessen's *The Snow Leopard,* I am struck by a line: "This worshipful or religious attitude is not impressed by scientific facts like figures of altitude, which are foremost in the mind of modern man." Matthiessen is speaking about the way primitive cultures respond to the natural world and the wild things that inhabit it, but you could say the "worshipful or religious attitude" is fully present in some modern human beings. It is in me. Not that I'm unimpressed with scientific facts like figures of altitude; I seek to know as much as anyone else born to an advanced, industrialized civilization. Nonetheless, Matthiessen's words reawaken my impatience and irritation with all the methods and paraphernalia with which Peyton and Craig are establishing scientific facts about the African lion. It strikes me as intrusive, setting up barriers between the animal and the human, closing off the part of our brains that might communicate with the beast, receive a message from it. And yeah, I know how silly that must sound. Yet that too is knowledge, albeit of a different kind.

June 5

OUR SECOND-TO-LAST day, and our final morning of work. Tomorrow will be devoted to striking camp. This afternoon, we're going to toss a party for Peyton, celebrating the completion of her research. Two days from now she'll be winging back to Minnesota to face the task of turning three years of observations, study, and data into a coherent thesis. Yesterday, she spoke of the drawbacks and attractions of her work:

"You spend 10 or 12 hours a day in a Land Rover all by yourself, listening to static and waiting to hear the *beep-beep* of a radio collar. You go to the same places over and over, and when you come back, you talk to the same people, who are basically doing the same thing you are, so you talk about the same things over and over. A lot of the elements of the job conspire to drive you crazy, and you crave stimulation from the outside world. But I love it, riding through the bush by myself. Looking for lions is like a treasure hunt."

Our treasure hunt yesterday netted three lions—a healthy lioness and two subadults, one male, one female, who occupied an unscenic feature, an abandoned gravel pit. They were quite shy and wouldn't allow us to approach closer than 50 yards before they moved. Finally, they pulled a Tsavo vanishing act.

Now, with Sammy driving, Peyton, Ogeto, and I are off to try to find them again, hoping a male is with them (though Peyton speculates that the lioness is a loner who left her pride after a takeover to protect her then-young cubs from infanticide by the new resident male). In dawn twilight, retracing yesterday's trek, we pass the strangest feature in Tsavo, the Shaitani lava beds. *Shetani* means "devil" in Swahili. It's derived from the Arabic *El Sheitan,* the root for the English word "Satan." Lava ridges 20 to 30 feet high run down the hillsides, with scrubby bushes sprouting from the sharp, black rocks. Lava flows, devoid of all vegetation, cover hundreds of acres, as if some mad contractor with an abundance of asphalt decided to pave the whole place over. It's a stark, barren, unsettling thing to look at it, and the cataclysm that produced it occurred only 200 years ago, when the Earth yawned and spewed fire and smoke and molten rock, burying villages and *shambas,* killing untold numbers of people. It must have seemed like the end of the world to the survivors, the wrath of some malignant demon. Legends persist that the people interred beneath the lava beds can be heard on certain nights making plaintive cries. Local people steal into the park, leaving food offerings to appease the restless spirits, lest they haunt the living. Shetani is thus a kind of vast, natural religious site, accursed, yet revered. That puts me in mind of Isak Dinesen's comment, in *Out of Africa,* that the African in his native creeds makes no distinctions between God and the devil; the two are one co-eternal majesty before whom man must submit. In exchange for his submission, the demon-deity allows the African to stay afloat in the continent's treacherous waters, while the Westerner, with his divided views of good and evil, thrashes, struggles, and ultimately drowns.

And that idea shunts my thoughts back to Matthiessen, which in turn leads me to inflict on Peyton and Ogeto my views about faith and science, about the "worshipful or religious attitude" toward nature versus the empirical. This is not the first time Peyton has heard this from me, and, though she listens patiently, I sense she's getting a little sick of it. Then, just at sunrise, we climb a rise through a notch in the hills and are presented a sight that shuts me up, stuns us all into a reverent silence.

Seventy-five miles away, across the oceanic expanse of the northern Serengeti plains, Kilimanjaro rises into a sinless sky. The veil of cloud that normally conceals its peak has lifted, and the snow and ice crowning the mythic mountain glimmers pale rose in the new day. Two layers of cloud, stretched for miles, obscure the middle and lower elevations, so that the summit and the slopes just below appear to rest on a gray and vaporous reef. Immediately before us, the grassy hillside flows down to the plains, sweeping away and away toward the base of the mountain and around it into what looks like eternity. To the north and northwest, more plains reach for an extinct volcano and, farther on, the foot of the Chyulu Hills. The wind blows as the wind blows at sea. The sun clears the hills behind us, and a flood tide of light washes over the dun grasslands specked with islands of acacia, and Kilimanjaro's peak grows ever brighter, becoming a white fire burning almost four miles high. A solitary wildebeest, dark hide painted beige by the sun, wanders southward toward the dry Serengeti sea, and a Cape buffalo bull stands stock still, turned to face us, his crescent horns gleaming.

In all the lands I've traveled, I've never seen anything anywhere to match this. Kilimanjaro towering above the African savanna, cradle of the human race. We sit on the Land Rover's roof and look without talking for half an hour, as wonderstruck as the first explorers and missionaries who beheld ice and snow on the Equator.

"I don't care what happens the rest of the day," Peyton says, breaking the silence. "There it is, looking down at us with all our little thoughts and petty insecurities. They don't seem to mean very much."

We drive on, westward. A giraffe raises its head from behind a tree and ambles on, looking amid the stunted acacia like a long-necked bird amid garden shrubbery. A herd of buffalo bulls eye us cautiously from the roadside. By midmorning we're driving through the deep forests along the Loosoito River, leopard rather than lion country, the green-barked fever trees overshadowing the river, and a crowned eagle, biggest of African eagles, perches in a branch, his crest feathers tipped in black.

Climbing out of the river bottoms, we cross marshland and savanna, nearing the spot where we'd seen the lion trio. A fine specimen of an oryx watches us, and Peyton takes his picture—it's the first one she's seen in the wild, three years in Africa notwithstanding. Turning off the road onto a faint two-track bordering another river, we continue the hunt, though again the tamarind and fever trees spell leopard. A great pod of hippopotamuses allow us to get incredibly close; one, lumbering out of the wallows, almost bumps the Land Rover. We push on, the track growing ever fainter, and suddenly the right wheel plunges into a hidden pothole, damn near a crater, the vehicle stopping as if it's struck a wall, my forehead meeting the rearview mirror with no damage to either. I swing my door open to see what sort of fix we're in now.

"Python!" shouts Ogeto from the backseat.

A second later, I see the grass moving as the huge serpent writhes away, but I never see it. Must remember you're in bloody Africa, Phil, where getting out of a car can have unpleasant consequences.

Sammy throws the Land Rover into low range and manages to extricate us. As we head back for camp, Peyton is in high spirits.

"Damn!" she says. "This is typical of Africa. Just when you feel that you've had enough of it and the bush and you can't wait to get home again, you have a day like this and feel like you don't ever want to leave."

I ask her if the expedition has been worthwhile. She nods and ticks off what it's accomplished. Before coming to Tsavo, she had only one statistically significant story out of the dummy tests—that males are scared of larger-maned opponents. Here, in the test with Burr Boy at Aruba, she added an eighth example to the seven she'd obtained in Tanzania. Now that was a really strong result. Then she tested the effect of color. Before, she had no real story with color, merely strong hints that females preferred dark-maned males. In the Serengeti, she'd done only two color tests involving males. In Tsavo, she'd added two more, so now she had four cases that males avoid adversaries with black manes. That by itself, she continues, isn't significant, but when added to the data from her tests with females, it gives her a story.

She sees how I react to this recitation of statistically significant facts and regards me for a moment.

"Phil, scientists don't want to demystify nature," she says. "We want just to clarify what the real mysteries are."

That strikes me as a wise statement; still, I feel divided, half of me hungry for scientific truth, the other half seeking to embrace the mythic. It occurs to me that I haven't come close to solving the mystery of Tsavo's lions, probably because my heart hasn't been in it.

June 6—Nairobi

DURING OUR TIME in Tsavo, one name came up again and again. If you want to hear about Tsavo lions, talk to Brian Heath. Brian will tell you, Brian knows: He's killed 500 of them. Talking to Heath was a piece of unfinished research business, so Peyton got hold of him when we returned here and arranged to have dinner with him.

She taxis from Karen, where she's staying with a friend of Craig's, and meets me in the lobby of the Norfolk, where we wait for Brian. He shows up 15 minutes later. A little above average height, stockily built, with fine, light brown hair and pale eyes, he's a soft-spoken man of 51 who neither looks nor acts like what you'd expect a formidable lion-killer to look and act like. No Hemingwayesque swagger, no boasting. He could be an accountant. Raised in Kenya, the son of up-country farmers, his main love has been wildlife, although, he adds with a vague smile, "you wouldn't think it."

We proceed to the Tamarind, a seafood restaurant downtown, and Kenya's ailing tourist industry is immediately apparent. We're the only customers and waiters flock to us. After we're seated, Brian tells us something else we never would have thought: Years ago, he worked for George and Joy Adamson, of *Born Free* fame, so no one can accuse him of being a man who enjoys shooting wild animals. It was his job, he says as drinks are brought. For 20 years, he worked for the Galana Ranch, which sprawls over 1.6 million acres east of Tsavo National Park, first as its game manager, later as its general manager. One of Brian's duties was eliminating lions that wandered out of Tsavo onto the ranch and began killing livestock. His career total isn't 500, but closer to 400 (which is still an awful lot of lions). He estimates that 300 were males in their prime—8 to 9 years old—and of those he can count the ones with manes on one hand.

This slaughter came about, ironically enough, as a result of the hunting ban instituted in Kenya in 1977. When the Galana began operations in the 1960s, it domesticated wild herd animals like oryx, eland, and buffalo for sale as meat. With its vast size, the ranch also supported a hunting concession, which brought in considerable revenue from trophy hunters. After the ban, the Galana stopped raising oryx and eland and other hoofed animals because there was no way to distinguish their meat from the meat of beef cattle. With the departure of professional hunting guides, who helped police the enterprise, Somali poachers moved in, killing elephant for ivory, rhino for their horns. By the mid-1980s, according to Brian, the Galana's elephant herd of 6,000 had been reduced to a few hundred, its 200 rhinoceroses wiped out.

"Since the ban, there's been a 50 percent decline in Kenya's wildlife populations. The ban, which was put into effect to enhance

Kenya's image among certain international conservation organizations, has had absolutely no positive effect on wildlife here."

This is an argument Peyton has heard before, and, as if sensing that she might disagree, Brian regards her for a moment, inviting her to offer her opinions. She declines, and Brian continues.

"Ken Clark was a ranch employee who tried to run photographic safaris on the property, but he found himself spending most of his time as a one-man anti-poaching unit. One night, on patrol with his tracker, he came upon two dead rhino with their horns removed. Driving farther on, he encountered a gang of shifta as they were cutting off the horn of a third rhino they'd shot just minutes before. Clark engaged them in a gun battle and killed three and then jumped back in his vehicle to pursue the rest of the gang, but they laid an ambush for him up the road and killed him instantly."

In the meantime, the consortium that owned the ranch turned to raising domestic cattle and was fairly successful at it. Nomadic lions, however, were killing an average of 250 to 300 head per year, that is, roughly one percent of its herd. That's where Brian was called in.

"The lions were wary of people because they'd been dealing with pastoralists for centuries, the Oromo people, herdsmen from the Tana River area who had hunted them with spears because they were a threat to their cattle."

The first course came and went, the main arrived, with a bottle of South African white. Brian made a few observations about his quarry.

"I found that the lions knew they were doing wrong when they killed a cow. When a lion kills a wild animal, it eats on the spot, then lays up near the carcass until it's hungry again and eats more. But a cattle killer will eat as much as it can and then leave, walking as far as ten kilometers, looking for a safe place to hide. You can see by the tracks that it inspects this bush and then that bush" —Brian mimics a lion peering into bushes—"until it finds the one it wants, usually the biggest bush around because it knows a man will be coming after it. If it isn't found, it will return to the kill to feed again."

He used two methods to kill them. In the one, he and a tracker would cover the cow carcass to keep vultures off and tie it to a tree. In the early evening, they would return and set up a blind 25 to 30 yards away. Any closer, they'd learned, and the lions would become aware of their presence, coming right up to the blind to sniff it and then roar to warn the men off (echoes here of Wayne Hosek's saga). Armed with a scoped .375 Holland & Holland and a spotlight, Brian and the tracker would wait. Almost every time, the lion or lions would show up around nine or ten at night. The tracker would switch on the light, freezing the marauders just long enough for Brian to shoot them. He says he didn't like this method if there were more than two lions.

"I could kill two easily, but it was difficult to kill three in such a short time, and if one survived, he became smarter and much more difficult to track down. And if you wounded him, you had real trouble." He pauses, then adds in his understated, laconic way, "You don't want to botch it. It's very important to get your lion the first time."

Brian wounded only a handful of lions in those 20 years, often when he had to get off a snap shot at a running target. Killing it then required icy nerve and courage, pushing into thick scrub to shoot the beast at point-blank range. In those instances, he exchanged his .375 for a .458, a gun capable of dropping an elephant.

The second method was the one he preferred.

"We would find the carcass and then track the lion in the morning to wherever he'd gone to sleep. We would follow the tracks for anywhere from two to six hours, and we could always tell where the lion was looking for a place to sleep because we could see the tracks meandering from one bush to another. When we got to the one he'd picked, we'd shoot him when he was asleep, before he knew what was happening."

Not very sporting, but recall that Brian did this for a living.

He pooh-poohs the myth of the ferocious, ever-dangerous king of beasts.

"In killing over 400 lions at Galana, I never once had a close shave. An unwounded lion isn't dangerous. I've seen Oromo herdsmen utterly fearless in the presence of lions, seen 'em track the lions into the bush and then part the branches to see where they were, staring right at them, face to face. The lion would do nothing or run away."

His close shaves came in the 1990s, when the Kenya Wildlife Service contracted him to kill lions that had been translocated to the Aberdares, where no lions had ever been before. The experiment was a disaster, as such experiments often are. The introduced lions went out of control, annihilating bongo and other indigenous animals, terrorizing tourists, two of whom were killed (indicating, I thought, that unwounded lions could be damned dangerous). Working in 6-week stretches, Brian went on a jihad against the offenders, and in 3 years reduced the lion population from 50 to a manageable 15.

"One time, with a KWS ranger, we saw two lions sunning themselves and I shot both dead. A third jumped, and she was hit by the ranger. He'd wounded her, but his gun jammed. The lioness vanished in thick bush and we went in after her, the ranger still trying to free the gun jam. Right ahead of us, we heard a very loud growl and she sprang at the ranger. He turned and ran and I shot her, almost literally off his back. She wasn't three, four yards from him when I killed her."

Dessert and espresso come to the table while Brian tries to think of another close call.

"Oh, yeah. There was another time when I shot and wounded a large male. A running shot at a hundred yards. The guy I was with and I spent five hours crawling on our hands and knees through the scrub, following the blood spoor. Our nerves were ragged." He describes this so phlegmatically that I wonder if he has any nerves to get ragged. "We took a break, then went back in. The lion had found the thickest bush he could hide in, and the guy I was with spotted it only two yards away. We'd sneaked up behind it, you see. As the guy pointed at it, the lion whirled around and growled and I shot it. We then called it a day. We'd had enough."

I ask about the lions of Tsavo. Does he think they're somehow a different breed of cat?

"Game is scarce there and the lions lead a hard life," he replies, echoing Marcus Russell, Iain Allan, and others. "Groups of males get together to kill big prey like giraffe and Cape buffalo because they can live off it for days."

And did tackling big prey make them more prone to injury and so more prone to turn man-eater?

He shrugs, saying that in all his 20 years at Galana, he knew of only two cases of unwounded lions attacking people, and both instances were nothing like the terrifying, cunning raids of the man-eaters of Tsavo. In the first, an old, starving lioness with worn teeth jumped a ranch hand and clamped her jaws on his throat, but failed to kill him before she was driven off by his friends. He died two days later of septicemia from the bite. The second case was not without an element of black humor. A herdsman was charged, again by an aging lioness. He drew his knife to battle her hand to hand, but when she knocked him down, he accidentally stabbed himself in his femoral artery and bled to death from the partly self-inflicted wound. His companion killed the lioness with a spear.

I pay the tab and the maître d' calls a cab for us. Standing outside waiting for it at ten at night in downtown Nairobi may be the most dangerous thing Peyton and I have done on this trip. On the way back to the Norfolk, where Brian has parked his car, he laments the fate of the Galana Ranch.

"The whole place has gone to seed. The roads are overgrown, buildings crumbling, machinery gone to rust. There's about 4,000 head of cattle still on it, but it's mostly gone back to bush, and the Oromo, the original inhabitants, have moved back in and are now poisoning the lions that raid their livestock." He pauses and again echoes Marcus. "When you poison, you kill indiscriminately. Hyenas, jackals, and vultures die along with lions. That's why you see few vultures in Tsavo. Thirty years ago, there were tons of vultures there." He pauses again. "When it all ended at Galana, it was a huge blow to me because I'd invested my life in it."

But Brian is a survivor if ever there was one. He's soon to take a job managing a wildlife conservancy project in the Trans-Mara, land of the Masai.

At the Norfolk, I say good-bye to him and Peyton, struck, as I always am, by the transience of the relationships writers develop. People come into your life, you into theirs, you get to know each other and it almost seems like friendship, but in the end it's a simulacrum of friendship. You go your way, they go theirs.

Having ended two acquaintanceships, I enter the lobby and renew another. Tom Gnoske is there, just arrived from Chicago and preparing to leave for Tsavo day after tomorrow.

He's cranked up, excited about running the transect from the Chyulu down to the plains, and he chain smokes as he outlines the project.* He interrupts himself to ask what was learned on the

---

* Data from the transect was analyzed in 2002. It supported the theory that climate and elevation affect mane growth. Gnoske and Kerbis Peterhans found that at elevations below 1,300 feet (400 meters), most lions were poorly maned or maneless. At mid elevations (600-800 meters), manes varied from horselike dorsals to sparse neck collars. Above 3,900 feet (1,200 meters), lions had thick manes.

Packer-West expedition. When I tell him that they have ruled out any relationship between Tsavo lions and Asian and primitive lions, he shakes his head.

"What Peyton doesn't understand is that Asian lions and mane-less lions, or lions with variable manes, have the same proportion of head to body size as Paleolithic lions, which could mean that these lions represent the ancestral condition of the lion."

There follows a long dissertation that I, tired and having drunk too much wine, have a hard time following. Ratio of cranial size to shoulder bone, Serengeti males have huge skulls, relatively short shoulder bones, Paleolithic lions have a longer ratio, as do hunting lions, that is, lions who do more hunting than fighting. Something along those lines.

Reluctant to get caught in a dispute among scientists, I steer him back to his upcoming project, and when he tells me that he and his team will be working mostly at night, when they'll be more likely to see lions hunting and killing buffalo, I'm briefly tempted to join him, for I'm still under the spell Kilimanjaro cast on me two days ago.

But only briefly. The truth is, I don't want to learn anything more about lions but am content to allow the mystery to remain, content to keep some blank spots blank; after all, those are what excite the imagination. I haven't captured the chimera. Rather, it's captured me, and so I cling to the image of Othello and Prince Hal, roaring under the slivered moon, beautiful in some terrible way, incarnations of all that's left in our world of the wild, the unknown.

WHY THE MAN-EATERS DID
WHAT THEY DID

When we camped for the night we were obliged to form a hedge of
thorn-bushes and circle the encampment with huge bonfires to keep the
wild beasts from attacking us. It was terrifying to hear the continuous
roar of lions resounding on all sides...and to see the glare of hyena eyes
in the darkness of the umbrageous surroundings. A sense of abject
helplessness momentarily possessed me.
—from an account of an 1892 journey
through Tsavo by M. French-Sheldon

AS RURAL TOWNS in Kenya go, Voi is fairly large and prosperous, boasting a modern bank, two large gas stations, bars, a busy marketplace, a couple of hotels, the Tsavo and the Red Elephant, an auto repair shop with a hip name, the Boyz-in-the-Hood Garage, even a shop run by an Indian couple where you can send e-mail and log on to the Net. Still, it's got plenty of the Third World blues: open sewers, run-down buildings, unpaved streets, a general look of disrepair that you know is going to stay that way. The most attractive feature in town is a small, fenced cemetery that lies just off the road leading to the park's Voi Gate. British soldiers who died fighting Germans in Tanzania (then Tanganyika) during the First World War are buried there, along with Indians and Africans who served in the colonial army (some killed by lions while on sentry duty). They lie under simple headstones with their names and the names of regiments. One marker, however, is of the grander sort. It bears this inscription: "To the Sacred Memory of John William O'Hara, of Madras, India. Killed by a lion on the road to Taveta, East Africa. 11 March 1899, aged 35 Years. Erected by His Loving Wife."

O'Hara was an engineer in charge of building a road between Voi and the mission station at Taveta. With his wife and two small children, he was encamped in the Taita Hills, some 12 miles west of Voi. On the night of March 11, the family were sleeping in their tent, O'Hara and his wife in one bed, the children in the other. The younger, a baby daughter, was feverish and restless, and Mrs. O'Hara got up to get her something to drink. As she was doing so, she thought she heard a lion prowling around the tent and woke her husband, who got up immediately and went outside with his rifle. He saw nothing and spoke to an askari who'd been standing watch by a campfire a short distance away. The askari reported that all he'd seen was a donkey. O'Hara returned to the tent and told his wife not to worry; she'd only heard a donkey.

Colonel Patterson, who was in Voi at the time and helped bury the engineer, interviewed his widow and records her description of what happened next in *The Man-Eaters of Tsavo*.

"The night being very hot, my husband threw back the tent door and lay down again beside me," Mrs. O'Hara (he doesn't give her first name) told Patterson. "After a while I dozed off, but was suddenly roused by a feeling as if the pillow were being pulled away from under my head. On looking round I found that my husband was gone. I jumped up and called him loudly, but got no answer. Just then I heard a noise among the boxes outside the door, so I rushed out and saw my poor husband lying between the boxes. I ran up to him and tried to lift him, but I could not do so. I then called to the *askari* to come and help me, but he refused, saying that there was a lion standing beside me. I looked up and saw the huge beast glowering at me, not more than two yards away. At this moment, the *askari* fired his rifle, and this fortunately frightened the lion, for it at once jumped off into the bush."

"All four *askaris* then came forward and lifted my husband back onto the bed. He was quite dead. We had hardly got back into the tent before the lion returned and prowled about in front of the door, showing every intention of springing in to recover his prey. The *askaris* fired at him, but did no damage beyond frightening him away again for a moment or two. He soon came back and continued to walk round the tent until daylight, growling and purring, and it was only by firing through the tent every now and then that we kept him out. At daybreak he disappeared and I had my husband's body carried here, while I followed with the children until I met you."

A physician named Dr. Rose was in Voi at the time and gave a sedative to Mrs. O'Hara. While she rested, he conducted an autopsy and was able to tell the widow the next day that her husband died instantly and painlessly. Dr. Rose concluded that O'Hara had been lying on his back, and that the lion seized his head in its mouth and drove its fangs through his temples into his brain.

The lion was killed a few weeks later by a poisoned arrow shot from a tree by a Taita hunter. Patterson doesn't give a description of the animal, whether male or female, maned or unmaned; but its attack on O'Hara showed that the deaths of the two man-eaters more than two months earlier wasn't the last word from Tsavo's lions.

In forensic medicine, a procedure known as a psychological autopsy is used to determine the motives of suicides who don't leave notes and of mass murderers who either kill themselves or are killed by police before anyone can ask them the reasons for their crimes.

The Field Museum's Tom Gnoske and Julian Kerbis Peterhans have conducted an analogous procedure with the Man-eaters of

Tsavo, which were mass killers of human beings, though not, of course, mass murderers. Why people and why so many? Early in this book, I presented the conjectures and assumptions that have been offered in the more than 100 years since the so-called reign of terror, but no one has answered the questions in a methodical way until Gnoske and Kerbis Peterhans completed a study in late 2001. They went about the task by reviewing the natural history of the lions, the first time that was done, by poring over hundreds of historical accounts, scientific texts, reports, and monographs, and by examining the lions' remains, chiefly their skulls and teeth. They planned to publish their findings in a lengthy article, "Causes of 'Man-eating' among lions (*Panthera leo*) with a discussion of the natural history of the 'Man-eaters of Tsavo' " in the *Journal of the East African Natural History Society.*

The study attempts to lay to rest the two most persistent myths about man-eaters, whether lions, leopards, or tigers: They're outlaws, behaving unnaturally, and they turn to people when they're too old, injured, or malnourished to catch "normal" prey. It turns out that we may be normal prey; there is nothing aberrant about eating us. As Kerbis Peterhans told me back in Chicago, big cats eat primates and we are primates. At an anthropological site in South Africa, it was discovered that *Australopithecus robustus,* one of our early ancestors, was the most common prey for prehistoric leopards. Detailed records of man-eating weren't kept till modern times, so we have to skip over two-odd million years of human evolution before we find facts and figures (those who continue to think that we're not on pantherid menus will not be encouraged):

– In India in the mid-1920s, 7,000 people were killed by tigers.

- Man-eating lions killed 128 people in southwest Uganda in 1927 and 1928.
- Between 1932 and 1947, in a 150-square-mile area of southern Tanzania, lions killed and ate an estimated 1,500 human beings, to date the all-Africa record.
- Tigers in the Kheri district of India killed 128 people between 1978 and 1984.
- Between 1975 and 1981, tigers in the Sundarbans Tiger Reserve in India devoured 318 people.
- Asian lions in the Gir forest attacked 193 people, killing 28, between 1977 and 1991.

Working from statistics compiled by Turnbull-Kemp, the South African game manager who showed that old and injured lions were in the minority among man-eaters, Gnoske and Kerbis Peterhans have concluded that healthy male lions between four and nine years old (subadult to prime age) are most likely to become cattle-killers and man-eaters. Examining the incident log books of the Kenya Wildlife Service, the two researchers found that of 110 recorded attacks in Tsavo on people and livestock between 1994 and 1998, 112 were committed by lions, 61 by males, 51 by females. The male lions killed two people, one in October 1994, the other in July 1998, and threatened three, whereas the females killed none but mauled one person and threatened two. The skulls of 29 problem lions shot by the KWS problem animal control unit were analyzed; of those, 24 were found to be subadults or prime-age adults and only 5 were aged. Nineteen of the 29 were males. So if you're in Tsavo, you're most at risk from a young to mature male lion in the pink of health.

Ghost and Darkness were in the prime of their lives. Their skulls, catalogued in the Field Museum as FMNH 23970 (Ghost) and

FMNH 23969 (Darkness), had lain around, hidden in the museum's storage rooms, for decades until Gnoske rediscovered them in the late 1980s. He and Kerbis Peterhans, by studying the condition of their teeth, were able to determine that the lions were between six and eight years old. Gnoske was the one who first observed that Ghost had a severely broken canine and that his skull had undergone cranial remodeling, indicating that he'd suffered an injury early in life, possibly from the horns or hoofs of a buffalo or zebra. Although this impairment could have hindered his ability to take animal prey, it's the least likely of his "motives" for turning to humans. Lions don't necessarily use their canines to kill zebra and large bovines. Strong limbs and powerful jaws are more useful than good dentures, because lions more often break their prey's neck by gripping the head with one forelimb while pushing the animal off its feet with the other; or they clamp down on its muzzle with a viselike grip and suffocate it. Neither method requires an impaling stab wound, like the kind that dispatched engineer O'Hara.

"Given that the two acted together," the preliminary article states, "there was no reason why the severely damaged canine and remodeled skull of one of them turned them both into man-eaters. Their social bond, immense size, apparently healthy limbs, and mature age would allow them to tackle 'normal' prey. Indeed, this prediction has been confirmed with the species profile represented by hairs extracted from their broken canines."

In a remarkable feat of forensic detective work, the two researchers extracted thousands of hairs lodged in the lions' teeth for more than a century and analyzed them to find out what species they came from. Most turned out to be lion hairs, which had gotten into the canine vacuities during periods of grooming; the rest were hairs of prey species: zebra, buffalo, warthog, impala, eland, and oryx, which showed that the lions were by no means dedicated, obligatory man-eaters. No human hair has been found so far, curiously enough—maybe not so curiously. As the report notes in a gruesome aside, lions don't like to eat our heads or pubes, preferring to rip our bellies open to get at viscera and internal organs, after which they consume buttocks and thighs.

So Ghost and Darkness didn't do what they did because they were incapable of hunting four-footed prey. They had other reasons, good reasons; every condition known to cause man-eating was present in Tsavo in the late 1890s, and we'll start with a lower life form, vegetation.

Tsavo then didn't look anything like Tsavo now. Photographs in Patterson's book show a nyika wilderness much more dense and extensive than today's. This condition was indirectly caused by man: The quest for ivory had almost eliminated elephants from all of eastern Kenya, and from most of Tsavo, and, because elephants are an ecosystem's gardeners, keeping undergrowth in check by browsing trees and shrubs, thorn thickets and woods proliferated. Thick cover favors ambush predators and, despite the pictures you see of lions bounding across open plains in pursuit of wildebeests, lions prefer to strike from ambush. Even on the expanses of the Serengeti, according to Schaller's study, 75 percent of all lion kills occur near thickets or in tall grasses or in stands of trees. Because human beings have keen eyesight and walk upright, giving them a wide field of vision, cover is important to a lion that stalks people, and there was an abundance of it in Tsavo in Col. John H. Patterson's time.

"Such an environment encourages man-eating behavior," Kerbis Peterhans and his colleague declare.

And in more ways than one. The "thornbush belt" in East Africa is scarce in prey in the best of times. As elephants diminished in Tsavo and its grasslands were overtaken by nyika, grazing animals like zebras and buffalos decreased, while browsing animals like dik-diks (too small for lions) and rhinoceroses (too big) increased. Gnoske and Kerbis Peterhans reviewed the field journals in which Colonel Patterson carefully noted the numbers and species of animals he encountered in 1898 and 1899. He saw only four zebras and four hartebeests, and records seeing no Cape buffalo (though a few must have been around, as indicated from the buffalo hair taken from the man-eaters' teeth).

Then as now the favored prey of Tsavo lions, buffalo had virtually disappeared from most of East Africa due to the devastating rinderpest epidemic. Buffalo are especially susceptible to rinderpest; their populations in British and German East Africa plummeted from hundreds of thousands to near extinction in the early 1890s. A few survived in Tsavo, but these holdouts were exterminated in another man-made disaster—the draining of swamps and wetlands to control malaria. Buffalo are highly dependent on marshes for graze, water, and mud in which to wallow and cool themselves.

Gnoske and Kerbis Peterhans chronicle outbreaks of maneating throughout Africa following rinderpest epidemics or other causes of prey depletion. Thirty-three people were killed in the Ankole region of Uganda during the first three months of 1924 after rinderpest swept through the country. The colonial government tried to eradicate the disease by destroying wild herd animals, aggravating the situation as far as lions were concerned. Deprived of their usual prey, they turned to cattle and man. One lion alone accounted for 84 people, another for 44.

Nobody learns from history. Only a few years later, authorities in Tanzania decided to establish a "game-free" corridor in the southern district of Njombe, again to protect livestock from rinderpest. A fence was constructed along 150 miles of the border with Zambia and teams of European hunters and African scouts ordered to shoot all game within 5 miles of it. Thousands of zebras, antelopes, and buffalos were killed. The campaign was successful; livestock were spared rinderpest. It was the people who paid a price. The slaughter of grazing game animals led to the all-Africa record, when the lions in the region killed an estimated 1,500 men, women, and children over a 15-year period. They were so fixated on human flesh that they ignored cattle, seizing herd boys from kraals while leaving the livestock alone.

As the attacks persisted from 1931 to 1947, it is believed that three leonine generations were involved and that the later killers were born and bred to hunt man. And that leads to the spookiest part of the researchers' findings. Lions can develop a "social tradition" of man-eating. They become specialists in hunting people, and pass their skills and knowledge on to their young. The Njombe lions had a lot to teach their progeny, having developed sophisticated techniques. Stalking people in a village beginning at sundown and taking advantage of cover, they would approach as close as possible before making a final rush. If two lions teamed up, two victims might be taken. Then, using relays, they would carry their prey up to a mile away. Much as Patterson's pair avoided striking the same camp on successive nights, so the Njombe man-eaters avoided attacking the same village twice in a row; their next raid could be as far as 15 miles away.

Gnoske and Kerbis Peterhans believe the Tsavo man-eaters grew up among lions accustomed to feeding on human flesh. The East African slave and ivory trades promoted consumption of people as dead or dying slaves and porters were left along the caravan routes that ran from the interiors of Kenya and Uganda to the coast. In 1874, a slave trader told a European traveler, one A. J. Swann, that any captive too weak to carry his load was abandoned or killed at once to discourage others from refusing to bear their burdens. Livingstone, in the mid-19th century, reported finding human remains all along the caravan tracks and estimated that only one in five slaves reached the coast alive. Working from rough figures of the number of slaves imported to Mombasa, Zanzibar, and other slave markets, Gnoske and Kerbis Peterhans calculate that as many as 80,000 lives were lost along the caravan routes each year. And that represented a cost-free banquet to any carnivore ready to take advantage, and lions, being both hunters and scavengers, most certainly did.

The Uganda Railway was built in part to discourage the slave trade. The emissaries of civilization and enlightenment thought it would make the ivory caravans obsolete, as, in fact, it did, though not as soon as they had hoped. The railroad was laid along a major caravan trail, which crossed the Tsavo River at a point two and a half miles from that river's confluence with the Athi. The ford was used for centuries as a rest stop by slave and ivory traders. It's obvious why. Even today, the rush of water and the deep shade of the doum palm groves is a welcome relief from the miles of surrounding scrub and arid thornbush wilderness. It must have looked paradisal to the caravaners and their slaves, both eager to camp under the palms with fresh water running alongside. The idyllic appearance was deceptive; come nightfall, nocturnal carnivores, hyenas, leopards, and lions, would approach, ravenous, keen of eye and smell. In the morning, some of the caravan's human cargo would be gone without a trace. Legends grew that the place was haunted by body-snatching demons.

That history is why Gnoske and Kerbis Peterhans are certain that the area around the ford had been plagued by man-eating for a very long time. The ford also happened to be where Colonel Patterson built the Tsavo River bridge. The lions must have regarded the workers' camps, crammed with thousands of men, as a caravan that didn't move. As we've seen, instances of man-eating in and around Tsavo continued after Patterson dispatched the marauding pair, right down to the present day; but they also occurred before he got there, a strong indication that man-eating was established practice, a tradition, if you will, among the region's lions. An expedition in 1891 lost a water carrier to lions. A party traveling through Tsavo in 1896 was warned by missionaries to stay out of one area because man-eaters were present; so the group, led by an explorer named A. J. Ansorge, detoured and camped on the banks of the Tsavo River. A porter was killed and carried off by a lion. Pursued by armed men, the animal dropped its prey and the man's body was recovered; the lion then attacked a Kamba caravan half an hour away and took one of its members. Just months before Patterson's arrival, railway surveyor O. R. Preston lost two workers to lions and found the remains of other people killed earlier.

As Gnoske and Kerbis Peterhans rather dryly note: "For a long-lived species with a long period of infant/juvenile dependency, any regularly practiced predatory behavior can become a cultural tradition, passed down from one generation to the next. To call such behavior 'aberrant' may be acceptable from an anthropogenic perspective but is normal behavior for the relevant predator."

Several other factors conspired to turn Colonel Patterson's nine-month stay in Tsavo into a nightmare.

One was the burial practices, or the lack of them, followed by indigenous peoples. The Taita of the Taita Hills inter their dead in the ground, but then dig them up and leave their skulls in rock shelters; the Kamba left the bodies of "peasants and women" out in the open and even tied the mortally sick to trees to be disposed of by hyenas. Of course, hyenas were not the only carnivores that did the disposing. At any rate, corpses lying exposed provided lions with ready-to-eat meals and accustomed them to human flesh.

Natural disasters also played a role. In 1897, a local famine caused hundreds of Kamba to die of starvation. Once again, the dead and dying were not buried, but desperate Kamba also raided, slaughtering isolated railway construction gangs to steal their food, and those bodies, some 340 all told, were left lying beside the railroad right-of-way. A smallpox epidemic in 1898 and 1899 killed thousands throughout Kenya, and the corpses provided a perpetual feast for scavenging carnivores, particularly hyenas. The plague also showed how predators habituated to eating already dead humans can turn their attentions to the living; when the epidemic abated and the ready supply of corpses ran out, hyenas started taking children at dusk and even attacked adults as they slept.

Finally, there was livestock raising, widely practiced in Tsavo during Patterson's time, as it is today. The Gnoske–Kerbis Peterhans study traces throughout history a pattern of lions, tigers, and leopards making a transition from domestic stock depredations, to conflict with humans (herdsmen defending their goats and cattle from lion attack), to predation on humans. Once again, the primary culprits are male lions, most commonly nomadic young males that have left their mothers and siblings to forage on their own until they're mature enough to lead a pride.

So, when John H. Patterson arrived in Tsavo that spring of 1898, all the preconditions leading to the development of man-eating behavior were there, waiting for him and his unfortunate coolies. Insofar as lions went, the natural world was about to give them a lesson in Murphy's Law: Everything that could go wrong was all set to go wrong, and it did.

"Although the human toll at Tsavo was thought to exceed 100 individuals," the researchers' study concludes, "it seems the total could have easily been far higher. Given the circumstances at Tsavo in the 1890's, instead of asking how so many humans could have been dispatched, we wonder why there weren't more."

The African lion is not endangered, but its range is shrinking as human populations swell and expand into its territories, building towns, transforming wild lands into farmland and cattle pasture. Tsavo, vast and austere, has been spared because it's unsuitable for agriculture or any other kind of human development. In the future, it could become one of the lion's last refuges.

As the Field Museum's Dr. Bruce Patterson put it to an interviewer: "The habitat that robbed the lion of his majestic rank, the mane, may give him something even more precious, a future."

ACKNOWLEDGMENTS

I would like to thank the scientists who made this book possible: Samuel Andanje, Thomas Gnoske, Dr. Julian Kerbis Peterhans, Ogeto Muwebi, Dr. Craig Packer, Dr. Bruce Patterson, and Peyton West. Thanks also to the staff of the Kenya Wildlife Service, to Wayne Hosek, and especially to my editor, Steve Byers, for all the angst and Sturm und Drang he endured on my behalf.